drug abuse

FOUNDATION FOR A PSYCHOSOCIAL APPROACH

EDITED BY:

SEYMOUR EISEMAN
JOSEPH A. WINGARD
GEORGE J. HUBA

Baywood Publishing Company, Inc.
Farmingdale, NY

To Joel, who tried but just couldn't make it.

Library of Congress Catalog Card Number: 83-7105
ISBN Number: 0-89503-039-X

Library of Congress Cataloging in Publication Data

Main Entry under title:

Drug abuse.

Includes bibliographical references.
1. Drug abuse–Study and teaching–United States–Addresses, essays, lectures. 2. Drug abuse–United States–Prevention–Addresses, essays, lectures. 3. Youth–United States–Drug use–Attitudes–Addresses, essays, lectures. 4. Youth–United States–Tobacco use–Attitudes–Addresses, essays, lectures. I. Eiseman, Seymour. II. Wingard, Joseph A. III. Huba, George J. [DNLM: 1. Substance abuse–Prevention and control. 2. Health education. WM 270 D7928]
HV5808.D782 1984 362.2'937'0880544 83-7105
ISBN 0-89503-039-X

Foreword

The Great Drug Abuse Epidemic in the United States is now almost two decades old. It has brought illegal drug use into all segments of American life for the first time in our nation's history. Marijuana, once an ethnically and geographically limited drug, has now joined alcohol and tobacco as truly a mass-consumed drug in the United States. The terrible effects of drugs in our society can hardly be overstated. Consider that roughly 30 percent of all Americans dying this year will die prematurely because of the use of alcohol and tobacco. Consider that the "new" drugs from cocaine and marijuana to PCP and heroin have been added without any reduction in levels of use of these two "old" drugs and that the "new" drugs are more toxic than alcohol and tobacco. Also consider that the only age group in twentieth century America to show a rising death rate has been Americans, fifteen to twenty-four years old, during the period of this drug epidemic.

For a clinician such statistics give perspective to more painful and purely human experiences with drug dependence. To live, with a drug dependent youth and his family, through a serious drug dependence problem, is one of the most humbling and harrowing experiences I have ever gone through. The hardest problem I face as a practicing psychiatrist is to get drug dependent patients (of all ages) and their families to face the enormity of the struggle they are required to make to overcome drug dependence. So many of my governmental and clinical colleagues, less directly involved with drug dependent people, have glossed over this anguishing and often terribly personal problem. Too many have thought the drug user simply needs to "quit his habit" without even beginning to grasp the dimensions of the struggle involved. To love someone with a drug dependence problem and to lose him (or her) is one of life's most painful experiences. This experience is now tragically common-place in America. Those so touched can be forgiven if they react angrily to the well-meaning friends and associates who treat drug dependence as a trivial, a political or a derivative problem.

We must face the stark fact that drug dependence is the nation's number one health problem. We must also face the fact that none of us escapes its impact.

Eiseman, Wingard and Huba are dedicated professionals who, through their writing and editing, have brought true leadership to the drug abuse prevention field. Their new book, *Drug Abuse: Foundation for a Psychosocial Approach* has brought together, for the first time, important and useful articles giving an excellent overview of the field—for the novice and the expert alike. Here we have a book which will be useful to students in many disciplines and to clinicians who are reaching out beyond their own direct experience, seeking to make sense out of the painful human experiences of their everyday practices.

As a clinician who daily treats drug dependent people and their families, and as a person concerned with public policy concerning drug abuse, I salute the editors for their contribution and urge you to read this book, and learn, as I have done.

Robert L. DuPont, M.D.
President, American Council on Marijuana
and Other Psychoactive Drugs, Inc.
Founding Director, National Institute on Drug Abuse

Preface

DRUG ABUSE: Foundation for a Psychosocial Approach is an attempt to educate teachers about one of the more serious health problems facing our society.

The purpose of this book is to offer a different approach to education about drug abuse. We have deliberately avoided the traditional model of substance physiology, metabolic function or even drug classification. To what avail is such information when the impact of this modality has not proven an effective deterrent? Teachers, school administrators, lawyers, parents and others have frequently been inundated with plastic hearts and lungs, as well as diagrams and other forms of visual materials describing differences and similarities in the actions and effects of licit and illicit drugs. Such data are readily available for anyone to obtain and use as the situation demands. We believe, however, that this knowledge base provides little information of great utility in actually planning programs which will significantly impact upon current levels of drug abuse in society. As an alternative, this book will focus on the state-of-the-art with regard to theory, research and practice pertaining to drug abuse using a psychosocial, rather than medical, perspective.

Over the past two decades, traditional and innovative or "experimental" approaches to solving the problem have not been as effective in reducing the incidence and prevalence of drug abuse among children and youth as it had been hoped. Furthermore, it is even possible that superficial approaches, as well as a reluctancy by many educators and parents to face the realities of drug abuse may have contributed to, rather than reduced or prevented the problem.

It is our belief that we have now learned much more about the etiology or cause of drug abuse than had been known even ten years earlier. A recognition of the general psychological and developmental factors influencing the individual's behavior is far better understood now than in the 1960's and 1970's and with some degree of confidence we can point to constellations of physiological, psychological, interpersonal, and societal forces as causes of youthful drug use initiation, maintenance, abuse, cessation, and relapse. The picture is now brighter than ever before for helping prevent and treat drug abuse throughout the lifespan.

Professionals in the disciplines associated with drug abuse no longer fear to admit that there is much more to learn about the theoretical aspects of preventing drug abuse. To theorize about causal relationships between and among a host of human and environmental variables gives credence to the proposition that no two persons are affected similarly to any one variable, and argues that our drug use prevention efforts must be multidisciplinary in building knowledge bases. Having viable theories of the phenomenon is critical if we are to make intelligent and cost-effective interventions in an attempt to prevent or stop drug abuse.

Research is a vital component of the problem-solving approach to drug abuse prevention. Research provides an objective way of testing theories. The outcome of such efforts can offer clues and trends to a more accurate portrayal of the human condition as it pertains to drug abuse and other behavioral disorders. The cycle may be completed by implementing theoretical models and research findings into less traditional but possibly overlooked modes of education, be they classroom exercises, treatment centers for individuals, or cost effective group counseling. It is by such careful attention to new knowledge that we can design new programs for maximum impact.

In Part I, we examine theoretical models proposed to address questions about education, school programs, and psychosocial factors affecting decisions to use or not use drugs. Various reflections on the value of research and program development will be discussed. This section provides the necessary framework and overview for grasping more specific issues discussed in later sections.

Part II will present selected research studies describing the attitudes of elementary and junior high school students toward smoking cigarettes and the use of drugs. The more known about the attitudes and interests of target populations, the less difficult it is to plan programs of prevention. In addition, we examine investigations about the awareness of substance abuse among preschool children. This age group is one in which general attitudes are formed about use or non-use of drugs – attitudes and behavior patterns which become established by age 9-13.

In Part III, we examine reports of some practices employed in a variety of settings which may be contributing to or serving as deterrents to drug abuse. The TV program which glorifies substance use and abuse will be discussed. We will look at meditation and Gestalt therapy as two models for rehabilitating the drug-dependent person. We also examine strategies for determining the effectiveness of such programs.

Throughout this book, the reader should be aware of the non-traditional approach to understanding the nature and factors associated with drug abuse. We believe that the content of *Drug Abuse: Foundation for a Psychosocial Approach* will provide the reader with a more global and subtle comprehensive approach to gaining insight about drug abuse behavior. As educated people, it is our responsibility to supply the fundamental ingredients to those whose lives we have in trust; as socially-concerned individuals we must use education, our most powerful tool, to combat the drug abuse problem our society faces.

Table of Contents

PART III PRACTICE

Part I
THEORY

Theory, in the drug abuse field, when cognizant of knowledge gain from the clinic, a community program, and/or empirical research study, can be a useful uniting summary. It is then an integration of the major principles uncovered through careful clinical and empirical study transcending the boundaries of uncovered facts. When basic principles have been discovered through careful analysis of a phenomenon and then integrated, they provide a reintegrative function examining logical interrelationships of primary principles and then generalize to new situations which have not as yet been studied. Thus theory constitutes a framework useful for stepping beyond the boundaries of what has been done, what is currently known, and practiced. This latter function of theory is the most important one for policy design.

Theory, then, is the sum total of what we currently know about the phenomenon and what reasonable theorists and researchers think we know in the absence of conclusive empirical data. As students, educators, and concerned professionals we need to be knowledgeable about the theories in the field so that we can understand the underlying assumptions that many professionals make in approaching drug abuse, and we can adopt the knowledge base to the many new situations we will face in our own experiences. Of course, it must be realized that there is no one totally accepted theory of drug use: if we had a theory which completely described the problem, we presumably would not have the problem. In the past decades, however, the field has transitioned from a primarily atheoretical one to one which has several major and dominant theories. This section provides a sample of some of the best theories in the field, and the simple act of placing them together for the student to read illustrates the fact that most of the theorists agree on the major points while each has something new and novel to contribute to the knowledge base. The accumulated ideas represented by the chapters in this section will lead the field into far more sophistication than it has had thus far.

The first chapter presents an overall framework for the entire drug abuse area which has been provided by Huba, Wingard, and Bentler. They present their theoretical model, a series of primary principles distilled from numerous research articles, and then go on to argue that their framework can be applied to different stages of drug use, the design of drug prevention programs, and the evaluation of social experiments. Of all the theoretical models examined in this part, theirs is the most general, although at the expense of presenting few specific details of exactly how individual forces work. Nonetheless, the model serves to tie the more specific formulations of other theorists together in an integrated framework.

Among the most important parts of the drug theory of Huba, Wingard, and Bentler are the relationships that adolescents have with their peers. Johnson summarizes existing psychological and sociological theories of adolescent peer relationships and distills existing knowledge into a set of general lines which will aid the practitioner in developing effective training strategies in cooperative relationships for youth. The types of principles espoused by Johnson assume that drug abuse and other maladjustment behaviors can be modified through the development of well-adjusted strategies for coping with the peer culture. Johnson's theoretical analysis has important applications to many peer pressure related problems and will prove useful to educators and parents.

Especially during the pre-teenage and early adolescent years when many lifelong attitudes about drug use are formed, parental figures play an important role. Eiseman provides a set of arguments in favor of parents assuming their correct place in the responsibility of drug abuse by their children and also discusses how parents can shape their child's behavior through supportive, warm relationships. Again the theoretical analysis is directly applicable to parent-adolescent confrontations and their resolution.

In addition to general theories which might be of interest to drug abuse program planners, it is important to consider different general theories of the overall drug education process. Eiseman, in a very early article in the drug abuse education field, argues that alternate strategies need to be considered by schools which chose to develop educational strategies for their pupils while cautioning the field against overly simplistic approaches, and stressing the great need then going largely unfilled by public and private educational systems. Eiseman shows us what goals must underlie all major drug education models no matter what their specific goals.

In related chapters Wepner and Goodstadt question the directions which have been tried in early experimental drug education programs. Both authors acknowledge that present drug education programs do not necessarily lead to a strong reduction in levels of drug abuse and instead ask if new approaches are required.

Chng presents some of the major principles of values clarification strategies of drug education. Since so many of the present drug education programs available are based upon this strategy, the student will gain important knowledge necessary to evaluate present programs from this chapter.

In a final chapter for this section, Dembo suggests that research on drug prevention has much to learn from the experience of the social programmer and that the social programmer has much to learn from accumulated results of empirical research. This chapter provides a bridge to the next part.

Overall this section provides a summary of the major theoretical models of drug abuse and their relationship to drug education programming. This new theoretical background will help current planners develop far more sophisticated approaches to alleviating and eliminating drug abuse problems in the future.

CHAPTER 1

Applications of a Theory of Drug Use to Prevention Programs

GEORGE J. HUBA
JOSEPH A. WINGARD
PETER M. BENTLER

INTRODUCTION

Our theory of drug use is one which centrally posits that drug-taking behavior is caused by several large constellations of intra- and extra-individual forces. These domains of influences interact to modify each other while determining the presence or absence of a large variety of lifestyle behaviors including drug and alcohol use. Many previous theories of drug-taking have provided valuable

* This research was supported by Grant Number DA01070 from the National Institute on Drug Abuse. This paper develops the implications of a theory reported in D. J. Lettieri, (Ed.), *Theories of Drug Use.* National Institute on Drug Abuse, Rockville, Maryland, 1980.

contributions to the field in that they are correct as far as they go; flaws in these theories stem less from incorrectness than from the pragmatic consideration that attention has been focused on one set of forces to the exclusion of other domains of influences. In order to provide a more comprehensive view of drug use than is typical, we will discuss the models or domains of influences which form major subsystems in our larger theory, and then present more specific ideas on how different influences work to modify each other as well as to determine the performance of behaviors.

The detailed theory we will consider is presented graphically in Figure 1. This diagram represents sets of influences as large boxes. We should point out quite forcefully that we believe each box contains many different variables, factors, or latent influences, some of which may be largely uncorrelated with one another. That is, we have presented relatively abstract *domains* of influences. In Figure 1 we have also drawn a large number of single-headed arrows to signify presumed causal influences. Where no arrow appears, we believe that there is not a strong direct effect. While the length of this paper precludes a detailed literature review, we should emphasize that most of the links have been empirically substantiated and are recognized as major conclusions by many researchers. The diagram can be viewed then as an abstract summary statement of our theory which permits detailed empirical tests using a variety of research and analytic techniques, including the new methods for causal modeling with latent variables, a variety of continuous and discrete multivariate methods, and experimentation. Within the framework, we will try to claim a rather modest role for ourselves, if such a stance is possible given the grandiose nature of our Figure 1.

FRAMEWORK

Having presented the model, we would like to digress somewhat and clarify several points about the framework we are suggesting for the development of a comprehensive theory of drug use. First, our general orientation has been to attempt to integrate various major themes of research developed by previous workers. While the labels chosen for various domains of influence may not be entirely synonymous with terminology used by specialists in different fields, we feel that the general set of domains can be differentiated into those variables addressed in studies that span disciplines from psychopharmacology to psychology, sociology, and economics. Second, the act of differentiation and greater specification in various systems is a desirable goal for both current research and future theory. We feel that systems of interest, such as personality, must be successfully charted by determining the major structural and dynamic components. Our current framework is a largely undifferentiated and unelaborated one which should naturally develop as more information about the various domains becomes available through basic and applied research in the major scientific fields of relevance to drug use. As a consequence, we expect

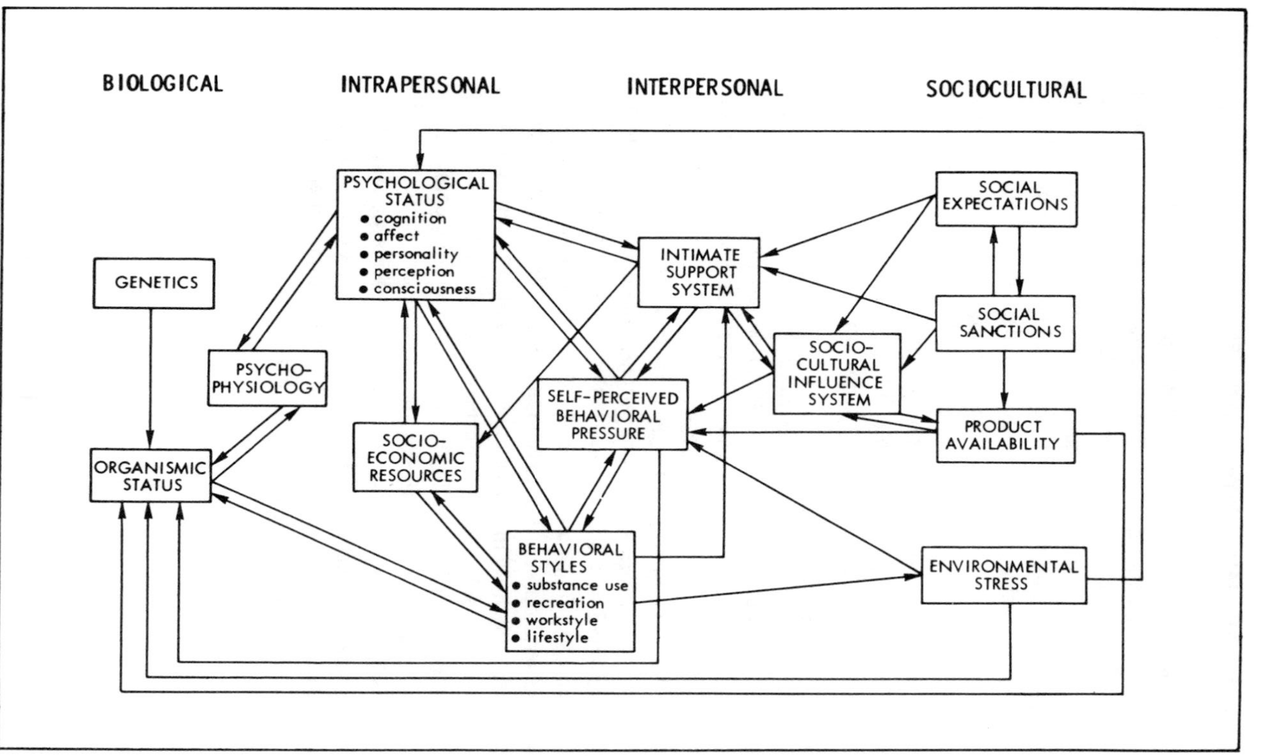

Figure 1. A model for presumed causal relationship to drug abuse.

that the future elaboration of our framework will possess some degree of ecological validity through empirical derivation rather than theoretical superimposition. Finally, we feel that the current framework allows the kind of differentiation which may permit confirmatory tests with such theory evaluation procedures as causal modeling with latent variables. That is, the current framework is explicitly designed to permit the comparison of various theories within a sophisticated, hypothesis-testing correlational methodology. While experimentation may well provide the best method for clarifying certain specific components of our model (e.g., the effect of certain products on various organismic variables), naturalistic research will be required to interrelate those many components that are not easily or ethically subject to manipulation (e.g., the effects of life stress on drug use) [1].

As this theory goes through successive generations of development in the future, there are several paths it must take. As a first task, we feel that there should be a clarification of the major variables within each domain that are relevant to understanding drug use. There are certain domains which traditionally have been the province of a given academic specialty, and we feel it is important to combine information from various disciplines so that the sphere may be generally charted with a consensual set of structural referents. Second, we believe that there should be a focus on the development of various submodels within the more general framework. Indeed, there is probably a lifetime of research productivity involved in determining the major structural personality characteristics related to drug use. As information accumulates within each specialty area, we would wish to see further elaboration of the component systems. Third, there should be an attempt to integrate alternative empirical and theoretical systems into our overall conceptualization. While we make no pretense of being able to explain all the phenomena of drug use, we propose the broad framework primarily because we hope that it has some potential for unifying more narrowly-based concepts of drug use.

THEORY

Turning away now from the abstract framework to the more detailed formulations we have chosen in our first attempt at theory, the reader will first note in Figure 1 that we have included construct domains which do not directly influence either drug taking or its alternatives. We feel that it is necessary to include these more contextual domains in a theoretical and empirical specification so that we can assess indirect effects and derive estimates of the amount of influence which are not biased because some important parts of the ecology are unmeasured. Furthermore, we must remember that many different domains are directly and indirectly changed as consequences of drug-taking and its alternatives. It is thus critical to consider the dynamic interactions of many different domains when considering drug-taking behavior.

A second major characteristic of our structural model is that the behaviors of drug and alcohol ingestion are embedded within a larger set of preferred behavioral styles which may complement or preclude one another. Indeed, it is necessary to speak of the psychosocial causes of drug taking *and its alternatives* because many of the alternatives share the same psychosocial causes and may bring the same consequences for the individual. The structural properties of individual behaviors must be considered within the interactive, ecological context of other characteristic behaviors performed and precluded so as to elaborate a theoretical network that has both convergent and discriminant validity.

At this time, we do not pretend to know whether it is more fruitful to approach a domain of Behavioral Styles from either dimensional or typological viewpoints. That is, we are not sure if there are delineable behavioral *types* or whether there are some major *dimensions* of behavioral preference and action. We do believe that it is important to know what other behaviors drug users also perform characteristically and to use co-occurrence with other behaviors as a way of differentiating among drug users. The present approach seems to open an avenue for conceptualizing other forms of habitual behaviors such as overeating, gambling, or obsessional shopping in relation to the dynamic causes of drug-taking. Our use of the phrase "Behavioral Styles" is meant to imply that the focus of our theory is on behavior that spans temporal and contextual effects. We are not particularly concerned with ad hoc and fleeting behaviors.

Presently, we continue to revise and expand the theoretical model. Consequently, the dynamic and structural properties implied by the Figure 1 should be perceived as a model in the process of evolution. Our goal is to develop and test many of the different submodels implied by the framework.

Proceeding to a detailed consideration of the figure, we have differentiated four major areas of interest at the highest level of abstraction. These areas are biological, intrapersonal, interpersonal, and sociocultural influences. At the very substratum of the biological area, we would place Genetic influences. We also wish to differentiate a domain which we call Organismic Status, and which includes such variables as health or efficient functioning as well as major anatomical and physiological systems. We also feel that it is necessary to specify those aspects of physiology which are directly influenced by the Psychological Status of the individual into a domain of Psychophysiology.

Dynamically, we have posited that Organismic Status is a function of Genetic influences as well as Psychophysiology and various behavioral and social forces. The dynamic lattice is presented in the figure as causal arrows. While there is residual, or unspecifiable, causation for each of the domains delineated, we have not indicated these in the figure. Specifying the nature of these residual influences is one of the major tasks to be completed in future generations of the present model.

Turning now to the intrapersonal sphere, as psychologists we have been most concerned with differentiating those systems which comprise Psychological

Status. We distinguish between subsystems of cognition, affect, personality, perception, and consciousness, each of which is a specialty area within the social sciences. Among the dimensions in the personality system which appear relevant to drug-taking and its alternatives are extraversion, law abidance, social adjustment, rebelliousness, anxiety, sensation-seeking tendencies, and autonomy and achievement strivings. We should note, parenthetically, that any of several sets of "second-order" personality factors are reasonable constructs, *in toto,* for describing relationships to drug use behavioral styles.

Within the affect subsystem of Psychological Status, it appears that Tomkins' derivation of positive and negative affects and their relationship to cognition, perception, consciousness, and personality may be the most elegant. This theory has already proven useful in differentiating types of cigarette smokers. Constructs which must be considered as the cognition system (or cognitive style) of the individual include the deployment of attention, memory capacity and organization, various intellectual ability skills such as reasoning, hemispheric dominance, and level of cognitive development. Perceptual constructs of interest include attention utilization, figure/ground relationships, distinctiveness, and ambiguity. Within the area of consciousness, it may be fruitful to consider the dimensions of content and structure outlined by Huba [2] as derived from the theoretical writings of Singer. We realize, of course, that the study of Psychological Status is a complicated one, including virtually the whole field of psychology, and we do not mean to oversimplify its importance within our diagram. On the other hand, when we try to conceptualize a very specific behavior such as drug use, or even a behavioral style which includes drug use, it may be necessary to use more abstract summaries of domains so that they might all be included.

It also seems important to consider the Socioeconomic Resources of the individual when considering a dependent variable of behavior. Financial resources are a function of the individual's psychological status as well as various social-system variables. Socioeconomic resources, or status, will also have an influence on the individual's psychological status.

Among the interpersonal domains, we differentiate Intimate Support Systems and Sociocultural Influence Systems. We consider the intimate support systems to be those individuals who are family, friends, and significant others for the individual. Among the important aspects of the intimate culture are providing relevant, valued models and reinforcers for various behaviors, as well as a sense of identity and belongingness. We believe that the sociocultural influence system is a set of more distal influences from the culture which includes subcultural norms, models, and impersonal socialization influences such as advertising. These influence systems are central to the government's belief in the efficacy of demand reduction methods through modifying the social environment of the drug user.

In the sociocultural domain, we prefer to distinguish Social Sanctions, Social

Expectations, Product Availability, and Environmental Stress. The domain of Social Sanctions includes such forces as laws, reinforcements or punishments, rituals, trends, fads, prevailing mores, and modal behavior patterns within the society. Within the domain of Product Availability we would include dimensions of cost and accessibility. While this domain does not appear as a central focus of psychological theories of drug use, the supply reduction strategy of dealing with drug use clearly implicates this domain in a central way as affecting behavioral styles. The domain of Environmental Stress has recently become one of wide interest. Among the dimensions which might be considered are the controllability, predictability, nature, magnitude, and duration of the stressors.

That most of the domains considered influence one another is something we take as given. Nonetheless, it is important to try to determine when one domain does *not* influence another strongly, or when some sources of influence are more important than others. While the general model is intended to explain the various stages of drug taking and cessation, we believe that certain domains exert more influence at different stages. For instance, it appears that the intimate support system influences may be particularly important in the initiation of drug taking while organismic status changes due to the drug may more fully account for continued drug ingestion. Additionally, we must ask when trait factors are more important in determining drug use than intimate support system factors, or when affective consequences of drug taking outweight legal punishments. Therefore, we would welcome individual research groups to include measures of our various domains in order to determine the most important influences, and consequences of drug use in a particular population.

STAGES OF DRUG USE

In the total phenomenon of drug-taking behavior, it seems useful to differentiate several different stages. Among the stages are initiation of use, continuance, cessation, and relapse. It seems to us that the current theoretical model can be applied to each of these different stages of use. Some implications of the interactive model for the different stages are presented briefly below.

Initiation

In our current conception, we believe that initiation of drug use, particularly when it occurs in adolescence, is almost entirely derived from self-perceived behavioral pressure resulting from the intimate support system. This support system plays a role in moving the individual to drug use through peer values, models, and reinforcers, and one of inadequacy in support of alternative, healthy behaviors and goals that would inhibit susceptibility to drug use. The personality system plays a much smaller role, with such dimensions as extraversion, leadership or autonomy strivings and rebelliousness needs seeking fulfillment in drug-taking behavior. This manifestation is particularly true when the majority culture defines drug-taking as illegal and dangerous, in which we posit that a negative psychological cycle may be instigated with initiation into use. The "backlash" effect is captured in the current model by the reciprocal arrows from perceived behavioral pressure to personality. The "backlash" may also be exacerbated when the individual's felt pressure to not use drugs is communicated to members of the intimate culture who convince him or her that drug-taking is desirable. It should also be noted that financial resources may preclude the initiation of certain forms of drug-taking, although this is unlikely within current youth cultures. During the initiation stage we do not think that organismic status plays any major role since the individual has had no direct experience with the mood altering properties of the drugs. To the extent that the individual self-attributes initiation to pharmacological properties, we may infer that he has been educated in drug effects by either the intimate culture or sources in the sociocultural influence system.

Continuation

Drug-taking is maintained primarily by its reinforcing effects, broadly conceived. These effects may be in the form of alleviation of pressure to perform undesirable behaviors, affect enhancement, a change in organismic status, or desirable consequences on the personality, cognition, perception, or consciousness systems. Thus psychopharmacological reaction to the drug is but one type of reinforcer. Systems which are directly affected by the ingestion of drugs may themselves secondarily influence other systems. For instance, changes in psychological status or of perceived behavioral pressure may cause an individual to redefine members of the intimate culture, alter family relationships, or change friends. To the extent that such direct and indirect changes are ultimately desirable to the individual, either in the short or long-term, drug taking will be maintained.

We would like to differentiate between early and later stages of maintenance, particularly for those drugs which foster either physical or psychological dependence. During the early stages, drug effects are probably evaluated by the individual as desirable because they change the systems in some psychophysiologically positive way. That is to say, the ingestion of the drug serves to enhance some positive psychological function for the individual. During the later stages of maintenance, or dependence, it is likely that the effects for the individual are primarily those of warding off unpleasant organismic effects associated with the cessation of the drug; these effects may operate directly on behavior without psychological mediation.

Cessation

We believe that the cessation of drug use is a less universal process than the initiation of use in that there seem to be groups of individuals for whom different influences are important. Nonetheless, these different groups of individuals may all be considered within the general framework of our theory and many different systems must be simultaneously studied.

One group of individuals seems to cease taking drugs because of behavioral pressure from the intimate support system. For this group, the major reason for stopping is that use fails to be valued within that set of individuals defined as important sources of modeling and reinforcement. A second group of individuals is perhaps more likely to quit of their own volition as a result of realizing undesirable changes in their psychological or organismic status. A third group of individuals may change their drug-taking behavior as a function of some intervention, usually arrest or forced treatment, caused by the sociocultural influence system. This process may operate in part because of product inavailability. Finally, some small group of individuals may cease taking a drug because of limited economic resources.

Relapse

Relapse into drug-taking may happen in much the same way as initiation occurs, with three major dynamic exceptions. First, since the individual has previously used drugs, it is expected that there will be both a direct and indirect effect (through behavioral pressure) of the organismic status systems on behavior. That is, there will be a craving for those drugs which have produced dependencies. In some cases, behavior may occur automatically as a result of the craving, although in most cases the indirect contribution through self-perceived behavioral pressure will occur. However, the craving may not be translated into drug-taking behavior, if the psychological systems, intimate support system, or socioculture influence system intervene through conscious deliberation, social disapproval, or socio-legal restraint. The self-perceived behavioral pressure may also be changed by product availability: cravings may diminish and disappear entirely when there is no product available for ingestion. Second, the personality system may exert more influence on relapse than it does on initiation. The individual may have developed coping and rationalization styles during prior drug use that serve to redefine intimate support, and because of strong prior behavioral tendencies, more minimal cues for rejection, loss of self-esteem, etc. may predispose further drug use. Finally, environmental stress is seen to have a more vigorous role in relapse than initiation, unless adequate counter-drug behavioral styles have been developed in the individual.

SIGNIFICANCE FOR EDUCATION

One important aspect of the current model is the set of the implications it carries for the design and implementation of drug education programs. We will briefly discuss some of these themes as they relate to different facets of the total drug education and prevention process.

Primary Prevention

In that our current model was designed to attempt to systematize the multiple influences which can cause an individual to initiate and maintain drug use, we believe that the model implies a certain strategy for primary prevention efforts. There is no single path to the initiation of drug use: many different domains of influences interact to lead to the beginning stage of experimentation. In designing primary prevention programs, we must look toward aspects of the intimate culture, the personality and affect systems, and the way the individual combines information into a judgment of perceived behavioral pressure. Any effective primary prevention program will have to address themes in many of the domains we have outlined since the influences combine together in many different ways to cause or preclude the initiation of use. An emphasis on one aspect of the total process (such as self-esteem training without training in resisting peer pressure) may at best only partially serve to lower rates of adolescent initiation. Notice that formal education, in the sense of cognitive or affective learning experiences, are expected in this model to provide inadequate inoculation against drug use, unless combined with efforts to modify other aspects of the intimate culture and an individual's psychological status. Furthermore, we must carefully chart how different interventions may be either compatible or incompatible with one another.

Secondary Prevention

In the design of treatment, we must consider the different ways that individual patterns of drug taking are maintained through reinforcement, affective benefits, the avoidance of withdrawal, and personality change. Our model predicts that drug taking influences many psychological systems within the individual as well as the intimate culture (through redefinition by the individual of the important persons with whom interactions take place). As in primary prevention, secondary prevention efforts must attempt to examine how different types of intervention will combine together to be effective. For example, we do not expect that individuals treated exclusively with therapies designed to change personality functioning will abstain from substance-taking unless alternate behavioral styles are developed which also serve to substitute for affective and interpersonal gains previously obtained from the ingestion of drugs. Similarly, we feel that successful abstinence will derive from reeducation in sources of behavioral pressure and stress management.

Professional Education

Our current model makes it clear that the phenomenon of drug-taking is a complex one which includes major constructs from many different disciplines of social and medical sciences. The complexity needed even to attempt to develop a first generation model of drug taking implies that professionals educated to undertake primary and secondary prevention will need training in such disciplines as psychology, sociology, psychotherapy, education, medicine, and pharmacology Currently, some programs contain components about these areas. What we must convey to our students, however, is not only the basic core knowledge in the scattered disciplines, but how sociological constructs of alienation, powerlessness, status, peer pressure, and the like combine with psychological knowledge about traits, social reinforcement contingencies, models, and therapy strategies. The knowledge of the various scattered disciplines must be integrated to inform the student of drug education about the complexity inherent in conceptualizing the psychological and physical aspects associated with coping and dealing with social realities. Drug taking is but a single behavioral style influenced in such a complex way, and we know that there are many different modes of adjustment that include drug-taking behaviors: students must be educated to try to design and implement programs within this true phenomenological complexity.

Evaluation of Programs

As has been noted elsewhere [1, 3, 4], a theoretical framework, such as that explicitly provided in our Figure 1, can also guide evaluation efforts using either quantitative or qualitative procedures for assessing causal models. The model we have provided makes explicit predictions about the linkages of certain sets of forces to drug-taking behaviors during different stages. Consequently, it is possible to translate our model into a form suitable for statistical assessment.

The theoretical model permits us to evaluate the effect of a program using criterion behaviors in addition to the obvious one of drug-taking. Certain interventions may be either relatively low in power or take a relatively long time to impact individual rates of drug-taking. These interventions can be validated and confirmed when a strongly supported theoretical model is available to provide the context for the tests. For instance, we may design a program to impact personality functioning in a certain way. If an empirically substantiated theoretical model indicates that relevant modes of personality are strongly related to drug-taking, then a demonstration that the intervention impacts personality in the desired manner can be taken as evidence that drug-taking will probably eventually be impacted by the intervention.

A theoretical model may also be used to help determine why certain intervention programs do not work. If we can show that other (uncontrolled) factors influence a domain more than the intervention does, it is possible to argue that one non-effective trial should not be considered sufficient justification to discard the potentially valuable program. Rather, it seems necessary under these circumstances to devise more sensitive measures of the impact of the program, or to control in some manner the concomitantly occurring extraneous influences. In varying situations one strategy may be more feasible than the other. For example, residential intervention programs afford a greater possibility of structuring the environment so that extraneous sources of influence are either eliminated or held constant across all program participants. On the other hand, in nonresidential, outpatient programs less control of the client's environment is possible, so more sensitive measures of the intervention effect may be the only viable alternative available.

Validation Research

In our current research program on young adolescents and their parents, we are seeking to interrelate the various domains through the use of structural equation models with latent variables [3] and various other hypothesis testing procedures. These new revolutionary procedures allow the theorist to posit various linkages between the important variables of a model and then determine, through the use of goodness of fit statistics, whether the model is sufficient for the data used to test the formulation. In our early empirical work preliminary to detailed causal modeling, a variety of findings on adolescent drug use have emerged. Perceived supply and support for drug use, important characteristics of the intimate culture and perceived pressure, seem much more important determinants of drug-taking than more general characteristics of the peer culture which are indicators of sociocultural influences [5, 6]. Sources of support and supply seem to be differentiated for various drug taking styles. Personality measures in addition to rebelliousness such as liberalism, leadership, extraversion, and the lack of deliberateness and diligence are important predictors of drug use [7, 8]. Logical introspection of the costs and benefits of drug use, as reflected in conscious decisions regarding drug use, are not strongly predictive of changes in subsequent use [9-11] indicating that behavioral pressures may not be purely logical functions of "objective" pressures. Drug use seems to cluster along lines pharmacologically related to mood alteration as well as legal penalties and availability [12]. Not only are drug-related behavioral styles quite stable in young adults, but previous drug-taking behavior serves as a major predictor of future drug-taking behavior [6, 8], and a behavioral style involving a dangerous drug like PCP is an organized consequence depending on prior substance use [13].

In an older sample of the mothers of our adolescent sample it has been shown that drug use is related to self-perceived organismic status as well as to various personality dimensions [14]. Two of the studies represent early applications of causal models with latent variables to drug use data [12, 14].

In the future, our work will consist of integrating various results into the framework of the model shown in Figure 1 as we seek to expand, elaborate, and revise the specific causal ideas pictured. It is our belief that utilizing such a sequential process allows a demonstration of ecological validity for the model by submitting it to periodic tests to establish or refute our specific claims. For example, our model proposes that the intimate support system affects drug use through perceived behavioral pressure, but not directly. Although we have demonstrated that perceived support for use is a major predictor of drug use, we have, as yet, no specific evidence on the mechanism or pathway by which the influence occurs.

REFERENCES

1. P. M. Bentler, The Interdependence of Theory, Methodology, and Empirical Data: Causal Modeling as an Approach to Construct Validation, *Longitudinal Research on Drug Use: Empirical Findings and Methodological Issues,* D. B. Kandel, (Ed.), Hemisphere, Washington, D.C., 1978.
2. G. J. Huba, Daydreaming, *Encyclopedia of Clinical Assessment,* R. H. Woody, (Ed.), Jossey-Bass, San Francisco, 1980.
3. P. M. Bentler, Multivariate Analysis with Latent Variables: Causal Modeling, *Annual Review of Psychology,* M. R. Rosenzweig and L. W. Porter, (Eds.), Annual Reviews, Palo Alto, 1980.
4. P. M. Bentler and J. A. Woodward, Nonexperimental Evaluation Research: Contributions of Causal Modeling, *Improving Evaluations,* L. E. Datta and R. Perloff, (Eds.), Sage, Beverly Hills, 1979.
5. G. J. Huba, J. A. Wingard and P. M. Bentler, Adolescent Drug Use and Peer and Adult Interaction Patterns, *Journal of Consulting and Clinical Psychology, 47,* pp. 265-276, 1979.
6. ———, A Longitudinal Analysis of the Role of Peer Support, Adult Models, and Peer Subcultures in Beginning Adolescent Substance Use, *Multivariate Behavioral Research,* in press.
7. J. A. Wingard, G. J. Huba and P. M. Bentler, The Relationship of Personality Structure to Patterns of Adolescent Drug Use, *Multivariate Behavioral Research, 14,* pp. 131-143, 1979.
8. ———, A Longitudinal Analysis of Personality Structure and Adolescent Substance Use, *Personality and Individual Differences,* in press.
9. G. J. Huba, J. A. Wingard and P. M. Bentler, Adolescent Drug Use and Intentions to Use Drugs in the Future: A Concurrent Analysis, *Journal of Drug Education, 9,* pp. 145-150, 1979.
10. ———, Intentions to Use Drugs Among Adolescents: A Longitudinal Analysis, *International Journal of the Addictions, 16,* in press, 1981.
11. P. M. Bentler and G. Speckart, Models of Attitude-Behavior Relations, *Psychological Review, 86,* pp. 452-464, 1979.
12. G. J. Huba, J. A. Wingard and P. M. Bentler, Models for Adolescent Drug Use, UCLA/NIDA Center for Adolescent Drug Abuse Etiologies, Los Angeles, 1979.
13. G. J. Huba and P. M. Bentler, Phencyclidine Use in High School: Tests of Models, *Journal of Drug Education, 9,* pp. 285-291, 1979.
14. J. A. Wingard, G. J. Huba and P. M. Bentler, Drug Use and Psychosomatic Symptomatology in Non-Institutionalized Adult Women, Paper presented at the meeting of the National Drug Abuse Conference, New Orleans, 1979.

ACKNOWLEDGEMENT

The authors wish to thank Janel Hetland for production assistance on the manuscript.

CHAPTER 2

Constructive Peer Relationships, Social Development, and Cooperative Learning Experiences: Implications for the Prevention of Drug Abuse

DAVID W. JOHNSON

CORRELATES AND CAUSES OF DRUG ABUSE AND USE

Although there is disagreement as to the definition of *drug abuse,* it is defined here as the chronic, excessive use of a drug to an extent that it interferes either with a person's social adjustment, career adjustment, or physical health. Thus, drug abuse includes addiction, habituation, and drug misuse. In searching for the causes of drug abuse and other socially dysfunctional behavior patterns researchers have found that the teenagers who are most likely to be treated for drug abuse, arrested for delinquency, treated for psychological illness, or expelled from school, are likely to [1-7]:

1. be from a family in which relationships are filled with stress, physical and psychological abuse, or indifference;
2. be socially alienated and isolated from their peers and lacking stable peer relationships;
3. be deficient in the social competencies necessary for building and maintaining stable relationships and for dealing with their emotions effectively;
4. have transient values and to be uncertain of their values, goals, and priorities and, therefore, have extreme difficulty in making responsible decisions;
5. have psychological problems relating to low self-acceptance and self-confidence, unstable self-identity, and low self-awareness of their own emotions and inner experiences;
6. lack self-control;
7. be, because of the above problems, unduly influenced by peers.

In studies specially aimed at drug use, Becker and Goode have stressed that friends are important in influencing others to start using drugs, not only by supplying the drug but by providing an example and defining the nature of the physiological experience [8, 9]. A number of studies have documented an association between adolescents' illicit drug use and their perceptions of drug use among their friends [10-12]. Jessor correlated a number of personality, parental influence, and peer influence factors with the use of marijuana and found that perceiving one's friends as being drug users and perceiving one's friends as approving of marijuana use, along with generally being influenced by one's friends, are highly related to the use of marijuana as well as other problem or possible transition behaviors such as experience of sexual intercourse, problem drinking, or participation in activist protest [5]. Kandel found a strong positive relationship between adolescent and best friend's use of marijuana which is far stronger than and relatively independent of demographic, personality, life-style, and family factors [13]. She also found that adolescents with high levels of peer activity are much more likely to be using marijuana than are adolescents with average or low levels of peer activity. And she demonstrated similar results for the use of illicit drugs other than marijuana. Adolescents' peer groups and friends, therefore, seem to have considerable influence on drug use patterns.

The findings on drug abuse point toward unstable family and peer group relationships as destructive influences on drug abusers' social development, inability to build and maintain constructive relationships within which values and goals are developed, and inability to manage negative feelings created by their alienation and the general stresses of living. In essence, drug abusers seem to lack the basic social competencies required for managing relationships and coping with interpersonal and intrapersonal problems. The findings on drug use indicate that adolescents may be strongly influenced by their peers when making decisions as to whether or not to use illicit drugs.

Many prevention programs have focused on:

1. viewing drug abuse as psychological pathology;
2. controlling children's and adolescents' behavior by instilling fear of the effects of drugs, punishment, and adult authority; and
3. giving information concerning the effects of various drugs.

An alternative approach is to view the prevention of drug abuse as depending on the socialization of children and adolescents into the basic social competencies that allow them to cope with life situations involving other people and their own inner experiences. This approach is a major divergence from the traditional preoccupation with pathology and psychological problems. A competence orientation to the prevention of drug abuse depends on conceptualizing social competence in a way that allows for prevention programs to be planned, implemented, and evaluated. In order to discuss such an approach to prevention it is necessary to review the basic processes of socialization, specify the social competencies resulting from healthy social development, outline the difficulties in relying on the family as an effective socializing agency, discuss the importance of the peer group for constructive socialization, and describe a prevention program that can be implemented within schools that utilizes peer relationships to promote the healthy social development of all students.

THE SOCIALIZATION OF SOCIAL COMPETENCIES

In order to develop social competencies children and adolescents must be involved in a series of relationships with people who care about them and who have social competencies that the children and adolescents see as desirable and want to acquire. It is within such relationships that socialization takes place. *Socialization* is the process of learning and internalizing the values, attitudes, roles, competencies, and ways of perceiving the world that are shared by one's family, community, and society [14]. There are three important aspects of socialization. First, the specific values, attitudes, roles, competencies, and perspectives that children and adolescents adopt are learned. They are not genetically inherited and they do not magically appear as children mature physically. Second, socialization has its origin in interaction with other people. It is the members of one's family and peer groups that provide socializing influences and it is within such relationships that children and adolescents are confronted with expectations as to what are appropriate values, attitudes, roles, competencies, and perspectives. Third, socialization is not a passive process; it is a dynamic process in which children and adolescents seek out and select how they respond to the expectations of the people around them.

Three of the most powerful processes through which socialization takes place are direct learning, identification, and role learning [14]. Some values, attitudes, competencies, and perspectives are directly taught. *Identification* occurs when children and adolescents try to incorporate the qualities and attributes of another person into themselves. Through incorporating the attributes of others, people transform themselves in new directions over a period of time. A great deal of identification takes place without full awareness of the extent to which one is adopting the attributes of another person. Identification can be positive or negative. Positive identification is based on liking for the other person and respect or admiration for the other person's competencies. Negative identification is based on anxiety and anger. Identifications result in the growth of people as they internalize aspects of external relationships. The affection and support one feels from one's peers becomes internalized and one feels similarly toward oneself. The rejection of parents can become internalized through identification and one will reject oneself. Healthy social development and constructive socialization depends on children and adolescents identifying with others primarily on the basis of love and a desire to become more competent, while avoiding identifications based on anxiety and anger. A *social role* is a set of expectations aimed at structuring interaction within a relationship. Examples of relationships in which social roles are learned are child-parent, brother-sibling or sister-sibling, student-teacher, customer-salesperson, male-female, friend-friend, and citizen-police officer. Through acquiring social roles children and adolescents learn large, integrated patterns of consistent behavior that they perform in relationships with other people.

In order for a society to continue, the children and adolescents living within it must be socialized. In order for parents, teachers, and other individuals involved in socializing others to model desirable social competencies, define social roles, and teach children and adolescents directly values, attitudes, competencies, and perspectives, they must have a general conception of what healthy social development is.

HEALTHY SOCIAL DEVELOPMENT AND SOCIAL COMPETENCIES

The prevention of drug abuse depends on the socialization of children and adolescents into the basic social competencies required to manage relationships and one's own inner experiences. Human development follows a pattern of expansion of interdependence with other people. Growing children are impelled to become aware of and interact with a widening social circle of people. From only having to relate to members of the family, they begin to interact with peers and other people in the neighborhood. Their social world is expanded dramatically when they start school. When they enter a career organization and become members of a community, young adults must build and maintain relationships with a larger and larger number of people. The expanded number of people with whom one must build and maintain relationships, along with the increasing specificity and necessity for cooperation, requires the development of certain social competencies [4, 14, 15].

The first is a generalized interpersonal *trust* that one can rely on the affection and support of other people [14, 16-18]. Distrustful attitudes that others are harsh and undependable have been posited to lead to habitual affective states of depression, anxiety, fear, and apprehension, and to beliefs that others are critical, rejecting, humiliating, inconsistent, unpredictable, undependable, and exploitative. This sense of trust begins in infancy when a person is totally dependent on the caring and commitment of others and it is reaffirmed or disconfirmed in all stages of a person's development and within the person's major relationships.

The second is *perspective-taking,* the ability to understand how a situation appears to another person and how that person is reacting cognitively and affectively. This competency is the opposite of egocentrism. Egocentric people see the world only from their self-centered point of view and are unaware of other points of view and of their own limitations in perspective. Both developmental and social psychologists have emphasized the importance of this competency for healthy social and cognitive development [4, 19]. Egocentric people tend to adjust poorly to social situations, are ineffective communicators, lack ability to make autonomous moral decisions based on mutual reciprocity and justice, act competitively, are closed-minded, manage conflict destructively, have a diffused identity and low self-awareness, and are unable to predict the effects of their behavior on others [4, 14].

The third aspect of healthy social development is a meaningful purpose and *direction in life,* a sense of "where I am going." Everyone needs a purpose that is valued by others and that is similar to the goals of the significant people in one's life [4, 17, 18]. Directionality includes such processes as directing one's attention towards desired future goals (intentionality and future orientation), believing that one is in control of one's fate and can take the initiative in applying one's resources toward the achievement of one's goals, feeling satisfaction when a meaningful goal is achieved, and developing and utilizing one's potentialities to achieve one's goals. Feelings of involvement, commitment, and meaning, and beliefs that life is worthwhile, challenging, and has purpose, depend on a sense of direction. People without a sense of direction flounder from one tentative activity to another, search for experiences to give their life meaning, refuse to assume responsibility for their choices, make little effort to achieve their goals, feel no satisfaction when they achieve a goal, fail to use their competencies, and have low aspirations.

Fourth is an awareness of *meaningful interdependence* with other people [4, 16]. All members of a society are highly interdependent. Other people make the cars one drives, the clothes one wears, the sidewalks one uses, the buildings one lives and works in, and the money one spends. In most situations there is no chance of achieving one's goals unless one combines one's efforts with the efforts of others. An awareness of meaningful interdependence includes perceptions that oneself and others will receive the same outcome (share a common fate), that the outcomes of a situation are mutually caused by the actions of both oneself and others, and that both oneself and others are dependent on each other's resources. In addition, a long-term time perspective is needed in order to plan long-range strategies for interaction and coordination of behavior. There is nothing more personally rewarding and satisfying than being part of a joint effort to achieve important goals and it is through such experiences that friendships and emotional bonds are developed. People who are unaware of their interdependence with others usually feel alienated, lonely, isolated, worthless, inferior, and defeated. Their attitudes reflect low self-esteem, an emphasis on short-term gratification, and the conviction that no one cares about them or their capabilities. Such people are often impulsive, have fragmented relationships, withdraw from other people, and are insensitive to their own and other's needs.

Finally, every person needs a strong and integrated *personal identity* [4, 17, 20]. An identity is a consistent set of attitudes that defines "who I am." It serves as an anchor in life. The world can change, other people can change, career and family life can change, but there is something about oneself that remains the same. During infancy, childhood, adolescence, and early adulthood, a person has several identities. The physical changes involved in growth, the increasing number of experiences with other people, the increasing responsibilities faced, and the general cognitive and social development, all cause changes and adaptations in one's self-definition. But the final result has to be a basic unified personal identity. A diffused and ambiguous identity results in dissociation from other people and an avoidance of growth-producing experiences [16]. People without an integrated and coherent self-identity will chronically feel anxiety, insecurity, depression, cynicism, defensiveness, unhappiness, self-contempt, and self-rejection. They will be unable to maintain relationships, will have transient values and interest, and will search frantically for a set of beliefs to cling to in order to superficially achieve a sense of unity.

Healthy social development and the acquisition of social competencies depend on the formation of meaningfully interdependent relationships with adults, older and younger children, and peers. It is within these relationships that socialization into an overall balance of trust rather than distrust of other people, the ability to view situations and problems from a variety of perspectives, a meaningful sense of direction and purpose in life, an awareness of mutual interdependence with others, and an integrated and coherent sense of personal identity, takes place. There are literally hundreds of studies demonstrating the superiority of cooperative (as compared with competitive and individualistic) relationships in promoting healthy social development [21, 22]. The overall results indicate that compared with competitive and individualistic experiences, cooperation promotes:

1. higher levels of interpersonal trust;
2. greater perspective-taking ability;
3. greater goal orientation, coordination of efforts, involvement in efforts to achieve goals, satisfaction from goal achievement, and success in achieving goals;
4. more mutual influence;
5. more frequent and accurate communication;
6. more mutual support, assistance, helping, and sharing;
7. more pro-social and less antisocial behavior;
8. more constructive management of conflicts;
9. lower levels of anxiety and greater feelings of personal security;
10. more positive self-esteem and greater unconditional acceptance of oneself;
11. positive interpersonal relationships characterized by mutual liking, positive attitudes toward each other, mutual concern, friendliness, attentiveness, feelings of obligation to and support for each other, and a desire to earn the respect of others.

The strength of this evidence indicates that a major avenue of intervention into the socialization of basic social competencies and healthy social development is the placing of alienated children and teenagers into cooperative relationships.

The development of the basic social competencies is vital to the prevention of drug abuse. There are two major settings in which children and adolescents may be socialized into social competencies—the family and the school. Since the children and adolescents most in need of constructive socializing experiences come from stressful, abusive, or indifferent families, the school is becoming increasingly important as a socializing agency. The difficulties in relying on the family for constructive socialization are briefly discussed in the next section. The importance of peer relationships and the ways in which schools can facilitate healthy social development are then outlined.

THE SOCIALIZATION CRISIS AND STRESS IN MANY FAMILIES

In order for children and adolescents to develop the inner resources and social competencies conducive to emotional growth and responsible decision-making they must be involved in relationships with other people in which they acquire (through direct learning, identification, and adopting social roles) the attitudes, values, roles, competencies, and ways of perceiving the world that are shared by their family, community, and society. Children and adolescents who are not involved in such socializing relationships become increasingly alienated in that they feel, and are in fact, disconnected from the people and activities in their family, community, and society. It is such alienation that leads to the abusive use of drugs.

There is considerable evidence that our society is in the midst of an alienation crisis caused by the failure of healthy socialization processes to occur in the lives of many of our children and adolescents. Besides the frequent abusive use of drugs, since 1960 juvenile crime has risen twice as fast as that of adults and more than half of all serious crimes (murder, rape, aggravated assault, robbery, burglary, larceny, and motor vehicle theft) in the U.S. are committed by youths aged ten to seventeen (*Time,* July 11, 1977). The frequency with which juveniles are involved in serious crimes increased over 200 per cent between 1964 and 1973. The suicide rate among teenagers has risen more than 250 per cent in the last twenty years, the ratio of illegitimate births per 1,000 live babies has gone up by 300 per cent in the last twenty years, the divorce rate has climbed steadily, and the average verbal and math scores of senior high school students taking the scholastic aptitude examination have steadily declined over the past ten years [23].

There is considerable evidence that the relationships in many families are such that they do not contribute to constructive socialization [14, 23]:

1. Marital disruption usually involves severe stress for children, and the parents of over one million children were involved in divorces in 1975, there have been dramatic increases in the number of mothers deserting their families, and more than 15 per cent of the nation's children live apart from one or both of their natural parents.
2. The amount of time parents spend with their children has direct effects on the quality of socialization that occurs. Over the past twenty years there have been decreases in the number of adults in the home, the amount of time parents (especially fathers) spend with young children, and increases in the percentages of mothers working. Even the increase in TV viewing and the construction of homes that separate children and adults into playrooms and dens or offices contributes to the lack of interaction between adults and children.
3. Abuse from parents increases the alienation of children and adolescents. The incidence of child abuse is rising dramatically and the frequency with which parents kill their children has jumped alarmingly, especially parents killing their teenage children.
4. The number of siblings in the home affects the opportunity for constructive relationships to be developed within the family. There are fewer children in each family now than ever before.
5. Any separation of children and adolescents from the careers of their parents and adult economic roles will increase alienation. Children have fewer opportunities to observe their parents at work or to see adults in economic roles now than has been traditionally the case in the past.

6. The mobility of families reduces the impact of relationships in the neighborhood and limits the influence of the community on socialization.

Over the past thirty years literally thousands of research studies have identified family disorganization as an antecedent to behavior disorders, lack of school achievement, and social pathology in children and adolescents [23]. Bronfrenbrenner believes that we are increasingly living in a society that imposes pressures and priorities that allow neither time nor place for meaningful activities and relations between children and adults, that downgrade the role of parents and the functions of parenthood, and that prevent positive relationships developing between adults and children where in the adult is a guide, friend, and companion to the children [23].

The breakdown of many families and communities as socializing units means that other organized activities (such as education) in children and adolescents' lives assume increased importance. Schools have been gaining in importance as socializing agencies, especially in the way in which learning experiences affect peer relationships. Children and adolescents are spending more time in school than ever before. It is within schools that interaction between students and adults and among students is most structured and most susceptible to influence. Yet the emphasis on interpersonal competition (where students work individually to outperform their peers) and individualistic efforts (where students work alone to meet set criteria) mitigates against the supportive relationships that are vital for constructive socialization. Compared with learning in cooperative groups, competitive and individualistic experiences create negative peer relationships and less positive attitudes toward teachers and other staff members [21, 22].

Many children and teenagers feel isolated, disconnected from their parents and peers, unattached to school and career, without purpose and direction, and lacking any distinct impression of who or what kind of person they are. At home, in school, and in their community, they feel like an alien in their own native land, estranged from themselves, their parents and peers, and the activities (such as school and career) that others of their own age are involved in. They are isolated both by their own feelings of alienation and because of the stress and lack of support and caring present in their family, educational, and community experiences.

THE IMPORTANCE OF PEER RELATIONSHIPS

One of the major roots of drug abuse is the failure of society to socialize its children successfully. Two of the institutions given the responsibility for socializing the younger members of our society are the family and the school. While it is a difficult if not impossible task to rebuild the family structure where it is needed, school practices could be modified relatively easily to promote more positive peer relationships among children and adolescents. The importance of positive peer relationships on healthy social development is frequently underemphasized.

Children and adolescents live in a social world. Quality relationships with other people are absolutely essential for all aspects of development; learning how to fulfill one's needs and potentialities; learning and internalizing the values, attitudes, competencies, and perspectives necessary for competently living within one's society; and avoiding dysfunctional patterns of behavior such as drug abuse. While the importance of parent-child relations on the development of the social and cognitive competencies associated with a lack of drug abuse is often emphasized, much less attention has been given to peer relations—to the child's acquisition of competence in encounters with other children and to the occupation of a comfortable niche within the peer culture. Most often when peer relationships are considered as an influence on drug abuse they are viewed as a subversive influence of the counter-culture that entices children and adolescents into experiences involving the abusive use of drugs. Yet there is considerable evidence that constructive peer relationships [24, 25]:

1. are centrally embedded in the socialization of the child and adolescent, providing models and reinforcement that shapes a wide variety of social behaviors, attitudes, and perspectives;
2. are prognostic indicators of future psychological health;
3. provide the context in which the competencies necessary to modulate aggressive and sexual impulses are acquired;
4. contribute to the development of sex-role identity;
5. influence the acquisition of perspective-taking abilities;
6. influence the acquisition of educational aspirations and achievement;
7. are related to patterns of drug use.

Peer relationships are not luxuries in human development, they are necessities; poor peer relationships in childhood and adolescence is among the most powerful predictors of later social and emotional maladies such as the abusive use of drugs [24].

Peer relationships are constructive when they promote meaningful interdependence; feelings of belonging, acceptance, support, and caring; acquisition of the social skills, roles, and sensitivity required to build and maintain meaningful relationships; the internalization of the values and goals needed for responsible decision-making; self-esteem; and the autonomy needed to resist social pressure to engage in drug abuse. Four of the steps to ensure that peer relationships are a constructive influence on the socialization of children and adolescents and are a preventive influence on drug use patterns are:

1. structure cooperative situations in which children and adolescents work with peers to achieve a common goal;

2. teach the interpersonal and group skills necessary for maintaining interdependent relationships;
3. require that peers hold each other accountable for constructive social behavior; and
4. encourage the development of autonomy.

Each of these steps are discussed below.

COOPERATIVE LEARNING EXPERIENCES

The majority of relationships in relating to peers in school come during instruction. It is while learning reading, math, science, social studies, and other academic subjects that students are placed in proximity to and interaction with peers. The effects of cooperative instructional experiences, compared with competitive and individualistic ones, have been discussed in the previous section on social development and psychological health. The first step in ensuring that peer relationships within school are a constructive influence on socialization and social development is to structure the majority of instructional experiences cooperatively. It is within cooperative situations that students interact with peers, share ideas and resources, give and receive help and support, and facilitate each other's efforts to achieve goals. It is within cooperative situations that friendships are formed and children and adolescents learn to utilize the resources of peers. Cooperative interaction promotes identification based on liking and admiration for superior competence, and the adoption of social roles within the context of completing a task. Without a cooperative context, constructive socialization cannot take place.

A cooperative learning situation exists when students can obtain their learning goals if and only if the other students with whom they are linked obtain their goals [16, 21]. Cooperative learning experiences structure a positive interdependence among students so that they benefit from each other's efforts to achieve. The essence of cooperative learning is assigning a group goal (such as completing a set of math problems, working as a group, and ensuring that all group members understand how to solve each problem), and rewarding all members of the group on the basis of the quality of the group's work according to a fixed set of standards. The teacher establishes a group goal and a criteria-referenced evaluation system, and rewards group members on the basis of their group's performance.

To complete assignments cooperatively, students are required to interact with each other, share ideas and materials, help each other learn, pool their information and resources, use a division of labor when appropriate, integrate each member's contribution into a group product, and facilitate each other's learning. Communication, conflict management, leadership, and trust-building skills become a necessity for basic academic tasks, not as something to suppress until after school. When teachers assign students to heterogeneous groups and assist them in learning the skills needed to work cooperatively, all students (including students who are alienated and isolated) become integrated into constructive, task-oriented, friendship groups. There is consistent evidence, for example, that compared with competitive and individualistic experiences, cooperation promotes greater feelings of acceptance, support, belonging, and caring, as well as higher levels of self-esteem and greater unconditional acceptance of oneself [22]. The specific procedures for teachers to structure, monitor, and evaluate cooperative learning groups are detailed in [21].

TEACHING SOCIAL SKILLS

The interpersonal and group skills necessary for maintaining interdependent relationships must be taught. In a cooperative relationship, whether it is the family or a learning group, children and adolescents need the social skills required for facilitating joint efforts to complete tasks and maintain supportive relationships [26-28]. Social skills are absolutely essential, as they are the keystone to the relationships with peers and adults within which social development and socialization takes place. They are also the keystone to building and maintaining a stable family a successful career, and a stable group of friends. Some of the more important social skills are those involved in communicating, building and maintaining trust, providing leadership, making decisions, and managing conflicts.

Children and adolescents are not born instinctively knowing how to relate to others. And interpersonal and group skills do not magically appear the first time children and adolescents are placed in contact with others. Social skills have to be taught just as purposefully and precisely as typing or reading skills. While many of these skills used to be learned in family and community experiences, many contemporary children and adolescents lack the basic social skills when they begin school. It is within task situations where students are positively interdependent that social skills become most relevant and, therefore, should ideally be taught. Procedures for teaching social skills are detailed in [26, 27, 28].

In learning social skills students may also learn important social roles that directly impact their socialization. Social roles structure interaction within a relationship. In cooperative interaction with peers, the role of "leader" becomes an important social role for children and adolescents to adopt. Being a "friend" may require competence in communicating feelings, building and maintaining trust, and resolving conflicts constructively. While being taught social skills children and adolescents are also adopting social roles that will structure their interaction in certain situations with their peers. And in addition, they are developing sensitivity to how to behave appropriately and in ways that will receive the approval of their peers.

PEER ACCOUNTABILITY

The third step in ensuring that peer relationships are a constructive influence on the socialization of children and adolescents is requiring peers hold each other accountable for appropriate and constructive social behavior. Two of the major benefits from being held accountable by peers for constructive social behavior are learning values and developing self-control [14]. In order to avoid socially dysfunctional behavior such as drug abuse, children and adolescents must internalize a set of values and utilize them in making decisions concerning social behavior; in addition, they must learn to control their impulsive actions.

Values are acquired through a process involving learning a set of rules and behavioral guidelines, being held accountable for following them, and internalizing the rules and behavioral guidelines so that one holds oneself accountable for following them, thus becoming self-responsible. More specifically, the acquisition of values begins when children and adolescents are taught a rule by their peers; "You should provide help and support to other group members when they need it," is an example of a rule. Children and adolescents must then be held accountable for following the rule by peers they like and respect. Through learning a rule and being consistently held accountable for following the rule, children and adolescents learn what is expected of them by others whom they like and respect, learn that failing to comply with the rule will result in its being enforced, and learn that complying with the rule will bring approval from other people whom they like and admire. Rules and behavioral guidelines provide predictability to the world of children and adolescents, thus allowing them to anticipate the consequences of their actions and providing the consistency necessary for planning to fulfill one's needs and achieve one's goals. It is only when rules and behavioral guidelines are consistently enforced, however, that such positive benefits result.

After children and adolescents are taught a rule or behavioral guideline and learn that they will consistently be held accountable for following the rule, the first two steps of acquiring a value are complete. The next step involves identifying with the peers who are enforcing the rule and internalizing it so that one enforces the rule on oneself, thus becoming self-responsible. When a group of supportive and competent peers consistently enforce a rule concerning appropriate social behavior, children and adolescents will identify with their peers, internalize the rule, and begin taking responsibility for their own actions by enforcing the rule on themselves. Thus, while a rule is, in the beginning, imposed by other people who give approval when one follows the rule, the rule becomes internalized into one's own value system and one feels satisfaction and self-approval when one follows it.

All children and adolescents must learn to control impulsive behavior and delay gratification of their immediate needs [14]. Young children tend to be centered on the present and lack the differentiated time perspective necessary for delaying gratification of their impulses; aggressive or sexual impulses are immediately acted upon, for example. The learning to inhibit undesirable behavior requires that children and adolescents develop some capacity to delay acting for immediate gratification, in order to avoid subsequent punishments or to obtain subsequent rewards of greater value than the ones forgone. Socialization involves the learning to control internally those behavior tendencies that potentially threaten the maintenance of relationships, such as unrestrained aggression or sexuality, cheating, deceit, thievery, and the abuse of drugs. It is within their relationships with adults and peers that children and adolescents become convinced to forego their immediate needs in order to avoid punishments and to obtain more valuable rewards in the future. The process for doing so is the same as for the internalization of values. Children and adolescents are given a rule to follow by their peers (such as "do not smoke"), their peers hold them accountable for following the rule, an identification process based on liking and a desire to become more competent occurs, the rule is internalized and self-enforced, and impulsive actions diminish.

ENCOURAGING AUTONOMY

The fourth step in ensuring that peer relationships are a constructive influence on the socialization of children and adolescents is through encouraging autonomy within each individual. Every child and adolescent ideally would both internalize a set of values to guide decision-making and acquire the social sensitivity to understand how to respond appropriately to the expectations of others and to the situational circumstances within which they find themselves [14]. *Autonomy* is the ability to understand what is expected from others within any given situation and to be free to choose whether or not to meet the expectations and situational requirements. It is derived from the internalization of values and the acquisition of social skills and sensitivity. And when one is under pressure to engage in dysfunctional social actions such as the abuse of drugs, it includes the ability to seek out peers who will support one's decisions concerning appropriate social behavior. To understand autonomy and how it is encouraged in children and adolescents, it is helpful to review inner-directedness, other-directedness, and the role of social support in independence from social pressure [29].

In discussing autonomy it is important to differentiate between the inner-directed and the other-directed person [29]. The inner-directed person appears to have incorporated a psychic "gyroscope" that is started by parental influences and is further influenced by other authority figures. *Inner-directed* people incorporate a small number of values and principles early in life which they rigidly adhere to in making decisions concerning appropriate social behavior. Other people, situational circumstances, and other external influences do not affect their decisions. *Other-directed* people receive guidance from others and are directed by whomever they are with. Approval from others becomes their highest goal, and they tend to invest all power in the actual or imaginary approving group. Insuring constant acceptance and pleasing others becomes their primary method of relating. Past learning, values, previous behavior, and other internal influences do not affect their decisions. Most alienated and drug-abusing children and adolescents tend to be other-directed in regard to their peers.

Autonomous people are independent of both extreme inner- and other-directedness. They have liberated themselves from rigid adherence to parental values or to social pressures and social expectancies. When making decisions concerning appropriate social behavior, autonomous people tend to consider both their internal values and the situational circumstances, and respond in flexible and appropriate ways. Autonomous people are free to choose a course of action based on their values, the situational social pressures and expectations, or a combination of both.

Without dynamic, flexible, and internalized values a person cannot be autonomous. The development of such a value system in children and adolescents who are alienated from their families depends on their being placed in cooperatively structured learning situations in which there is a high degree of peer accountability for appropriate social behavior. Without the ability to sense and meet the expectations of other people within a given situation, a person cannot be autonomous. The development of social sensitivity depends on accumulated social experience in which there is an emphasis on learning the social skills and competencies needed to ensure the achievement of joint goals and the maintenance of cooperative relationships.

When children or adolescents find themselves in a situation in which peers are pressuring them to use drugs in abusive ways, they need the autonomy to resist successfully. A vital aspect of an autonomous decision in such a situation is the ability to seek out peers who also resist social pressures to engage in dysfunctional behavior such as drug abuse. Especially when children and adolescents are members of multiple peer groups, pressures to use drugs in abusive ways within one peer group can be countered by adhering to the expectations of another peer group that one would not engage in such behavior. Awareness of another person or persons who hold values or make judgments that agree with one's own is a powerful liberator from conforming to the expectations of others [30]. Teaching students to seek out social support for resistance to inappropriate peer pressure facilitates the development of autonomy.

CONSTRUCTIVE PEER RELATIONSHIPS

Within instructional situations peer relationships can be structured to create meaningful interdependence through learning cooperatively with peers. Within cooperative learning situations students experience feelings of belonging, acceptance, support, and caring and the social skills and social roles required for maintaining interdependent relationships can be taught and practiced. Through repeated cooperative experiences students can develop the social sensitivity of what behavior is expected from others and the actual skills to meet such expectations if they wish to. Through holding each other accountable for appropriate social behavior students can greatly influence the values they internalize and the self-control they develop. It is through belonging to a series of interdependent relationships that values are learned and internalized and social sensitivity and autonomy are developed. And it is through prolonged cooperative interaction with other people that healthy social development with the overall balance of trust rather than distrust of other people, the ability to view situations and problems from a variety of perspectives, a meaningful sense of direction and purpose in life, an awareness of mutual interdependence with others, and an integrated and coherent sense of personal identity, takes place.

SUMMARY

A major strategy for preventing the abusive use of drugs by children and adolescents is socializing them into the social competencies necessary for psychological health and responsible decision-making about the use of drugs. Such socialization is achieved through direct learning, identification based on love and admiration for superior competence, and the adoption of social roles within meaningfully interdependent relationships with adults, older and younger children, and peers. It is within such relationships that socialization into an overall balance of trust rather than distrust toward other people, the ability to view situations and problems from a variety of perspectives, a meaningful sense of direction and purpose in life, an awareness of mutual interdependence with others, and an integrated and coherent sense of personal identity takes place. While adult-child relationships have long been emphasized, there is increasing evidence that constructive peer relationships are a necessity for successful socialization. There are two major settings in which socialization occurs—the family and the school. Since the children and adolescents most in need of constructive socializing experiences come from stressful, abusive, or indifferent families, the most promising avenue of intervention is within the school, maximizing the constructiveness of peer relationships. This may be done through structuring the majority of learning experiences cooperatively so that students will work jointly to achieve mutual goals and be meaningfully interdependent in task situations. What results from such experiences are feelings of belonging, acceptance, support, and caring; acquisition of social skills, roles, and sensitivity; peer accountability for appropriate and constructive social behavior with its resulting internalization of values and development of self-control; and the gaining of the autonomy necessary to resist social pressure to engage in socially dysfunctional behaviors such as drug abuse.

REFERENCES

1. R. Blum, et al., *Society and Drugs,* Jossey-Bass, San Francisco, 1969.
2. G. Braucht, D. Brakarsh, F. Gollingstad, and K. Berry, Deviant Drug Use in Adolescence: A Review of Psychosocial Correlates, *Psychological Bulletin, 79,* pp. 92-106, 1973.
3. J. Cornacchia, D. Bentel, and D. Smith, *Drugs in the Classroom,* Musby, St. Louis, 1973.
4. D. W. Johnson, Cooperative Competencies and the Prevention and Treatment of Drug Abuse, *Research in Education, 11,* Eric Number ED 108066, 1975.
5. R. Jessor, Predicting Time of Onset of Marihuana Use: A Developmental Student of High School Youth, *Predicting Adolescent Drug Abuse,* D. Lettieri, (Ed.), National Institute on Drug Abuse, Washington, D.C., 1975.
6. S. Pittell, *Drug Abuse Treatment Referral System,* Contemporary Problem Consultants, Inc., San Francisco, 1971a.
7. ______, Drugs and the Adolescent Experience, *Journal of Drug Issues, 7,* 1971b.
8. H. Becker, Marihuana Use and the Social Context, *Social Problems, 3,* pp. 35-44, 1955.
9. E. Goode, *The Marihuana Smokers,* Basic Books, New York, 1970.
10. B. Johnson, *Marihuana Users and Drug Subcultures,* Wiley, New York, 1973.
11. L. Johnston, *Drugs and American Youth,* Institute for Social Research, Ann Arbor, Michigan, 1973.
12. E. Josephson, Trends in Adolescent Marijuana Use, *Drug Use: Epidemilogical and Sociological Approaches,* E. Josephson and E. Carroll, (Eds.), Haldsted-Wiley, New York, pp. 177-205, 1974.
13. D. Kandel, Some Comments on the Relationship of Selected Criteria Variables to Adolescent Illicit Drug Use, *Predicting Adolescent Drug Abuse,* D. Lettieri, (Ed.), National Institute on Drug Abuse, Washington, D.C., 1975.
14. D. W. Johnson, *Educational Psychology,* Prentice-Hall, Englewood Cliffs, N.J., 1979.
15. D. W. Johnson, and R. Matross, The Interpersonal Influence of the Psychotherapist, *Effective Psychotherapy: A Handbook of Research,* A. Gurman and A. Raxin, (Eds.), Pergamon Press, New York, pp. 395-432, 1977.
16. M. Deutsch, Cooperation and Trust: Some Theoretical Notes, *Nebraska Symposium on Motivation,* M. Jones, (Ed.), University of Nebraska Press, Lincoln, Nebraska, pp. 275-320, 1962.
17. E. Erikson, *Childhood and Society,* Norton, New York, 1950.
18. S. Freud, Introductory Lectures on Psychoanalysis (1916-1917), *Standard Edition of the Complete Psychological Works of Sigmund Freud, 15 and 16,* J. Strachey, (Ed.), Hogarth Press, London, 1963.
19. L. Kohlberg, Stage and Sequence: The Cognitive-Developmental Approach to Socialization, *Handbook of Socialization Theory and Research,* D. Goslin, (Ed.), Rand-McNally, Chicago, pp. 347-480, 1969.
20. L. Breger, *From Instinct to Identity,* Prentice-Hall, Englewood Cliffs, New Jersey, 1974.

21. D. W. Johnson, and R. Johnson, *Learning Together and Alone: Cooperation, Competition, and Individualization,* Prentice-Hall, Englewood Cliffs, New Jersey, 1975.
22. D. W. Johnson, and R. Johnson, Social Interdependence in the Classroom: Cooperation, Competition, and Individualism, *Journal of Research and Development in Education, 12,* Special Issue, Fall, 1978.
23. U. Bronfenbrenner, Who Cares for America's Children, *The Family–Can It Be Saved?,* V. Vaughan and T. Brazelton, (Eds.), Year Book Medical Publishers, New York, pp. 3-32, 1976.
24. W. Hartup, Peer Interaction and the Behavioral Development of the Individual Child, *Psychopathology and Child Development,* E. Schopler and R. Reichler, (Eds.), Plenum, New York, 1976.
25. D. W. Johnson, Group Processes: Influences of Student-Student Interaction on School Outcomes, *The Social Psychology of School Learning,* J. McMillan, (Ed.), Academic Press, New York, 1980.
26. ______, *Reaching Out: Interpersonal Effectiveness and Self-Actualization,* Prentice-Hall, Englewood Cliffs, New Jersey, 1972.
27. ______, *Human Relations and Your Career: A Guide to Interpersonal Skills,* Prentice-Hall, Englewood Cliffs, New Jersey, 1978.
28. D. W. Johnson, and F. Johnson, *Joining Together: Group Theory and Group Skills,* Prentice-Hall, Englewood Cliffs, New Jersey, 1975.
29. D. W. Johnson, *Contemporary Social Psychology,* Lippincott, Philadelphia, 1973.
30. V. Allen, Social Support for Nonconformity, *Advances in Experimental Social Psychology, 8,* L. Berkowitz, (Ed.), Academic Press, New York, pp. 2-43, 1975.

CHAPTER 3

An Approach to Primary Prevention of Drug Abuse Among Children and Youth-Parental Influence

SEYMOUR EISEMAN

To seek uniform answers to questions about individual drug-related behavior is an unrealistic goal. For each youngster taking the "drug route" there are an infinite variety of variables, such as personal motivation for using drugs, and beliefs held concerning the personal short and long range psychological and physiological effects of drugs on himself (herself) and society. These variables are complex and individually unique. Behavioral scientists have claimed that "we must keep constantly in mind that individual behavior is determined by *his* motives and by *his* beliefs regardless of whether the motives and beliefs correspond to our notion of reality or our own notion of what is good for him [1]." If one accepts this hypothesis, then surely the foundation(s) upon which each person perceives his world of reality, becomes central to the concept of parental influence and effectiveness in directing the basic behavior patterns of their child(ren).

Parents have always exerted strong influences on the behavior of their child(ren). Such influence can be described by a variety of terms, e.g., example, pressure, threats as well as rewards, and can be traced back to the days of early childhood. Ostensibly, such influence cannot be discounted nor ignored during a child's formative years when decision-making about specific behaviors becomes vital to *normal* development. It is safe to speculate that each parent is deeply concerned about the kinds of decisions that their child(ren) may arrive at, pertaining to the use of drugs as *the* way of coping with the responsibilities of daily living.

Hopes, wishes, fear, and even worry will do little if nothing at all to stem the tide of drug-related behavior among children and youth of school age.

Perhaps parents in the United States today are a viable source of influence in directing young people away from drug use. This influence, however, has been questioned and subject to serious doubt. On the other hand, mothers and fathers may not have lost their potency to direct behavior of their children, but are in a temporary state of *paralytic hysteria*, unable to cope with, understand, nor take appropriate steps toward preventing such situations from occurring initially.

Selected Reasons for Drug Use Among Children and Youth

Many writers in the fields of medicine and psychology have attempted to explain the etiology of drug-directed and drug-related behavior among the younger members of the population in this country. Brotman [2] suggested that drug use may be fashionable among certain peer groups. He further suggested that drug use might be a developmental phase in the life of the user. Ausubel [3] stated that the drug user may be "motivationally immature." Another writer inferred that one's socio-economic status and minority background was correlated to drug use [4]. Bruyn [5] wrote that "the so-called permissive era has resulted in a generation of young people who have no experience with controls and regulations and who also have witnessed the hypocrisy of the adult world and its attitude toward alcohol and other mind-altering drugs." "Marijuana smoking" according to Smith [6] "among a majority of teenagers is interwoven into their daily rounds of activities. It is but one facet of adolescent style that emphasized clothes, music, friendship, sexuality, freedom from restraint, and violence." Halleck [7] felt that drug abuse among college students may be the result of "unwillingness to conform to adult standards, basic mistrust of the adult over-thirty population." The college student, said Halleck "demands instant gratification of his impulses and is not satisfied to accept the restrictions placed on him by society."

Naturally, one must acknowledge the existence of causes other than those stated which may be contributory to obtaining mental and/or physical gratification from the use of drugs. Examples of such variables as, *peer pressure*, *religious meanings*, and *mind expansion* may be the factors which affect one's decision to use specific chemical substances. It is acknowledged that the use of specific drugs, e.g., CNS stimulants, CNS depressants, and the variety of hallucinogens may be representative of a wide range of motivational responses among specific as well as general segments of the pre-adolescent and adolescent population in this country today.

Perhaps the aforestated explanations can provide clues about "drug behavior" from which further research studies can be designed to shed additional light on *why* young people employ a variety of drugs in the general categories stated previously.

It is not the intention of this paper to place blame on those parents whose children are chronic drug users. It would be highly presumptious to suggest that parents alone are the culprits, causing their child(ren) to abuse drugs.

Realistically, we live in a drug-oriented society. This orientation, unfortunately, is not coupled with an awareness of the benefits to mankind which specific drugs under special circumstances can provide, nor the inherent dangers to life and health when the same drugs are utilized improperly or not supervised adequately by trained professionals.

It is rather pointless to offer broad-based explanations *why* a youngster of school age uses drugs, particularly *after* he has started. The terms *experimentation*, *alienation*, *rebellion*, *thrill-seeking*, *peer pressure(s)*, *euphoria*, *mind expansion* and a host of other terms seem inadequate for those parents who wish to influence their child(ren) against the use of chemical substances which have the ability to alter the *regular* functioning of mental and physical processes.

There aren't any "pat" answers to the question of this highly complex behavior of children and youth. Some of the intervening variables have been identified. The determinants of drug-related behavior as stated above are highly individual and unique.

At this point in time we seem to be offering fragmented approaches to prevent, control or even minimize the incidence of drug use among children and youth in schools today. This is in reference to the kinds of educational programs offered in schools as one way of affecting decisions about drug use. Psychiatric services and psychological counseling are available to families of children who are so involved. Law enforcement officials tend to approach the problem *after* laws have been broken. Social workers see youngsters *after* they are in trouble. Parents, on the other hand are in a position to "fertilize the soil" before any "seeds" are planted.

Possibly all that is required for some parents are guidelines for developing and implementing personal programs of primary prevention as a way of influencing their children to decide against the use of drugs as a lifestyle.

Guidelines for Parents

DEVELOPING DECISION-MAKING SKILLS AMONG CHILDREN

Decision-making by children should not be misinterpreted to imply an abrogation of parental responsibility and obligation to decide anything more for their children [8]. A skillful parent can and should allow children to arrive at decisions for themselves, those which are within their area of competency to make. For example, a five year old *can* choose whether he will eat or how much he will eat of a particular food offered him by his parent. Should the child fail to choose wisely, he will, no doubt, experience the outcome of his decision and then later might choose an alternate approach at the next meal. In this way the child can learn from his experience. On the other hand, it would seem foolhardy for a parent to grant the child the privilege of a decision to cross the street in a traffic congested area.

It is inconceivable that one can accept the notion that a child who is denied the opportunity to participate in decision-making will be prepared adequately to make the kinds of decisions as an adult can in a mentally healthy fashion.

Adolescents cannot be expected to have the skills necessary to weigh alternatives with regard to the advisability or inadvisability of drug abuse if such opportunities to weigh alternatives were denied him in the earlier years of development. The concept of decision-making is not uniform at all age levels. If we can envision a confined area within which the child can function freely without causing harm to himself or others, then decisions within this area of restriction will offer a realistic basis for further decision-making in a less restricted environment. As a child matures physically and psychologically he should be capable of building on his previous experiences.

Decision-making skills cannot be conferred on children by parents. It is a *threatened* parent who would deny his child the opportunity to acquire this all-important component of the maturational process. A child's mental health, according to authorities in the mental health field "is influenced and determined by all that goes into his existence [9]."

Logically, it might follow that the concept of "motivational immaturity" as stated by Ausubel [3] can be prevented if and when children are encouraged to make decisions for themselves as a normal function of the maturational process. Parents must decide for themselves which behaviors their children can make decisions about as individuals. Coupled with the decision-making process is the responsibility factor which accompanies the outcome of the decision itself. Parents should be aware that being too restrictive or too permissive will negate the effects of such a process.

GIVING AND RECEIVING LOVE

Parental love is a qualitative phenomenon. It is an emotion which is without qualification nor condition. To love a child conditionally is not the foundation upon which healthy parent-child relationships are built. One can only learn to give love or feel loved when one has himself been the recipient of such love. Thus feelings of security are engendered by a significant adult and is essential to good mental health.

A "loving" situation cannot be started during the child's formative years. It must be initiated and sensed by the child from birth on. Conversely, parents must not allow themselves to be placed in the awkward position of allowing their child's love to be conditional, and expect positive outcomes of such behavior. Particular meaning attached to the term *love* will vary from parent to parent. For example, if parents do not wish their child(ren) to use drugs, such regulatory messages must be physical and/or psychologic harm and distress. Total permissiveness is not an accurate indicator of parental love. Youngsters might consider permissiveness as a sign of emotional immaturity or apathy on the part of the parent. Love can be demonstrated or projected in non-verbal or verbal fashion. Parents and children *feel* this qualitative phenomenon. As such, children need not employ drugs of any kind to find this pleasurable feeling of being loved and wanted.

CREATING A POSITIVE SELF-IMAGE

Parents project self-images to their children. A feeling about oneself can be, and often is transmitted by a significant adult. Here again, the communicative process can be verbal or non-verbal. Judd felt that "the basic tasks of the adolescent is to develop a "positive self-image [10]." This writer is of the opinion that the positive self-image is akin to a positive level of self-confidence. Because parents are the significant adults in the early lives of most children, it would follow that the impression(s) created by parents for their children can serve as the foundation upon which the "image" is created. Role expectations established by cultural and familial norms are usually transmitted from parent to child. Role performances, especially in families are subject to critical review by one or both of the significant adults. Thus the process must commence early in a child's life. In some instances the significant adult may well be an adult other than the biological parents. Hence the perceived attitude of adults by children becomes the focal point about which one's self-esteem can be developed.

During moments and even periods of frustration, parents often assume the role of *predictor analyst*. For example, a father or mother who communicates to a son or daughter that "you are no good, and will never amount to anything" in one sense is actually predicting the direction the youngster's life will be taking. Although parents may have been attempting to influence a particular behavior by their children, the perceived message may have taken on a meaning for the child other than that which was intended in the original message offered by the parent(s). Possibly a youngster may attempt to live up to the predicted image created by his or her unwitting parent and turn to drugs as a primary lifestyle. Conversely, the use of drugs by children and youth may be an attempt to conceal the reality of the "predicted direction" provided by the parent(s) during an earlier period of maturation. Informing an adolescent that what was said or inferred for any number of years was said in jest or "for your own good" does nothing more than create an exercise in frustration for both parents and children.

CARING—PERCEIVED AND DEMONSTRATED

The extent to which children perceive their parents as caring about them is best characterized by an educator who wrote as follows, "while children appreciate parents who set rules and limits, they do not care for parents who are overly strict or overly lenient. Children interpret such extreme behavior, and rightly, as parents who do not care about them [11]."

One dilemma in setting behavior limits is in the ability to find a comfortable middle ground from which to function as an "effective parent." The acceptable limits set by one or both parents vary considerably from family to family and even within families. Parents might be well advised to establish clearly defined lines of demarcation for expected and acceptable behavior by their children. For example, of parents do not wish their child(ren) to use drugs, such regulatory messages must be given early and clearly in the developmental years so that no doubt is left in the mind of the youngster receiving such messages. The communication process will vary, no doubt, e.g., casual conversation among parents with their child(ren) present, or indirect messages with facial expressions being interpreted.

Caring, coupled with the concept of love is an interchangeable phenomenon. Surely one who is capable of giving love is most capable of caring about himself and others. Thus the transference of "caring behavior" is a variable which is difficult, if not impossible, to measure in a quantitative manner. However, there are moments in time when a child may consider the quality of caring in quantitative terms. This is best characterized by the youngster who is caught by the police for using or selling one or more kinds of drugs. The child might expect his parents to be "cool" about it. Children can sense the "caring phenomenon" when parents will stand by their children even though the parent(s) might not agree with the outcome of such drug-related behavior. Probably one of the most difficult tasks parents will face is the task of supporting their child(ren) without supporting nor condoning the act itself. Offspring might tend to reject this concept of caring, but eventually will concede that caring is not synonymous with "giving in" to emotional wishes of their children. Caring for one's child does not mean abrogation of parental responsibility for the welfare of the child(ren).

POSSESSING ACCURATE KNOWLEDGE ABOUT DRUGS

Information becomes knowledge when the information itself is synthesized and internalized by both parent and child in order to modify the existing behavior of such persons. Too often, parents and children exchange different levels of ignorance rather than accurate information about drugs. The credibility gap between youngsters and parents can be bridged by information which is understood and acknowledged by both parties to be accurate, and from which wise decisions can be made. Instead, we see an emotional chasm being widened as a result of failure to seek out the "truth." Myths, stereotypes, and half-truths held by both parents and children do little if anything to establish credibility among parties concerned.

Naturally, cultural beliefs will cloud the acceptability of scientific data. Regardless of these basic differences, facts about drugs per se, remain unchanged. Facts must not be clouded to meet the emotional needs of both parents and children. It would behoove parents and children to read and study as much as they can about drugs and their effects on the human body as well as their collective effects on society. Clearly this attempt to gather accurate data together can change the attitudes of parents and youngsters toward drugs. One fact does remain clear, there doesn't seem to be a preponderance of evidence that the existing mode of dealing with inaccurate or no information is any more successful than what was offered as an alternative. Indeed, the panacea will be attained when both parents and children can respect each other while disagreeing with one another. Accurate information can serve as a cementing factor to a potentially destructive relationship between parent and child(ren).

What Does the Future Hold?

The use of drugs in our society today is a source of continuous concern to many, if not all people, young and old alike. Patterns of drug abuse have been traced throughout recorded history. With all the available knowledge, technical know-how, and scientific discoveries we have yet to understand the nature of individual choices with regard to drug-related behavior. Certainly the future cannot be foretold. The extent to which young people will choose between the use of drugs as a way of life and the abstinence therefrom is difficult if not impossible to predict.

There is a world of difference between playing at living and living itself.

Parents cannot protect their children against all the frustrations attendant on growing and developing as human organisms. The path that life will take for each person may not always be a smooth one. This concept was best stated by Maslow [12] who wrote the following,

> growth has not only rewards and pleasures but also many intrinsic pains and always will have. Each step forward is a step into the unfamiliar and is possibly dangerous. It also means giving up something familiar and good and satisfying . . . It often means giving up a simple and easier and less effortful life, in exchange for a more demanding, more responsible, more difficult life. Growth forward *is in spite* of these and therefore requires courage, will, choice and strength in the individual, as well as protection, permission and encouragement from the environment, especially for the child.

Summary

To the parents of the present and the future, the guidelines for effective parent-child relationships are offered as one of many possible ways by which children can be influenced to avoid drugs as a way of life. The concept of such guidelines is subject to review, acceptance, rejection, or even modification by concerned parents. The pathways are rocky and somewhat dangerously uncertain, however the potency of the family has not been reduced to a state of sterility. Time, patience, courage, and determination may be those ingredients vital as a successful catalyst to the positive future of our nation's children and youth.

REFERENCES

1. Irwin M. Rosentock, Godfrey M. Hochbaum, and S. Stephen Kegeles, "Determinants of Health Behavior," p. 2, Golden Anniversary White House Conference on Youth, Washington, D.C. (mimeograph).
2. Richard M. Brotman, Ph.D., "Drug Abuse: The Dilema of the Criminal Sick Hypothesis, *in* Perry Black (ed), *Drugs and the Brain*, pp. 371-377, Johns Hopkins Press, Baltimore, Md., 1969.
3. David P. Ausubel, *Drug Addiction: Physiological, Psychological and Sociological Aspects*, p. 41, Random House, New York, 1958-1968.
4. George E. Vaillant, Parent-child cultural disparity and drug addiction, *Journal of Nervous and Mental Diseases*, 142(6): 534-39, 1967.
5. Henry B. Bruyn, M.D., Drugs on the college campus, *Journal of School Health*, p. 93, February, 1970.
6. Roger C. Smith, "U.S. Marijuana Legislation and the Creation of a Social Problem," in David E. Smith (ed.), *The New Social Drug*, pp. 115-16, Prentice-Hall, Inc., Englewood Cliffs, N.J., 1970.
7. Seymour L. Halleck, The roots of student despair, *THINK*, IBM publication, Vol. 33(2): 21-24, 1967.
8. E. James Anthony, "The Reactions of Parents to Adolescents and Their Behavior," *in* E. James Anthony, M.D. and Therese Benedek, M.D. (ed's.), *Parenthood Its Psychology and Psychopathology*, pp. 307-8, Little, Brown and Co., Boston, 1970.
9. Report of the Joint Commission on Mental Health of Children, *Crisis in Mental Health*, p. 139, Harper and Row, New York, 1970.
10. Lewis L. Judd, M.D., "The Normal Psychological Development of the American Adolescent" *California Medicine*, Vol. 107, pp. 466, Dec. 1967.
11. David Elkind, *A Sympathetic Understanding of the Child Six to Sixteen*, p. 24, Allyn & Bacon Co., Boston, 1971.
12. Abraham H. Maslow, *Toward a Psychology of Being*, (second edition), p. 204, Van Nostrand Reinhold Co., New York, 1968.

CHAPTER 4
Education about Narcotics and Dangerous Drugs — A Challenge to Our Schools

SEYMOUR EISEMAN

Introduction

Never before in the history of this nation's schools have we been faced with the problem of open drug use by students, both in and out of class. It is difficult if not impossible to assess the extent of this drug use activity with any degree of certainty. Attempts by individual schools or school districts to determine the actual numbers of students involved in drug use can only be estimated. There are few empiric data to support estimates of student drug use that can provide clues to the questions "who?" and/or "how many?" Allegations that from sixteen to thirty or more per cent of students are using drugs have been heard from a variety of sources, but these allegations are without supportive evidence. One can only hope that for each student engaged in drug activity, there are many more who have decided against using drugs as a way of facing life and its problems. The question now before us is, how can the school, as an agent of society, assist in preventing this problem from reaching epidemic proportions.

The Role of the School

Our schools are charged with the responsibility for helping students to arrive at wise decisions about matters pertaining to their immediate and future welfare. In one sense, these decisions can have positive or negative consequences with regard to the ultimate welfare of our society. Those *forces* that have an effect on the lives of youngsters today may well be observed in changes in cultural modes of living in the years to come. Hence, a commitment to this idea by our schools will serve to acknowledge the potential impact that daily living has in store for all persons, teachers, and students alike. As a social institution, the school cannot afford to isolate itself from the mainstream of individual, family, or community life. The health problems of all people become the central issues which the school is committed to solve through the process of education. Consequently, education *per se* must hold a deeper meaning for each person than the acquisition of cognitive skills. Facts alone do not modify one's behavior. Possession of information alone is self-defeating to the central purposes of education.[1] *Real* meaning allows for a personal commitment to modify one's behavior, and is more easily attainable through the process of active inquiry.[2]

The extent to which education becomes an efficient tool for society, rests in the personal meaning(s) that each individual perceives for himself. "Each child," wrote Gilchrist and Snygg, "must be given the opportunity to develop to his greatest potential, not only to increase his own success and happiness, but to also make possible his optimal contribution to the society of which he is a part."[3] Hence, the goals of education must be directed toward optimal individual growth and development. The direction that education must take to prevent narcotic and dangerous drug use by students is clear. Students must be prepared to recognize, face, and hopefully, cope with those particular challenges that are common for all human beings. They must be given the opportunity to investigate, analyze, and evaluate which attitudes and/or alternatives available to them are necessary to face life without resorting to the chemical substances used by many, as *the* way of solving problems.

However, before the school can work toward developing sound educational programs of prevention, acknowledgement of the problem must be forthcoming. No longer can school administrators smugly reject the possibility that a drug use problem is present in and around school grounds. The questions now facing the school administrator is, "What can be done to prevent or even control the existing problem?" No one can afford to live with an *ostrich-like* attitude about the presence of a contagious disease bordering on epidemic proportions. It would be wonderful if this disease had a known etiology, for then a vaccine could be developed, produced and utilized in a program of mass immunization. Unfortunately, such a vaccine does not exist in fluid or solid states. But the *vaccine* of education does contain all the necessary ingredients for successful results. These ingredients include such items as *thought*, *inquiry*, *analysis*, *evaluation*, and *decision-making*.

Health education classes, with realistic and dynamic programs of instruction can serve as effective deterrents to drug use by students. In the effective health education setting, decisions can be made by young people to live their lives in a satisfying manner without employing *synthetics* as a mode of life.

One could argue that experimentation with drugs is a reflection of youth's natural curiosity about things they have not experienced before. This is a weak excuse to explain away the actions of the curious person(s), especially where drugs are involved. The "curiosity syndrome" is an unacceptable rationalization. How many younger and older persons alike would risk placing their fingers into an open wall socket, knowing full well that strong currents of electricity await the curious. Certainly no one would attempt such a foolhardy act merely to satisfy a whim. If one youngster is involved in the act of "placing a finger into the wall socket," isn't this enough to warrant some educational program for the prevention of such acts by others? Who, among the parents of children in school today, teachers notwithstanding, can lay claim to the knowledge that their children are *not* the ones to whom educational programs are directed? Providing instruction about narcotics and dangerous drugs in the health education setting is likely to be as effective as the quality of instruction by individual teachers. Together with a determined attitude by all school personnel, an *all* school instruction program can augment the efforts of the health education program in a most effective fashion. Yet it should be realized that any educational program directed at controlling and preventing narcotic and dangerous drug use, will be as effective and meaningful as students, teachers, and administrators wish it to be.

An Approach to Planning a Program of Prevention

Close cooperation and planning are essential to a well-designed program of prevention. Administrators must be willing to give the necessary time for planning and working, while teachers must be willing to take the time to plan and work in their own individual areas of instruction, e.g., Health Education, Business Education, Home Economics, English, Languages, Mathematics, Art, Drama, Physical Education, Music and so on. When all school personnel, together with students, are willing to expend their energies as one unified body of concerned citizens, the initial step toward active inquiry has been taken.

The variables attendant on designing and implementing a short-term program for the prevention of narcotic and dangerous drug use are complex and varied in nature. A well-planned program reflects the kinds of objectives that have been set forth by those persons planning the program. These objectives must also reflect the kinds of behavior to be modified as a result of the program and measured insofar as attainment of the stated objectives are concerned. An example of program objectives and evaluation is offered as a guideline to program development (Figure 1). Evaluation is a process for assessing the extent to which each objective is attained at each level. This process serves to determine points of intervention at specific levels for the clarification and re-organization of specific objective levels.

The Instructional Program

The following list suggests a variety of content resources for planning a program within an existing curriculum framework

- *Art*—approaches to visual communication: a study of color perception affected by drugs
- *Business*—the economics of a drug manufacturing program: the cost of drug use and abuse to society in terms of

Program Objectives	*Evaluative Criteria*
Commitment by students not to experiment with, or use narcotic or dangerous drugs as ways of seeking solutions to the problems of everyday living.	Action programs initiated by students against the use of narcotic or dangerous drugs with a concomitant reduction in the use of these substances.
An increase in the levels of knowledge about narcotic and other drugs held by members of the student body.	Increases in test scores as demonstrated in the pre-test minus post-test scores.
Develop a program of instruction directed at preventing narcotics or dangerous drug use by students.	Implementation of the instructional program about the effects of narcotic and other drug use, utilizing all instructional areas in the school curriculum.
Student commitment to assist in identifying specific areas for further instruction in each of the instructional areas in the school curriculum.	Utilization of those areas identified by students for inclusion in the instructional program.
Faculty participation in developing a program of instruction within individual subject areas as it pertains to preventing narcotic or dangerous drug use by students in school.	Faculty-developed program of instruction to be conducted as part of the total curricular pattern of instruction.
To increase levels of knowledge about narcotic and dangerous drugs held by teachers and administrators alike.	Active participation by teachers and administrators in an in-service program about narcotics and drugs.
Active cooperation from school administrator by providing the time and school facilities from the instructional program for the development and implementation of an educational program directed at preventing the use of narcotic and other drugs by members of the student body.	Acceptance of the idea for an educational program, and provision of the necessary time and facilities for the development and implementation of the instructional program.

Figure 1. Example of program objectives and evaluative criteria for an educational program about narcotic and dangerous drug use.

dollars lost due to absenteeism, manpower needs: the cost of maintaining services and facilities for cure and rehabilitation of the drug dependent person

- *Driver Education and Training*—the effects of drugs: the skills required for safe driving
- *English*—a review and analysis of written articles about the effects of drugs on man and society: discussion(s) about authors who used drugs and their writings
- *Health Education*—a study of the behavioral components of drug use by people: physiological effects of drugs on the human body: the effect of drug use on society as it pertains to the total health and welfare of a community: coping with problems of daily living with an analysis of available alternatives to living without resorting to drugs as a way of facing life
- *Home Economics*—a study of the effect(s) that drug use may have on the structure of a family
- *Music*—an analysis of sound(s) perception and musical skills: the effect(s) of drugs regarding music appreciation and communication
- *Physical Education*—the effects of drugs on motor skills and motor performance
- *Science(s)*—a study of the chemical properties of selected drugs: their effect on plant and animal life
- *Social Studies*—a study of social trends, population mobility and changing value systems as factors in drug use in a population: an analysis of legislative patterns dealing with the problem: suggestions for action by different levels of government

Suggested Procedures for Initiating the Educational Program

The following procedures are offered as a guideline for initiating the first steps in program development.

1. School administrator(s) develop a point of view that reflects the philosophy of the school and can serve as a guide for the development of program objectives: to hold a faculty meeting and approach the topic of an all-school program of education directed at preventing drug use by students

2. School principal to meet with all department chairmen to seek ways by which each instructional area in the school curriculum can contribute effectively to the development and implementation of the program
3. Department chairman to meet with teachers in their respective departments to explore ways to utilize group and individual competencies for a successful instructional program
4. Student committees to work with teachers to identify each instruction area that can serve as an information source
5. Plan and develop a program of in-service training for teachers and administrators in the area of narcotics and dangerous drugs
6. Implement the all-school instructional program.

Evaluation

The attainment of objectives is central to any program in the educational setting. "The measure of success," wrote Knutson, "is how well it achieves its intended purpose. This principle applies no matter what the purpose, whether it is to raise curiosity, to inform, or to produce action."[4] In Figure 1, the stated objectives are accompanied by specific evaluative criteria. The final assessment of the program's effectiveness can be found in the measurable changes in the behavior of those students participating in the program. To this extent, one might consider the feasibility of two overall objectives of the program. The first is to increase the levels of knowledge about narcotics and other dangerous drugs held by students following the instructional program. The second objective is concerned with the kinds of decisions that students might make with regard to either experimental or committed drug use. The first objective could be evaluated by developing and administering a pre-test of knowledge about narcotics and other dangerous drugs, with questions drawn from all the instructional areas of the all-school program. Following the instruction program, a post-test could be administered, and the results quantified. With respect to the second objective, the procedures for evaluation become uncertain and difficult. Here the qualitative behavioral results are more important than the quantified results of knowledge tests. Counseling students on an individual or group basis could provide one source of evaluation for student decision-making. From this counseling program, information about socio-economic factors as well as demographic data can be obtained for future planning of programs related to student needs. Parent-teacher meetings could also give clues to the effectiveness of the instruction program on student attitudes and behavior. A positive quantitative and qualitative analysis offers hope for the educational process as the positive affector of wise decision-making by both students and teachers alike.

Summary

The school as one of the oldest social institutions is in a position to help young people to find positive direction for their lives. Personal meaning is more emphatic when students can inquire actively and participate in programs that affect their personal lives. Students can be counted on to make wise decisions about matters that affect them directly or indirectly when they find the *truth* for and by themselves. Should the school fail to accept the responsibility and the challenge for this direction, then certainly it will be the educators who must shoulder the responsibility for shortsightedness and for lack of courage to face social problems in a realistic manner.

REFERENCES

1. Educational Policies Commission. *The Central Purposes of Education.* Washington, D.C.: The National Education Association, 1961.
2. Seymour Eiseman, "An Approach for Student Involvement in Health Education Classes." *The Journal of School Health*, 39 (6) 409, June 1969.
3. R. Gilchrist and D. Snygg, "The Case for Change," (Gladys Unruh, ed.) *New Curriculum Developments.* Washington, D.C.: Association for Supervision and Curriculum Development, 1965, p. 2.
4. Andie L. Knutson, "Evaluating Health Education," *Public Health Reports*, 67 (1) 74, January, 1952.

CHAPTER 5
Which Way Drug Education?

STEPHEN F. WEPNER

From 1973 to 1978 ten states enacted laws that reduced the penalties for possession and/or use of small quantities of marijuana. Even New York State, which until 1977 had some of the toughest statutory "drug laws" in the country, subsequently softened its position on marijuana. On the national level, President Carter called on Congress to enact legislation which also diminish penalties for violations of federal anti-marijuana laws.

It requires little imagination to recognize an inexorable trend. While the pharmaceutical and liquor industries jockey for position to determine who will manufacture and retail legal "soft" drugs, those in the still embryonic field of youthful drug abuse prevention/education are struggling to adapt to constantly changing social mores.

HISTORICAL PERSPECTIVE

Historically, drug education had gone through several identifiable but overlapping evolutionary periods. The late fifties and early sixties saw minimal attention paid to education. Junior and senior high school education classes were exposed to didactic instruction on the sources and types of drugs and the evils of drug abuse. Lack of knowledge by instructors coupled with an over-zealousness to discourage drug experimentation led to frequent instances of misinformation, i.e. the addictive potential of non-addictive substances and the now classic "marijuana to heroin" syndrome are representative examples.

As recognition of drug abuse as a nationwide problems began to emerge in the late sixties, the educational establishment responded with a plethora of bulletins, pamphlets and teacher guides. Often nothing more than restatements of earlier curricula, some did incorporate the concept of needed sensitivity to the problem on the part of school administration and teachers. The pamphlets did promote teacher knowledge of drugs and pedagogical techniques useful in discouraging drug abuse. A combination of the recognition coupled with a desire for improvement by pedagogues and constant mass-media attention to the problem produced an enormous increase in the number of inservice courses offered throughout the country.

The end of the decade saw the first truly innovative techniques in a Baltimore City Public Schools Bulletin that detailed a drug abuse education program in that city [1]. In the program, unit plans were developed for grades five, seven, and nine which outlined curricular content and learning activities. The objectives for grade five were to acquaint the students with harmful and beneficial durgs. Grade seven dealt with the sociopsychological problems of drug use as well and stressed interpersonal relationships in preventing drug abuse. By grade nine the students studied the use and abuse of stimulants, depressants, narcotics, and hallucinogens; drug dependence, drug laws; rehabilitation and decision-making. Throughout the program the students were active participants and the stress was on sharing ideas, thingking logically, and arriving at valid decisions.

Winston described a program in the South San Francisco Unified School District [2]. The program was created to deal with students who had violated narcotics laws. These secondary school students were not considered hard core users or sellers. Drug counseling workshops using a number of techniques were provided two hours per week for four weeks. The sessions involved the students and their parents. If either student or parent refused to attend, the student was expelled from school. The session leader was a psychologist or qualified staff member.

Geis and Gilbert detailed a program in two junior high schools in Los Angeles which employed former addicts to present worshops to teachers and students [3]. The results indicated increased knowledge on the part of students regarding drugs and attitude changes in the desired direction.

Daniels described the Glen Cove, Long Island Drug Education Program which began drug education for students in kindergarten of that system's public schools [4]. The ultimate objective of the experimental program was to involve all pupils for a period of time in each school year throughout the twelve grades. An important part of this program were the parent education workshops in which the parents were told that they should be concerned about potential teenage drug problems even before their child entered school. The parents were taught more effective means of communicating with their children and the students in the lower grades were given instruction aimed at developing respect, understanding and responsible behavior.

The Gribbin School in Glen Cove utilized this curriculum from 1967 to 1969. As a result of a seminar on drug abuse held at Glen Cove High School in 1967, ex-addicts were invited to participate in the new program as counselors to high school students. Reality aspects of drug abuse experience were stressed. The unique aspect of the Glen Cove drug education program was its emphasis on educating elementary school children and their parents about drugs.

Freedman, Stolow, and Lewis described a program utilizing drug experienced youth which was begun in the silver Lake Regional High School of South Boston [5]. The program exployed ex-addicts and began with the help of the local Junior Chamber of Commerce. A former addict would speak to groups of fifteen students for 45 minutes with a teacher present. A central information and service center was set up for private counseling.

A Nation's Schools article described drug eduation programs in various states [6]. One of the earliest drug education programs was started in Montgomery County, Maryland in 1963. A six week course was given as part of the health education curriculum to provide drug information to ninth grade students. In 1969, Prince Georges County, also in Maryland, has a similar program, with one difference in that the course was offered as an elective.

The Ann Arbor, Michigan School District conducted a structured drug program since 1966. Units on drug abuse were included in science, social studies, and physical education. In the elementary school, warnings were given against household drugs. In the junior high school, the effects of stimulants, depressants and hallucinogens were discussed. In the high schools, drug abuse and social problems were explored. The entire program also involved an inservice course for teachers.

In Houston, Texas, a program extending from 1967 to 1970 was given for ninth grade girls one day a week in the physical education class. A local pharmaceutical company sent representatives to discuss various drugs in one period lectures which were followed by teacher led discussions.

The Los Angeles school system has a program completely run by former addicts and did not require the presence of school personnel. They presented differing viewpoints which allowed students to weigh alternatives. During 1969, the program reached 150,000 students in Los Angeles and 360,000 throughout Southern California.

The Oklahoma City School District had implemented a program in 1970 in which a series of meetings were conducted for parents, students, teachers and principals of elementary, junior and senior high schools.

As greater awareness of youthful drug involvement developed, varying opinions appeared about the nature of Drug Education.

According to Brill, drug prevention should focus on peer group "counter cultures" [7]. Embracing a preventive thrust, a successful drug abuse program should begin in the elementary grades, should involve a total health framework, and should increase the student's ability to develop opportunities and alternative behaviors.

Bedworth stressed that the goal of drug education should be not to eliminate drug use but to provide individuals with the ability to make a choice regarding such use [8]. To do this, drug education must be taught both inside and outside of the classroom.

Dohner suggested that to stem drug abuse, positive alternatives must be presented to children [9]. Such alternatives might include personal awareness, interpersonal relations, self-reliance development, vocational skills, and aesthetic and creative experiences. To avoid drug involvement, children must experience a viable alternative. Programs which involve growth, according to Dohner, are effective in preventing drug abuse.

A report of the Bureau of Narcotics and Dangerous Drugs revealed some interesting insights into drug abuse prevention programs [10]. According to the report, alternative school patterns must be established if drug abuse is to be ameliorated.

To accomplish this: programs should build positive self-concept in children; develop in the child the concept of self-respect and respect for others; teach them to take responsibility for themselves; teach the child to handle his emotions; make the child aware of his surrounding influences; teach the child to develop his own set of values; teach him to take risks intelligently; teach him how to make decisions and to solve problems; enable him to understand peer influences; and teach the child to understand the nature of drugs.

According to Baker scare techniques are not effective in drug abuse prevention [11]. Rather, programs should deal with the psychological factors of drug abuse. These include peer pressure, alienation, and curiosity.

Perkel and Zink also supported the idea that scare techniques do not work. An effective drug abuse prevention program should be process-oriented and should relate to the human aspects of drug abuse. Moreover, it should provide accurate, objective information about drugs and their effects and it should address itself to the legal, social, and psychological implications of drug abuse. Further, it should have a referral capacity and have a research component which is designed and implemented by children to examine not only the incidence of drug abuse but also the differences between perceived drug abuse and actual use among peers.

Horan stated [12, p.; 207]:

> In terms of methodology, unlike addiction treatment, drug education is essentially a holding battle. Its function is not so much to eliminate

> ongoing drug abuse as to prevent the future use of illegal drugs. Behavioral evaluation, then, requires a longitudinal design. . . . The drug educator must wait several years after conducting his program, when the reducing influences of history and maturation have taken their toll before collecting behavioral data capable of being analyzed in a meaningful manner.

Kaminsky and Demak reviewed several principles upon which to base a drug program [13]. All important, according to the authors, is the philosophy that drug abuse is a symptom of some inner unrest. It is not a disease and it is not external to the user. According to the authors, the prevention of drug abuse depends on facilitating communication among adults and children and among peers themselves; presenting an image of the program which reflects the youth culture and norms; using members of the youth culture in treatment and prevention programs; developing an alternative peer group; a subculture of non-use; and educating the adult culture and reducing the culture shock of moving between the adult world and the world of peers.

According to Bard, most didactic, content-oriented drug programs are actually counterproductive. In summary, Bard stated [14, p.; 255]:

> Perhaps the schools would better serve teenagers if they chucked their scare movies, narcotics, "curriculum guides," and exhibts of drug paraphernalia into the furnaces. Fewer kids would get hurt.

A recent Education Daily article indicated that early identification approaches do not work in the case of drug education programs [15]. Rather than trying to spot high risk individuals, school programs should be established that maximize the total personal development of all children, thereby offsetting some of the factors that incline them toward deviant behavior.

The Ex-Addict Epoch

The early seventies might be called the "ex-addict epoch." Recognizing that traditionally trained middle class teachers possessed neither the ability nor the inclination to "get down" with drug abusing students, school districts sought out street wise ex-addicts who "knew the scene." The New York City public school system, the largest in the country, is a notable example. From 1971-73 graduates of drug free theraputic communities were sought after and hired by the hundreds because of their alledged ability to more effectively communicate with and relate to students considered vulnerable to drug abuse or who were already involved with drugs.

The use of ex-addicts in schools, piloted by Los Angeles in 1969, received widely mixed responses in New York City. Parental resistance was encountered in many quarters. "I don't want my child exposed to some "junkie" was a refrain heard often throughout the city. School administrators and teachers greeted their new colleagues with enormous skepticism and a degree of anxiety, fear and anger. How could these often bearded and/or long haired jean clad "hippies", including few college graduates and proportionately many more minority group members than the existing pedagogic population, accomplish anything in a school system built on formally trained professionals and the merit system.

Great support for the inclusion of ex-addicts was provided by the Assistant Commissioner of the New York City Addiction Services Agency, Rick DeLone who stated [16]:

> In New York the prevention programs have forced some schools to abandon the notion that only licensed personnel can contribute directly to a student's growth. A teacher's license does not necessarily mean that its bearer cannot "get down" with students, but the crucial element is not certification - students in the city report that as a rule ex-addicts and former drug users are the most credible staff for drug prevention programs. The introduction of non-licensed personnel, including ex-addicts, as the peers of certified professionals is a major and important modification in a number of New York School districts.

Within a period of two to three years, the rehabilitated ex-addicts had achieved the distinction of gaining not only broad acceptance as integral parts of pupil-personnel teams, but also a degree of envy of their ability to communicate and relate to students. During this evolutionary period, the ex-addicts as well as teachers, guidance counselors and other staff members of the drug abuse prevention/education programs received extensive training in a myriad of skills necessary for their work with students. Instruction in values clarification, group dynamics, problem solving skills, group process, individual counseling, sensitivity training and other techniques were implemented in the training plans of many programs.

Program implementation varied widely from community to community. In some quarters didactic instruction on the evils of drug abuse still persisted. In other programs "scare tactics" including parading children past a coffin containing a "victim" of drug abuse made newspaper headlines. At the other end of the spectrum there were broad attempts at community education, parent workshops, teacher training in humanistic approaches and extensive counseling with children to provide them with greter awareness of their own values, feelings and worth to themselves, their familes and society. The latter approach treats drug experimentation or abuse as symptomatic of a more severe problem and not as the problem itself. Commonly observed manifestations that are also treated as symptomatic phenomena include truancy, violent disruptive behavior, vandalism and rapid academic deterioration.

The Present

From the first year of program implementation to the present there has occurred a coalescence of approaches and the development of a relatively uniform philosophy. In essence, one might conclude that drug abuse is a fixture of our society. In fact, it is a widely expanding phenomenon. Abstinence by children is a desirable but unrealistic goal. Let us help children recognize the reasons for their behavior, and then by understanding themselves, equip them to better cope with their problems, let us provide them with alternatives to their existing behavioral patterns, help them to identify their strengths and successes and then hope that the attitudinal changes they have experienced as a result of program participation translate into prolonged behavioral changes. It is important to note that the desired attitudinal change from this writer's perspective does not necessarily mean abstinence. Rather, it indicates that whatever decision is made should be arrived at by careful consideration of the ramifications, and understanding of why the decision is being made and, most importantly, that the decision is not being made for the individual by his/her peers in an attempt to gain an identity as part of a peer group. To go along with a crowd to avoid ostracism or being alone on a Saturday night is a decision that some readers of this article have probably made as youths and may continue to do so long into their adult years. Conformity reaches all levels. It may mean straight legged jeans, bell bottom jeans, wide flared jeans, moderately flared jeans ad infinitum ad nauseum. The impact of media on the citizens of this country has been well documented. We have reached a point where we buy half the car we might have purchased ten years ago for twice the price and think we are getting a "great deal."

Yet it is precisely the need of the average individual to fit in, or to belong that this writer hypothesizes is the future thrust of drug education. Numerous other approaches have been suggested and are in fact being implemented. Providing alternatives to drug abuse, such as channeling youths into previously unexplored activities and triggering their interests for creativity and expression have and will continue to work with certain young people.

Counseling families as an entity rather than working with individual children in a vacuum also holds promise and is in the forefront of not only drug abuse prevention but also in programs servicing youths who have become involved in the juvenile justice system.

It has been proposed that equipping drug education/prevention service providers with more extensive clinical skills to develop more effective counseling techniques in the approach of the future.

What we have seen then is a distinct shift in the emphasis of drug education programs. Initially they were designed to provide prevention/education services to a broad student population. But, as the number of reported instances of youthful drug abuse grew, the programs were put under great pressure to address the special needs of the abusing population. Prevention became a logistically impractical task. Early intervention, intensive counseling and referral to clinical settings rapidly replaced prevention efforts.

The Future

To be sure, many of the approaches described earlier and numerous others suggested by practitioners have worked and will continue to impact favorably on some young people, there are still several undeniable facts: Drug abuse among the young is commonplace; it reaches into every socioeconomic stratum, and each and every effort described has not extinguished it or decreased it to any significant degree.

What impact can be expected from school services which try to offset every negative societal influence? It is unrealistic to expect programs with limited resources operating for approximately five hours each day for less than half the days in the calendar year to overcome the influences of "hip' 'pot smoking parents, movies, television, a plethora of 'head shops," open and blatant sales and use of drugs in public places and the legislatures of ten states that have implied through their actions that using marijuana is not really as serious a problem as it once was. Jousting at windmills is valiant but not terribly rewarding.

What joy does a young marijuana user experience besides the mild "high"? He/she gains acceptance, fits in, belongs, identifies with and is, in effect, accepted into a sub-society which is rapidly replacing the "straight" culture from which it is rebelling. The user is "bad" which a few years ago was "cool." How can using drugs be made into something "uncool"? What is implied is a massive thrust to invert a cultural more. Yet on closer inspection it is not mearly as insurmountable a goal as it appears. The resources to do this monumental job are for the most part already in place and can be approached on several different levels.

In the schools where drug programs already exist, the peer group concept is a frequently used process. It is often built on positive students with strong leadership abilities who are drawn from the natural leadership pool of students, i.e.: the student government's kitchen cabinet made up of former gang leaders, athletes, political radicals and others who students often emulate and follow. The individuals in these groups have often gone through a developmental process resulting in recognition of their self-worth and responsibilities to themselves and others. They have learned to make decisions that are in their own best interest, and can say "no" when saying "yes" is something that contradicts this belief. This type of group can, through its actions do much to repudiate the notion that drugs are "in." In their unofficial leadership capacities these students can impact strongly on those that follow their leaders. It takes little peer influence to change the dress style of a school. The type of leadership proposed will begin the process, but as pointed out earlier, school is only part of the life of a young person. The youth centers, settlement houses and after-school centers that young people frequent, represent a natural network for reinforcement. Whether operated by churches, boards of education or social service agencies, the agenda is often the same - a safe healthy outlet for energies providing varying degrees of opportunity for creative expression. Often mobilized and unified over community issues, these agencies represent a formidable non-school base for perpetuating the theme that drugs are "out." It is possible to visualize on local levels, a sustained low-key community campaign echoing that refrain.

Parent Teacher Association, medical societies, business associations, charitable groups, and local governmental agencies through their combined resources provide another vehicle on several levels for reinforcing the theme.

Individual states and the Federal government have initiated and combined campaigns to diminish the incidence of youthful drug abuse. It would not be logistically difficulty for the emphasis of the campaigns to shift from, "drugs are harmful," to "drugs are out." Still unexplored is the role of the most important element in this process of involution - the mass audio-visual media that serves to shape much of our lives. Spot public service commercials during prime viewing times will reach millions of young viewers. The contributions of socially minded performers, both in the fields of entertainment and athletics would be of enormous value.

The music that young people listen to is often undecipherable by adults. Yet the same youngsters who have difficulty memorizing a list of vacabulary words or a part of the Declaration of Independence have no trouble at all remembering the words of the latest hit rock record. Just as *Lucy in the Sky With Diamonds* conveyed two messages in the late sixties so could songs by today's "hot" artists entertain while conveying the idea that drugs are "out."

What has been presented then is an outline, not a blueprint of a multi-level strategy which , if sustained over a period of time could in the opinion of this writer do more to shape the behavior of young people than all of the drug education programs currently operating.

To be sure, much coordination and communication is implied and the logistics will be difficult. Yet mobilization of resources in this country during times of crisis has been one of the benchmarks of our two centuries of history.

There is, of course, an inherent weakness in this strategy if it is successful. While it may significantly decrease the incidence of youthful drug abuse, it will be accomplishing this goal for all the wrong reasons. It's appeal is essentially no different than the blue jeans syndrome described earlier. It is based on conformity, fitting in and being "in." It does not rely on individual decision making and the pursuit of goals that enhance a sense of self worth. But it will buy the time needed by drug educators to reach out with a variety of approaches to a manageable population of young people and help them to explore and understand their motivations and needs. It has been estimated that fully one fifth of the population of the U.S. has tried marijuana. Estimates of high school students experimenting with soft drugs run to 50 percent of higher. How can one or two drug educators effectively cope with half the population of a two to three thousand student high school. In fact, they cannot. However, if the enormous number of recreational, "going along with the crowd" users could be effectively reached by other means, the drug educators could stand a real chance to succeed with the population that has not yet gone beyond "a few "tokes at a party." The stage will be set for those in the field of prevention/education to get out of the intervention/treatment business and return to their original mission, primary prevention. This approach has in fact been mandated by the State of New York Commission on Alcohol and Substance Abuse Prevention and Education in 1978. This policy recognizes that validated, proven prevention strategies must become the prime functions of the drug educator.

To accomplish such a redirection will require that a price be paid. It is politically desireable to report on reductions in levels of adolescent drug abuse since that kind of data is well received by legislators who appropriate program funds. The effects of prevention efforts are harder to explain, more difficult to comprehend and are certainly less "marketable" in the political arena. The lessons that we have learned from public health must be used as examples. The cost of eradicating smallpox from the face of the earth by preventing its occurence has certainly been enormous. Yet it could never be as costly to humanity as allowing the disease to exist and intermittently treating its victims after each outbreak.

Drug educators have been successful with hundreds of thousands of children. This success is attested to by the many people they have aided, by teachers and supervisors, by parents and other concerned citizens. Yet the task is too large for them, given their current resources. This is not an indictment but rather an observation. In fact the job is too big for all the law enforcement agencies in this country. Constant arrests of pushers, interception of shipments of illicit drugs and international agreements have not stopped the flow into this country. Instead millions of dollars are spent annually on drug law enforcement, prosecution, incarceration and rehabilitation. The flow of drugs continues because there are buyers. The market perpetuates the business. The business perpetuates human suffering, misery and destroyed futures. Much has been said in recent years about the priorities of this country. We have become ecologically conscious and conservation minded. We protect our forests, our water and our air, but the greatest natural resources of any nation are the minds and bodies of its young. Only through the acceptance of this precept and a commitment to the lives of our next generation can we truly expect to reverse the trend of a generation that is growing up "turning on" to "turn off."

REFERENCES

1. Drug Abuse Education Program, *Drug Abuse Education*, grades 5, 7, 9, Baltimore City Public Schools, Maryland, (ERIC Document No. ED 038 660), 1969.

2. S. L. Winston, Drug Counseling Workshops: A New Resource for Schools, *Journal of Secondary Education, 44,* pp. 352-353, 1969.
3. J. Geis, J. Gilbert, et al., *Addicts in the Classroom: The Impact of an Experimental Narcotics Education Program on Junior High School Pupils.* California State College, Los Angeles, California, 1969.
4. R.M. Daniels, Drug Education Begins Before Kindergarten: The Glen Cove, New York Pilot Program. Paper presented at the annual meeting of the American School Health Association, Philadelphia, Pennsylvania, November, 1969.
5. M. Freedman, A. Stolow, and D.C. Lewis, Utilizing Drug-Experienced Youth in Drug Education Programs. *National Association of Secondary School Principals Bulletin, 53,* pp. 45-51, 1969.
6. Drugs and the Educational Antidote: Programs Give the Facts Without Stings. *Nation's Schoold, 85,* pp. 49-52, 1970.
7. L. Brill, Drug Abuse Problems: Implications for Treatment. *Abstracts for Social Workers, 7,* p. 4, 1971.
8. D.A. Bedworth, Toward a Rational View of Drug Education. *Journal of Drug Education, 2,* pp.371-381, 1972.
9. V.A. Dohner, Alternatives to Drugs - A New Approach to Drug Education. *Journal of Drug Education, 2,* pp. 3-22, 1972.
10. Bureau of Narcotics and Dangerous Drugs, U.S. Department of Justice. *Proceedings on the Alternatives to Drug Abuse Conference.* Washington, D.C., 1973.
11. R.J. Baker, Drug Education: Is It Doing Any Good? *Education Digest, 5,* pp. 38-40, 1973.
12. J.J. Horan, Outcome difficulties in Drug Education. *Review of Educational Research, 44,* pp. 201-211, 1974.
13. K. Kaminsky and L. Demak, Edu-Caring: A Response to Drug Abuse. *The Clearing House, 48,* pp. 402-405, 1974.
14. B. Bard, The Failure of Our School Drug Abuse Programs. *Phi Delta Kappan, 57,* pp. 253-255, 1975.
15. Watch Drug Abuse Early Identification, Educators Told. *Education Daily, 34,* p. 6, September 24, 1976.
16. R.H. DeLone, Ups and Downs of Drug Education. *Saturday Review of Education, 2,* p. 18, 1972.

CHAPTER 6
Drug Education—A Turn On or A Turn Off?*

MICHAEL S. GOODSTADT

Drug education has received much criticism within the past decade. Some of this critical attention has been directed to indirect negative consequences, for example, the raising of parents' anxiety or the occurrence of "false flashbacks." [1,2] More damaging is the possibility that drug education has produced effects counter to those intended–increasing drug use or pro-drug attitudes. Such an indictment has been suggested by both lay and professional people. The present paper will examine the research evidence associated with the contention that drug education is counterproductive.

PROBLEMS OF DEFINITION

Concern with the negative consequences of drug education assumes an understanding of "negative," and by implication "positive," in this context, which, in turn, depends upon: 1. the *intended* outcomes; 2. the priorities of

*Based on Paper presented at The 10th International Conference on Health Education, London, England, September 2-9, 1979.

these outcomes; 3. the *observed* outcomes; 4. the balance of positive *versus* negative outcomes; and 5. the nature of the evidence supporting conclusions regarding outcomes. Differences of opinion can exist in interpreting the impact of any drug education program according to this framework.

No initial assumptions about the desirable objectives of drug education will be made in this paper; focus will be directed to *intended* and *observed* outcomes as stated in the relevant research reports. "Negative" consequences will, in this empirical fashion, be defined or inferred on the basis of discrepancies between intended and observed outcomes and in the context of the authors' discussion of their findings. Such an approach does not remove all definitional problems, since ambiguity frequently exists concerning a program's intended objectives, and evaluations do not always assess the achievement of intended objectives. Later discussion will clarify some of the issues and problems inherent in current approaches to establishing and evaluating program objectives.

EVIDENCE OF NEGATIVE EFFECTS OF DRUG EDUCATION

Type of Evidence

As suggested above, views differ concerning the acceptability of alternative forms of evidence in assessing the impact of drug education. Emphasis will be placed here on evidence from research studies employing conventionally admissable research techniques. Such studies should be selected on the basis of their use of scientific procedures which maximize confidence in drawing conclusions, including the use of adequate experimental design features (e.g. control/comparison groups, random assignment etc.), adequate measurement techniques and appropriate statistical analysis. The majority of studies of the impact of drug education have been less than adequate in these respects [3] ; selection of studies for this review will, however, give weight to those employing at least the framework of scientific experimental design and procedures.

Less emphasis will be given to quasi-experimental studies which lack some of the elements of more rigorous experimental design. Such studies are capable, however, of permitting insightful investigation of important questions and the evidence thus obtained can be of special value in the absence of more rigorous research.

Better than an individual's opinion are data obtained from systematic opinion surveys, which, however, incorporate few of the scientific procedures designed to permit more confident testing of hypotheses and conclusions. Surveys can, of course, be better *or* less well conducted and analyzed and can be more *or* less informative; but their position in the hierarchy of scientific procedures should be clearly recognized. This is especially important in considering the negative impact of drug education: much of the relevant evidence is of a survey or quasi-survey nature. Some of this evidence will be reviewed, but appropriately less weight will be given to its conclusions. This review will consider the evidence from any drug education program except those dealing exclusively with tobacco use, but will include those few which have dealt exclusively with alcohol.

Non-Experimental Evidence

The non-experimental evidence cited in the debate concerning the impact of drug education has taken various forms. Much of the data is derived from single survey studies [4–7] providing observations at only a single point in time. Other studies have repeated the same survey at successive time-points [8–10] allowing for examination of temporal change including the influence of intervening exposure to drug education.

Studies have sometimes asked respondents specifically about their views on the effectiveness of drug education programs [4–6, 11]: these studies have reported little effect on drug education in "stopping use of drugs" [4] or in "affecting drug use" [5], or have shown mixed effects [9,10, 11 Study II]. Examination of these procedures, however, suggest attention should be given to the types and validity of questions (see Goodstadt, for example, for a more detailed critique of the Macro Systems Inc. research [12]). Little data exist from such survey studies to show that drug education has *increased* drug use; more commonly, respondents feel that exposure to drug education does *not decrease* drug use.

Another approach taken by survey studies has been to correlate reported exposure to drug education and reported drug use or other relevant outcome measures [5,7,10]. Of greatest concern has been evidence of a correlation between exposure to drug education and reported drug use, such that those reportedly exposed to more drug education are likely to report more drug use. These findings have not been entirely consistent either within or between studies. Cook et al. reported that soldiers exposed to drug education programs reported a "negative" effect (i.e. more drug use) only with respect to alcohol use [5]. Berberian et al. found such a correlation to hold for grade 7 students' cannabis and, to a lesser extent, alcohol use; opposite trends were demonstrated for the older student cohorts [10]. Goodstadt et al. found a "negative" association between drug education and drug use only for tobacco among grade 7 students, and marijuana among grades 7, 9 and 11 [7].

It is important in considering this evidence to recognize: 1. that the data is correlational not causal; 2. that several alternative explanations of the relationship may exist (e.g. that drug education is directed towards those who are judged to require it on the basis of their drug use [10]; and 3. that the data itself may be flawed by selective attention and/or recall [5].

Survey data relating to the impact of drug education is interesting and sometimes instructive; it usually, however, raises more questions than it answers, even when it is conducted in a well designed quasi-experimental fashion [9,10]: little control of exposure to drug education is possible and too many competing explanations of the data are available.

Experimental Evidence

Consideration of the non-experimental research evidence has deliberately been expository rather than exhaustive. An attempt has been made, however, to accumulate all available data from experimentally designed studies which suggest a "negative" impact of drug education. This search has been curtailed, nevertheless, by restrictions on publication of negative findings and limitations on the availability of such reports; it is likely, therefore, that several other instances of negative impact exist. As indicated earlier, "negative" has been understood to include results contrary to either the intended outcomes of those considered to be desirable by the program researchers.

Relatively few scientifically conducted studies have demonstrated a negative impact of drug education programs—Although a large number of studies have suggested that drug education programs have had minimal "positive" effect, only fifteen experimental studies are available which have reported negative effects. It is difficult to estimate the proportion of all studies that this finding represents, but an examination of 127 drug education evaluations by Schaps et al. revealed only seven instances of negative impact, and some of these effects arose within the same study [3]. Fifteen studies were identified and obtained [13-17, 18 Studies I & II, 19–26]. Not included in our considerations, due to lack of availability, were two studies identified by Schaps et al. [3] (personal communication, Stoessel [27] and Weimer [28].

The majority (i.e. nine) of reported negative findings have involved a significant increase in reported drug use among those receiving experimental drug education programs [13–16, 19–21, 23,26]—It should, moreover, be recognized that not all studies examined impact on drug use [17].

The majority (i.e. nine) of reported negative findings have included a significant liberalization in attitudes towards drugs or drug use among those receiving experimental programs—These studies were not always identical to those which reported negative behavioral effects [15,17,18,21–25]. Again, attitudes were not measured in all studies [1,2].

All reported negative findings have been associated with the reporting of positive findings in the same study—These "mixed" results have been of two forms: 1. negative findings for one sample subgroup (either experimental or demographic) and positive findings (on the same dependent variable) for other subsamples: alcohol and drug related behaviors [15], drug use [16], and attitudes [18]; 2. negative findings as measured by one dependent measure and positive findings on other dependent variables: positive knowledge gains [19,21,23–26], improvement in self understanding [17], positive self concept change and problem behavior improvement [20], drug use changes [25], reduced tendency to become intoxicated as frequently [26], reduce "spread" in frequency of drug use [13,14], positive shifts in attitudes [15], positive alcohol use changes [18] and positive changes in expectations regarding future use [18,19].

From these mixed results it can be seen that negative findings have rarely been unambiguous even within the same study, although the majority of mixed findings include, on the positive side, an improvement in knowledge which is outweighed by negative impact on attitudes and/or behavior.

Few of the studies from which negative findings have been reported have been free from major experimental design problems—an earlier review provided a detailed critique of five of the fourteen studies [12]. The same general criticisms apply to all fifteen, notably:

1. Non-random assignment of subjects [18,20];
2. Uncertainty regarding random assignment [15–17, 21,22];
3. Small sample sizes [17,20,22];
4. Large sample attrition, especially among studies employing extended follow-up periods, [13,19,23,26];
5. Unknown validity and reliability of outcome measures: this applies to most studies, especially those employing self-reported indices of drug use, but also applies to affective measures of values and decision-making impact [19];
6. Absence of follow-up, other than immediate post-program assessment. Exceptions to this were: Stuart [23] (4 months); Swisher et al. [24] (3 months); Blum [13,14] (2-2½ years); Carney [16] (2 years); Goodstadt et al. [19] (6 months); Williams et al. [26] (1 month and 1 year);
7. Low "intensity" programs: as measured against Schaps et al's criteria [3], few of the fifteen programs would have rated highly in terms of program intensity (i.e. duration and intensity of interventions, duration and intensity of staff training, scope of the variables addressed by intervention, the likelihood that program services will persist).

Schaps et al., found more than 50 per cent of the 127 studies they reviewed to be weak in intensity, only 20 per cent being of strong intensity.

It is estimated that of the fifteen reviewed here only Blum [13,14] and perhaps Carney [15,16] would qualify as being of strong intensity, matching the proportion found by Schaps et al. Several programs would probably have been rated as weak by Schaps et al's. criteria [18,21,22].

Schaps et al. identified only eight of their 127 studies as being exemplary, having both high intensity programs and rigorous evaluation methods. These eight studies tended to show positive results, with only one exhibiting negative effect. Probably only Blum's two studies would qualify as being exemplary in program content and research design, although lack of clarity in analyzing and reporting results (especially Blum) clouds interpretation of his results [14].

No common program characteristic (content and process) was detectable in the "negative" programs–The fifteen programs included the full range of program styles from the most completely factual to the most purely affective. This finding is similar to Schaps et al's. who, although finding that more intensive and more vigorously evaluated programs were more likely to show positive effects, were unable "to identify any useful patterns or commonalities in program design or implementation procedures" among the ten studies that were both most positive in outcome and were well evaluated.

IMPLICATIONS

It is clear from both the non-experimental and the experimental evidence that "negative" program effects are not isolated phenomena, but occur frequently enough and affect self-reported behavior often enough to require more careful scrutiny. Some of the questions and implications raised by these findings will be considered here.

It is essential to: 1. provide better definitions of program objectives; 2. ensure that the programs are designed to achieve these objectives; and 3. match evaluation measures to the stated objectives. The most common failing in this regard was the statement of objectives as being to reduce or prevent "drug abuse," while program impact was frequently measured in terms of changes in reported drug *use* and attitudes towards drugs–without a clear conceptual link being made between drug use measures and reduction in drug abuse.

It is usually not clear from the results of these studies, or from the associated discussion, why an increase in drug use or more liberal attitudes toward drug use is *necessarily* a negative or undesirable outcome. Common sense might suggest that movements in these directions would be counter-productive, with the end state worse than the initial state. There are however reasons which could be proposed for believing that such changes are not entirely negative.

There are studies in which shifts towards more liberal attitudes are found in conjunction with less reported drug use and lower expectations regarding future drug use [18]; this would suggest that more liberal attitudes are not in themselves always "negative" as measured by their behavioral implications. Such an assessment of attitudinal shifts is reinforced by the generally poor correspondence between measures of attitudes and behaviors, and between attitude-change and behavior-change((see [29] for a fuller discussion). Secondly, in interpreting negative attitude shifts, it is possible that the facts (and the absence of highly emotional content) presented by more unbiased programs can result in a removal of *unjustified* anxiety regarding drugs and hence lead to an attitudinal shift in a liberal direction [23]. Thirdly, the outcome of programs which have emphasized the role of decision-making and values may have had the effect of decreasing negative feelings or attitudes towards drug substances or use *per se*, and shifted the focus to individual responsibility in using drugs; this process might, again, lead to an apparently more liberal attitude towards drugs and drug use, which need not necessarily imply negative consequences with regard to individual drug use.

With respect to "negative" program effects on reported drug use, several observations are in order. Firstly, as discussed in an earlier review [12], one of the confounding effects of program assessment techniques is the possibility that a good program will result in a greater openness on the part of students regarding their drug use [23] and hence more *reported* drug use on post-program measures—such an effect would lead to the spurious conclusion that a program had increased drug use. A second possiblity is that programs "destabilize" drug use, resulting in more use of drugs, but that better programs can simultaneously result in less extreme drug use [13,14]. The one aspect of this phenomena might be interpreted as negative while the other aspect would be positive. Blum suggests from his results that drug education programs might be more appropriate for those who are likely to use drugs or be exposed to drug use, in which instance a drug education program has the effect of producing a "negative" effect (i.e. more experimentation with drugs) which was in any case highly likely, but has the benefit of controlling the extent and hence consequences of this use. If it is accepted that drug use may increase or attitudes may be more liberal as a result of drug education programs, it might be both feasible and appropriate to include such expectations in defining program objectives. Such objectives might, for example, (a) not aim to reduce drug use or produce more opposed attitudes, but (b) allow for drug use and attitudes to shift in either direction and (c) aim to discourage "inappropriate" drug use and associated attitudes (e.g. drinking and driving, drinking to reduce tension, etc.)—see Dorn and Thompson for a more extended discussion of problems and criteria associated with choosing drug education objectives [30]. Difficulties with such an approach are obvious:

"inappropriate" begs for definition; any increase in drug use would be negatively interpreted by some program developers and researchers; finally, as with most of the issues being considered here, the *long term* effects of immediate "negative" program effects are unknown—does an increase in drug use, for example, resulting from a well designed balanced program lead in the long term to an increase in drug problems, or can it be handled so as to reduce problems at a later stage of development?

It is possible that some "negative" impact of drug education programs has to be tolerated as the price for programs which are more broadly beneficial (e.g. decision-making programs). It might be argued that the benefits from such programs to the majority of recipients (including those who increase their drug use) are greater than the negative consequences resulting from a small (though statistically significant) increase in drug use; such benefits might include improved decision-making skills, even though the decisions may not meet with society's approval, or greater awareness of the importance of individual responsibility. The same problems and arguments apply to many "enlightened" educational efforts.

It is evident that the use of improvements in levels of knowledge cannot be validly used as a measure of program effectiveness. Previous reviews [29] have shown that while many programs have demonstrated positive changes in knowledge, far fewer programs have been associated with positive attitudinal or behavioral changes. The present analysis similarly shows that several programs have shown both knowledge improvements and negative behavioral or attitudinal effects.

The last implication of the present review is that more and better program research is required. This recommendation is almost self-evident, but is certainly borne out by each of the fifteen studies included here. Detailed recommendations for such improvements can be found in previous reviews [3,12,29]. A summary of these recommendations would include:

1. Greater clarity and rigor in the conceptualization, development, implementation and evaluation of drug education programming, this includes concerns related to:

   a. Program objectives,
   b. Program audiences,
   c. Program content and processes,
   d. Explicit psycho-social dynamics (e.g. cognitive, affective, etc.) of programs,
   e. Outcome measures,
   f. The interrelationships between the above five issues;

2. Greater emphasis on research which increases understanding of dynamics, the "whys," of successful drug education programs; process evaluation is especially relevant in this regard;

3. Greater attention to the scientific quality of drug education research, including greater emphasis on:

    a. Experimental and quasi-experimental designs,
    b. The quality of dependent measures,
    c. Behavioral outcome measures,
    d. Long-term outcomes;

4. Greater emphasis on research of alternative program modalities especially as they relate to divergent audiences–particularly as defined by current drug use and "risk levels,"–for example:

    a. Peer-oriented programs,
    b. Family-oriented programs;

5. Greater attention to the timing of drug education, from the perspective of the psychological and behavioral developmental stages of the audience;
6. Greater concern for teachers' mediating roles in implementing programs.

REFERENCES

1. R. M. Levy and A. R. Brown, Untoward Effects of Drug Education, *American Journal of Public Health, 63,* pp. 1071-1073, 1973.
2. A. Stickgold and A. Brovar, Undesirable Sequelae of Drug Abuse Education, *Contemporary Drug Problems, 7,* pp. 99-115, 1978.
3. E. Schaps, R. DiBartolo, C. S. Palley and S. Churgin, *Primary Prevention Evaluation Research: A Review of 127 Program Evaluations,* Pacific Institute for Research and Evaluation, Walnut Creek, California, 1978.
4. Macro Systems, Inc., *Evaluation of Drug Education Programs,* Macro Systems, Inc., Silver Spring, Maryland, 1972.
5. R. F. Cook, A. S. Morton and A. D. Little, *An Assessment of Drug Education–Prevention Programs in the U.S. Army,* U.S. Army Research Institute for the Behavioral and Social Sciences, Technical Paper 261, 1975.
6. R. Dembo et al., *Drug Abuse Prevention: The Awareness, Experience, and Opinions of Junior and Senior High School Students in New York State, Report No. 2 of Winter 1974/75 Survey,* New York State Office of Drug Abuse Services, Bureau of Social Science Research and Program Evaluation, 1976.
7. M. S. Goodstadt, M. A. Sheppard, K. Kijewski, and L. Chung, *The Status of Drug Education in Ontario: 1977*, Addiction Research Foundation, Toronto 1978.
8. California State Department of Education, *A Study of More Effective Education Relative to Narcotics, Other Harmful Drugs and Hallucinogenic Substances,* A Progress Report, Submitted to the California Legislature, 1970.

9. B. Swift, N. Dorn and A. Thompson, *Evaluation of Drug Education: Findings of a National Research Study on Secondary School Students of Five Types of Lessons Given by Teachers,* Institute for the Study of Drug Dependence, London, 1974.
10. R. M. Berberian et al., The Relationship Between Drug Education Programs in the Greater New Haven Schools and Changes in Drug Use and Drug-Related Beliefs and Perceptions, *Health Education Monographs, 4,* pp. 327-376, 1976.
11. F. S. Tennant Jr., S. C. Weaver and C. E. Lewis, Outcomes of Drug Education: Four Case Studies, *Pediatrics, 52,* pp. 246-251, 1973.
12. M. Goodstadt, *Myths and Methodology in Drug Education. A Critical Review of the Research Evidence,* M. S. Goodstadt, (ed.), *Research on Methods and Programs of Drug Education,* Addiction Research Foundation, Toronto, 1974.
13. R. H. Blum, *Drug Education: Results and Recommendations,* D. C. Heath and Co., Lexington, Mass., 1976.
14. R. H. Blum, E. F. Garfield, J. L. Johnstone and J. G. Magistad, Drug Education: Further Results and Recommendations, *Journal of Drug Issues, 8*, pp. 379-426, 1978.
15. R. E. Carney, *An Evaluation of the Effect of a Values-Oriented Drug Abuse Education Program Using the Risk Taking Attitude Questionnaire,* Coronado Unified School District, Coronado, California, 1971.
16. ______ , *Final 1972-1973 Report on the Use of the RTAVI to Evaluate the Effects of a Values-Oriented Drug Abuse Prevention Program in the Tempe, Arizona Schools,* Educators Assistance Institute, Santa Monica, California, 1975.
17. J. F. D'Augelli, *Brief Report: Initial Evaluation of a Televised Affective Education Program as a Primary Prevention Strategy,* Pennsylvania State University, Addictions Prevention Laboratory, 1974.
18. M. S. Goodstadt, M. A. Sheppard and S. H. Crawford, *Development and Evaluation of Two Alcohol Education Programs for the Toronto Board of Education,* Addiction Research Foundation, Toronto, Substudy #941, 1978.
19. M. S. Goodstadt et al., *Alcohol Education: A Comparison of Three Alternative Approaches,* Addiction Research Foundation, Toronto, 1979.
20. M. B. Lynch, *"US": Primary Prevention, Para-Counselling Research Project,* Rogue Valley Council on Aging, Medford, Oregon, 1976.
21. M. L. Mason, *Drug Education Effects: Final Report,* Young Adult Services, Gainesville, Florida, 1972.
22. H. G. Morgan and A. Hayward, The Effects of Drug Talks to School Children, *British Journal of Addiction, 71,* pp. 285-288, 1976.
23. R. B. Stuart, Teaching Facts About Drugs: Pushing or Preventing, *Journal of Educational Psychology, 66,* pp. 189-201, 1974.
24. J. D. Swisher et al, Four Approaches to Drug Abuse Prevention Among College Students, *Journal of College Student Personnel, 14,* pp. 231-235, 1973.

25. J. D. Swisher and A. J. Piniuk, *An Evaluation of Keystone Central School District's Drug Education Program,* The Pennsylvania Governor's Justice Commission, Region IV, 1973.
26. A. F. Williams, L. M. DiCicco and J. Unterberger, Philosophy and Evaluation of an Alcohol Education Program, *Quarterly Journal of Studies on Alcohol, 29,* pp. 685-702, 1968.
27. R. Stoessel, *A Cross-Modality Evaluation of Drug Abuse Prevention Program Effectiveness,* Addiction Services Agency, New York, 1974.
28. J. M. Weimer, *The Effects of Film Treatments on Attitudes that Correlate with Drug Behavior,* Dissertation, University of South Dakota, 1976.
29. M. S. Goodstadt, Alcohol and Drug Education: Models and Outcomes, *Health Education Monographs, 6,* pp. 263-279, 1978.
30. N. Dorn and A. Thompson, An Exercise in Choosing Educational Goals, *International Journal of Health Education, 19,* pp. 260-269, 1976.

CHAPTER 7

A Critique of Values: Clarification in Drug Education

CHWEE LYE CHNG

INTRODUCTION

Values clarification is today widely used in drug education programs in the United States [1]. With the recognition that the mere dissemination of information about drugs is grossly inadequate to influence drug-using behavior; values clarification has gained increasing acceptance among drug educators [2]. Simon and deSherbinin, strong advocates of the approach, have readily endorsed it as a viable method for influencing drug "use." They content [3, p. 679]:

> . . . Drug educators across the country increasingly use values clarification techniques. Drug educators report reaching students by examining their values. Instead of focusing exclusively on drugs, they involve young people in looking at their total lives. The young discover what they prize and cherish and begin to think about the consequences of their actions. Eventually, they learn techniques for examining the harder issues of their lives, such as whether or not to use drugs. . .

The premise for employing values clarification in drug education programs is that decisions pertaining to whether to use drugs or to abstain are predicated primarily on non-cognitive factors like attitudes, feelings and, in part, a direct function of a confused values system. The purpose of values clarification is to assist individuals both to structure and operationalize a value system which is personally satisfying and socially acceptable [4–8].

Unfortunately, there is no concensus on the efficacy of values clarification to effectively influence behavior. Some scholars–like Simon, deSherbinin, Blokker, and Kirschenbaum [1,3,5]–are avid proponents of the approach, while others–like Lockwood, Stewart, Goodlett, Loggins and Goodstadt [9–13]–have expressed some reservations and misgivings. In an attempt to raise questions regarding the potential of values clarification to influence drug use, a few criticisms of the approach will be offered in this paper: the role of content in valuing, the position of "ethical relativism," the dange of "values teaching," and the social pressure to conform. Before exploring these problem areas, a brief description of values clarification will be presented.

VALUES CLARIFICATION

Values clarification, an approach founded on the study of Louis Raths and his associates [14–16], claims not to be concerned primarily with the ultimate product–the content of values–but with the valuing *process,* with the means through which values are acquired and exercised. They explain that values are a direct function of three processes: choosing, prizing, and acting. Accordingly, a value emerges when all seven of the criteria listed below are satisfied: choosing one's beliefs and actions freely, choosing them from alternatives, choosing after thoughtful consideration of consequences; prizing and cherishing one's values and actions, publicly affirming one's values, when appropriate; acting on that choice, and acting repeatedly, in some pattern of life.

In values clarification, the role of the teacher is not to impart predetermined values but rather to guide the students through the seven aforementioned processes of valuing, as they respond to an array of value issues. Raths and his associates maintain that this sequence of processes will assist individuals to structure and operationalize a personal value system. The final product is an individual who is "less flighty, less conforming, more zestful, more energetic, and more likely to follow through on decisions." [16]

CRITIQUE OF VALUES CLARIFICATION

The Role of Content

One of the sharpest criticisms of values clarification is its excessive preoccupation with the *process* of valuing, which creates an illusion that it is devoid of content and consequently, free of any moral communications. This focus on the process of valuing relegates the role of information and knowledge in decision-making to insignificance. In reality, a drug educator, like other instructors, cannot communicate any content without a process and similarly, cannot employ any process without some committment to content. For example, consider the value implications involved in this question, often posed in drug education classes using the approach, "Should marijuana be decriminalized?" Before anyone can commence to discuss the question intelligently, a large body of relevant information must be made available: facts about the health hazards of the drug, the impact of legal prohibitions on the supply and demand of marijuana, a profile of users of the drug, the legal ramifications of decriminalization, *ad infinitum*. The meaning is clear: it is blatant deception to suggest that a mere committment to the process of valuing alone will help individuals successfully resolve their value concerns. Simply to appreciate an issue, let alone take a position, requires access to a considerable amount of factual data. Forcinelli points out that "values do not simply come from within. . . Environment, behavior patterns, conceptions of justice are types of affective and cognitive forces which influence personal choices." [8] The failure of advocates of values clarification to recognize this is both myopic and regrettable.

Ethical Relativism

Another objectionable element of values clarification is its position of "ethical relativism" which advocates that all values are equally valid and morally defensible. Accordingly, this position prescribes that in matters of morality, no opinion can be presented as superior than others. "Ethical relativism" may be, in fact, a misnomer because in most cases where values clarification is used, no moral foundation is required of the students to justify their value reponses. Their judgemental statements are called forth without any discussion of moral criteria. The students are regrettably dependent on such factors as dynamics of groups, social and moral influences, perceived pressures from the educator to guide them in proffering an opinion. However, despite both the inadequacy and inaccuracy of the term "ethical relativism," because of its wide currency in the literature and the lack of any available acceptable substitute, we will use it in this paper advisedly.

It is apparent that in inconsequential matters involving non-moral values, (e.g., "Shall I wear my red or blue dress?") "ethical relativism" may be harmless and acceptable. However, it would be naive to believe that decisions to use drugs or to refrain from drugs have no moral implications. Here is the problem. Values clarification neither engages the individual in abstract thinking about his or her choices nor assists in identifying the moral dimensions of value conflicts. Rather than encouraging the individual to appraise critically his, her or another's values, it promotes unquestioning acceptance of the dominant norms and values of society. For the individual grappling with conflicts involving a dispute of moral values, "ethical relativism" offers little help. For example, a high school boy who has been educated from childhood to value both loyalty and honesty, observed his friend drinking beer in the school parking lot during break. Subsequently, he is questioned by his coach–whom he respects–whether he knew about the incident? Should he be loyal to his friend and say nothing? Should he be honest and confess what he has seen? Or should he consider another alternative? How does he decide? Values clarification not only provides little help for the individual to evaluate his or her judgements and actions in such moral predicaments, it even fails to acknowledge the issue of the conflicts of moral values.

"Ethical relativism" has extensive consequences for drug education programs. For instance, if "ethical relativism" is extended to a logical conclusion, students who are educated in values clarification will believe that there is no "morally" relevant criterion. Conceivably, some of them may even steal to feed a drug habit but rationalize that they have committed nothing "morally" objectionable. This is because their own "clarified" valued system, which might be incompatible with those of the law enforcement officers, made it "morally" expedient for them to steal. Their "values," in fact, have been merely articulated, not clarified. Values clarification in this instance has unwittingly promoted a socially "questionable" ethical position. Unless its proponents confront this problem of "ethical relativism," values clarification in many cases will be little more than the easy exchange of personal prejudices.

The Danger of Indoctrination

Although the advocates of values clarification have vehemently opposed authoritarian, indoctrinatory techniques in the classroom, some critics appraising the approach emphasize the risk of indoctrination. Those individuals whose values are incongruent with the "desired" values of the drug educator or program, become easy targets for "values teaching." In this instance, values clarification is, in fact, a kind of oblique indoctrination. For example, the Coronado Program, a leader in the values clarification approach to drug education, espouses to help students "develop a personal value system," but declares unequivocally that the values clarified student should "opt against drug misuse." [4] This hidden agenda of drug abstinence is replete throughout drug education programs in the country [17–19]. Obviously, the assertion to promote personal, free, informed value choices in drug education is more illusionary than real. Values clarification is not altogether "value free."

Furthermore, the available literature has not established conclusively that drug users or abstainers can be differentiated on the basis of the clarity of their values [5,16,20]. Even if such a correlation has been established, it is quite different from proving a causal relationship between unclear values and drug use. These hidden, unproven assumptions of values clarification certainly should receive careful scrutiny before the approach is implemented extensively in drug education programs.

Peer Pressure

An obvious shortcoming of the approach is its proclivity toward conformity to the detriment of the personal development and clarification of values. Theoretically, each individual is free to act and express as he or she feels appropriate. Despite the abundant references to relativism and individualism throughout the literature, however, several of the recommended strategies and exercises, covertly or otherwise, rely on peer pressure. This is especially significant and detrimental, given the social context of a normal company of young people who are vulnerable to the influence of their peers. Apparently, only the most psychologically secure are willing to express their candid feelings and views on value issues publicly, without fear of ridicule or censure, particularly if they do not fall into the mainstream of peer opinion. The following example will demonstrate this predicament. One of the most popular exercises of the approach is "values-voting" which involves having students indicate publicly their position *vis-a-vis* drug related issues. For example, they may be asked to respond to the question, "How many of you think it is alright to smoke a pack of cigarettes a week?" Consider the dilemma of a middle school girl who is very concerned about her status with her peers and the teacher. Although her position on this question may be evident, because the probability of being scoffed is so awesome and real, she may decide to "pass" or express an opinion more consonant with socially acceptable standards. This girl's true values are certainly not clarified or affirmed. In reality, therefore, there is no genuinely "free" context in the classroom, such that all students are unafraid and uninhibited from openly expressing non-conforming values. Given the dynamics of social relationships within the classroom, this insistence for frequent public affirmation of a value position can all too easily degenerate to a case for social conformity.

CONCLUSION

While the need to clarify the values of students cannot be denied, there are still several issues in values clarification which remain unclarified; an ironic circumstance for an educational approach professing to seek clarification. This brief critique is presented to encourage drug educators and others to formulate a more comprehensive and defensible position on the role of values clarification in drug education. Meanwhile, educators who are convinced about the efficacy of the approach to influence drug use, should employ it fully cognizant of its inherent problems and limitations.

ACKNOWLEDGEMENT

The author wishes to record his appreciation to Gordon Giles for proofreading an earlier version of the manuscript.

REFERENCES

1. S. Simon, Sid Simon on Values: No Moralizers or Manipulators Allowed, *Nations Schools,* p. 40, December 1973.
2. P. Cimini, Humanizing as a Teaching Strategy, *School Health Review, 5:*1, pp. 15-21, 1974.
3. S. Simon and P. deSherbinin, Values Clarification: It Can Start Gently and Grow Deep, *Phi Delta Kappan, 55,* pp. 679-683, June 1975.
4. M. Bensley, *Values Education: A Promising Approach to the Drug Problem,* Croft Educational Services, Inc., New London, Conn., p. 9, 1971.
5. W. Blokker, B. Kirschenbaum, and H. Kirschenbaum, Values Clarification and Drug Abuse, *Health Education,* pp. 6-8, March/April 1976.
6. Coronado Unified School District, *Teachers Guide to the Coronado Plan for Preventative Drug Abuse: Kindergarten through Grades Twelve,* Value Education Publication, Campbell, California, 1973.
7. R. Carney, *A Report on the Feasibility of Using Risk Taking Attitudes as a Basis for Programs to Control and Predict Drug Abuse,* Coronado Unified School District, Coronado, California, 1970.
8. J. Swisher and A. Piniuk, Factors to Consider in Planning a Drug Education Program, B. W. Corder, R. A. Smith, and J. Swisher (eds.), *Drug Abuse Prevention,* Wm. C. Brown Company Publisher, Dubuque, Iowa, 1975.
9. B. Corder, Values Clarification in Drug Abuse Programs, B. W. Corder, R. A. Smith (eds.), *Drug Abuse Prevention,* Wm. C. Brown Company Publisher, Dubuque, Iowa, 1975.
10. M. Forcinelli, Values Education in the Public School, *Thrust,* pp. 4-6, March 1974.
11. A. Lockwood, A Critical View of Values Clarification, *Teachers College Record, 77:*1, pp. 35-50, September 1975.
12. J. Stewart, Problems and Contradictions of Values Clarification, *Phi Delta Kappan, 55,* pp. 684-687, June 1975.
13. D. Goodlett, Values Clarification—Where Does It Belong?, *Health Education,* pp. 10-11, April, 1976.
14. D. Loggins, Clarifying What and How Well? *Health Education,* pp. 2-5, March, 1976.
15. M. Goodstadt, Myths and Methodology in Drug Education: A Critical Review of the Research Evidence, M. S. Goodstadt (ed.), *Research on Methods and Programs of Drug Education,* Addiction Research Foundation, Toronto, Ontario, p. 126, 1974.
16. L . Raths, H. Mernie, and S. Simon, *Values and Teaching,* Charles E. Merril, Inc., Columbus, Ohio, 1966.
17. J. Raths, Clarifying Children's Values, *The National Elementary Principal, 42,* pp. 35-39, November 1962.
18. S. Simon, L. Howe, and H. Kirschenbaum, *Values Clarification: A Handbook of Practical Strategies for Teachers and Students,* Hart Publishing, New York, New York, pp. 17-21, 1972.
19. S. Halleck, The Great Drug Education Hoax, *The Progressive,* (reprint pages 1-17), 1970.

20. M. Deardon and J. Jekel, A Pilot Program in High School Drug Education Utilizing Non-Directive Techniques and Sensitivity Training, *Journal of School Health, 41,* pp. 118-124, 1971.
21. G. Braucht, D. Follingstad, D. Brakarsh, and K. Berry, A Review of Goals, Approaches and Effectiveness, and a Paradigm for Evaluation, *Quarterly Journal of Studies on Alcohol, 34,* pp. 1-6, 1973.
22. P. Wald and A. Abrams, Drug Education, P. M. Wald and P. B. Hutt (eds.), *The Drug Abuse Survey Project Dealing with Drug Abuse,* Praeger Publication, New York, New York, 1972.
23. F. Amendolora, Modifying Attitudes Toward Drugs in Seventh Grade Students, *Journal of Drug Education, 3:*1, pp. 71-78, 1973.
24. L. Gagnon, An Analysis of an Experimental Methodology for Teaching, Thinking and Clarifying Values, Ph.D. Dissertation, Wayne State University, 1965.

CHAPTER 8
Substance Abuse Prevention Programming and Research: A Partnership in Need of Improvement*

RICHARD DEMBO

INTRODUCTION

The fields of drug abuse prevention and research into substance use have become increasingly sophisticated in recent years. Initially designed to prevent all non-medical drug use, prevention efforts gave considerable emphasis to the moral and social values that were violated by the use of various substances. This moralistic stress gradually shifted to the development of programs that provided scientific information in regard to the effects of drug taking; the rationale of these efforts was that as a result of being presented with such information, people would rationally decide to avoid drug taking. More recently, programs geared to providing individuals with non-drug use alternatives to deal with their

* Presented at the Second Annual Meeting of the National Association of Prevention Professionals, Denver, Colorado, February 1979.

personal and interpersonal difficulties, as well as gaining satisfaction, have received considerable interest. Such a prevention program thrust is consistent with a main recommendation of the landmark Second Report of the National Commission on Marijuana and Drug Abuse [1] : that the phenomenon of drug use be examined from the perspective of the needs the user seeks to satisfy from substance taking, rather than focusing attention on particular substance(s) of preference or the physiological effects of drugs.

On the research side, theoretical and methodological sophistication has also increased in the drug field. Theoretically, an increased understanding has developed that drug use must be examined in the context of the attitudes, beliefs, and social and cultural experiences of the people taking them; and that the psychological features of the lives of many users are a necessary but not a sufficient basis for understanding their drug taking. Just as the view of the factors relating to substance use has expanded, so, too, has the focus on the drugs individuals use. There has been a shift from addressing attention to one drug or another to examining more comprehensively the legal (prescription, over the counter drugs, alcohol and tobacco) as well as illicit drugs the same groups of individuals may use. Certainly, detailed inquiry into these two areas has expanded the frame of reference of any assessment of drug taking within any population group; however, such a line of analysis is necessary if we are to be able to capture the scope and complexity of the drug use experience.

In terms of research methodology, we have witnessed an increasing use of sophisticated analysis techniques that enable us to gain greater insight into the complex patterns of drug use among different life experience groups. Assisted by work published by the National Institute on Drug Abuse [2, 3] , applications of such multivariate analysis procedures as factor analysis, path analysis, discriminant analysis, multiple regression analysis and multivariate analysis of variance in research into drug use have become common.

In spite of the progress in drug abuse prevention and research in the drug field, much remains to be accomplished before these two areas of activity can become better integrated. The issues facing drug abuse prevention I shall now discuss are not exhaustive, but they cover some salient concerns related to the theoretical naivete of much drug prevention programming and problems in researching the experiences and effects of these programs. The discussion will suggest ways to improve these areas of work and their relationship.

ISSUES FACING DRUG PREVENTION PROGRAMMING AND RESEARCH

Theoretical Issues

A key theoretical issue facing the field of drug abuse prevention is that many programs continue to regard the individual user as the focus of concern.

Secondary interest is usually given to the social and cultural experiences of users, although research has consistently indicated these are critical factors in people's reactions to drugs and to prevention programs [4, 5].

A second, related point is that many drug prevention programs take place in institutional settings, such as the school, with relatively few program activities occurring in the community. This situation exists in spite of the fact that research, particularly among young people, has indicated that many drug users, especially those whose substance use reflects deep personal and socio-cultural commitments to the community, would be more effectively reached in their neighborhoods. Program efforts here would be able to capitalize on the social, cultural and environmental factors relating to individuals' drug use by using respected persons and groups as role models to prevent users from becoming fruther involved in substance taking [6, 7]. In emphasizing the need for this development, a recent review of 127 primary prevention program evaluation studies completed in the last ten years (85% were published or issued between 1973 and 1977) prepared by Schaps, DiBartolo, Palley and Churgin found that 81 per cent of the programs were school or school-district based, whereas only 13 per cent were located in the community [8].

Third, there is a need to develop drug prevention programs for non-youths and non-white, middle-class persons. As Schaps, DiBartolo, Palley and Churgin found, 90 per cent of the programs they reviewed addressed target audiences of college age or below [8], and no program was seen to serve senior citizens. In addition, the reviewers uncovered that only three of the programs examined served populations with more than 50 per cent minority representation. Such a youthful, white, middle-class thrust in drug prevention programming is in marked contrast to research results indicating a need for these efforts among other target groups [9–11]. We have scarcely scratched the surface in these program development areas; but, it is necessary that we devote attention to this challenge if our work is to be relevant to the drug use experiences and prevention needs in our society today.

Fourth, an emphasis on preventing drug use still prevails. This program stress continues in spite of the growing body of research findings indicating high and increasing prevalence rates of the use of a wide range of legal and illicit substances – especially among youths and young adults [10–12].

Fifth, drug prevention programs tend to be given to large audiences, such as those in the classroom or assembly, and emphasize one-way communication techniques, like talks by "experts" and films on drugs. Schaps, DiBartolo, Palley and Churgin found, for example, that informational strategies were the most commonly employed among the 127 primary prevention programs they reviewed [8]. This program stress is in marked contrast to the lessons to be drawn from research findings in this area. The results of a 1974/75 New York Statewide survey of public, junior and senior high school students showed the classroom and school assemblies to be the most frequent mentioned settings, and films on drugs to be the most often noted program technique, to which they had been exposed during the year prior to the survey. However, these program exposure rates were in marked contrast to other findings of this survey which highlight that most of the youngsters prefer drug prevention programs that involve interaction techniques – such as rap sessions and individual/group/family counseling [5]. In particular, substantial discrepancies were found to exist between student ratings of the effectiveness of prevention programs and the rates of participation in these activities. Classrooms and school assemblies, for example, were claimed as prevention program sites by large numbers of the youths surveyed; however, these sites were judged to be low in effectiveness ("helped turn young people away from drugs") by their participants. As a case in point, 22 per cent of the students surveyed indicated they had been exposed to talks by ex-addicts; but, this technique was rated as effective by 63 per cent of those who had experienced it. In this vein, Schaps, DiBartolo, Palley and Churgin found that, among the programs they reviewed, those whose services were delivered by parents or by peers had more positive outcomes than those which were delivered by teachers, program staff or others [8]. Further, only six programs were found to rely upon peers to deliver program services and only one program relied upon parents as service deliverers.

Research Concerns

The state-of-the-art in prevention program evaluation is uncertain. Developed out of a sense of urgency to do something about the drug abuse problem, examinations of these program efforts have not been marked by their sophistication. In their review of the literature in 1976, Randall and Wong pointed out that meaningful evaluations of prevention programs that could provide data for future efforts were lacking [13]. Perhaps the most useful recent analysis of the research quality of evaluation of prevention program efforts is reported by Schaps, DiBartolo, Palley and Churgin [8]. Their findings suggest the road that needs to be travelled before examinations of the impact of drug prevention programs can match the growing theoretical sophistication of these programs. Here is a listing of their main findings in this area:

1. Of the various types of measurement techniques that could find a place in examining the effects of prevention programs (questionnaires, interviews, archival records, direct observation or trace measures, such as counting beer bottles), only one technique, questionnaires, was relied upon to gather program outcome information. More than 90 per cent of programs evaluated used this method, and only 12 per cent employed any of the other methods. It can certainly be argued that, whatever the strengths relating to the use of questionnaires, there are problems associated with their use (such as response bias) and the use of other data gathering techniques would be a fine supplement to the use of questionnaires.

2. A majority of the program evaluations (57%) used pre-post test testing schedules, a much preferred strategy over post tests only or retrospective designs. However, one would like to see a more widespread use of this procedure.
3. Only 31 per cent of all the program evaluations used randomly constituted comparison groups, with an additional 9 per cent of the programs involving group comparisons free of confounds that could call the results into question. In contrast, 60 per cent of the evaluations involved poor comparison groups or lacked any comparison group at all.
4. In regard to various measures of prevention program impact, drug use, intentions to use drugs and attitudes toward drug use, attitudes toward drug use were most commonly employed among the 127 evaluations (65%). Measures of drug use were employed in 57 per cent of the program evaluations, and 13 per cent of the evaluations used measures of intentions to use drugs. (Percentages total more than 100%, since some studies used more than one measure.) Yet, however important they may be, attitudes to drug taking and claimed intentions to use drugs are much weaker measures of program impact than actual substance taking; and, one would hope that such an outcome measure would find its place in even more prevention program evaluations in the future.

The above noted research issues relating to prevention program evaluation have important implications for our understanding of what prevention programs work for what groups and how they are effective. Such an implication is apparent in the finding of Schaps, DiBartolo, Palley and Churgin that weak research methods, such as retrospective only studies, come up with higher average outcome ratings than do studies using the three more rigorous testing schedules (post-test only, pre-post-test and follow-up with pre-post or post-test) [8]. In calling for more rigorous research designs incorporating the use of multiple measurement techniques, the use of both pre- and post-tests (with avoidance of retrospective only studies) among randomly assigned comparison groups and the gathering of data on actual drug use, in addition to information on intentions to use drugs and attitudes toward drug use, Schaps, DiBartolo, Palley and Churgin have performed a valuable service for the field [8].

BUILDING A MORE EFFECTIVE PARTNERSHIP

It should be clear from the above discussion that effective prevention program efforts can best be planned and put into operation by working in close coordination with research activities that are sensitive to the needs and aims of these programs, closely linked to program events and relevant to the needs and interests of the target groups to whom these programs are addressed. Building such a relationship is difficult, and there are few ongoing experiences from which to draw.

Prevention program personnel are intensely concerned with providing service, and their interests often conflict with those of researchers who are concerned primarily with methodology and instrument design issues. Program workers are often deeply involved in the settings in which they work, usually having devoted considerable effort to putting their programs into place. The researcher, infrequently part of the prevention program team, is less community involved and is often viewed as an outsider whose concern is with following the scientific canon rather than helping people; and, researchers are often accused of taking off with the research data, never to be heard from again. From the researcher's perspective, prevention program workers are often seen to have a very narrow focus in not appreciating that a sophisticated research examination of the aims of the program and what the program is accomplishing can serve to improve its effectiveness. In discouraging the use of rigorous research procedures, prevention program personnel are seen to fall victim to their own biases and, perhaps, misleading assumptions about what they are trying to accomplish and how effective their program is in this regard. Such a conflict between the researcher and program personnel is not unique to the drug field [14].

Whatever the cause(s) of this difference in viewpoints, it is necessary to build bridges between researchers and drug prevention program activities. As a modest contribution to this process, I should like to review some experiences we had in developing and carrying out a survey of South Bronx, New York City junior high school youths that was completed in 1976, which suggests how researcher, community and program officials can work together in pursuing work that is relevant to school and community. We were engaged in work that could lead to the development of prevention efforts to serve different target groups of youths in the school, rather than evaluating any programs. However, our experiences are instructive and translatable to issues regarding the relationship between evaluation researcher and prevention program personnel.

A Brief Natural History of the South Bronx Survey

The N.Y.S Drug Abuse Control Commission, for which I worked in 1974, had as one of its interests gaining a greater understanding of the substance use patterns of various population groups. Since arriving at the agency in late 1973, I had participated in, among other things, the development of a statewide survey of the attitudes, values, drug prevention program experiences and substance use behavior of public, junior and senior high school youths. While I appreciated the value of such a large scale survey effort, I also realized that the findings must necessarily be rather gross in that the social, cultural and geographical diversity represented in this work made control of social context impossible. There was a feeling that more focussed survey efforts in particular areas would be of considerable value in helping to tease out the background, attitude, value and social behavior characteristics that relate to specific patterns of drug taking, as well as permit the examination of various hypotheses regarding drug use.

Reflective of a continuing concern over the relationship between drug use and crime in New York City, a major interest of the agency centered on the substance use of young people in the inner city. In response to this interest, a few members of my research section and I began to search for a setting in which we could carry out this kind of research.

Preliminary inquiries among various agency treatment and prevention personnel, and school and community contacts, led us to focus our attention on the South Bronx. Not only had this location witnessed rapid population changes, it was generally acknowledged to contain some of the most severe social and economic problems of any area in New York City.

In the spring of 1974, I had the good furtune to meet Bill Burgos, my major collaborator on the South Bronx project. He was introduced to me by a former agency aftercare officer who was employed as a drug prevention worker in a Bronx junior high school. Bill was a social worker, who had grown up in the South Bronx and had worked there for some ten years. At the time we met, Bill was working on a research project in a South Bronx therapeutic community drug program. He was well respected in the community and had extensive contacts in the area.

Bill and I began doing some preliminary fieldwork in a number of different South Bronx neighborhoods, interviewing individuals and groups of youths in youth clubs and street corners. Our open-ended discussions covered the following agenda:

1. relationships with parents, peers and school;
2. vocational aspirations;
3. orientations to the environment;
4. leisure-time behavior, including the use of the mass media;
5. self-concepts;
6. perceptions of various styles of life that existed in the neighborhood;
7. social behavior – including substance use;
8. motivations and rationalizations relating to the experimentation and use of drugs;
9. symbolic meanings held in regard to drug use; and
10. suggestions concerning drug abuse prevention efforts and the efficacy of new approaches.

We were usually permitted to tape record these interviews.

Several New York City school districts served the South Bronx in 1974. Our first contact was with a large district, which had fairly well developed drug prevention program activities in most of its schools, and a concerned, open-minded staff. District officials were supportive of the research we had in mind, but were reluctant to have the project pursued for at least a year. Major administrative changes were in progress, and officials wanted to let time pass so things could settle into a routine.

In the fall of 1974, we contacted another large school district serving the South Bronx. Our research idea was favorably received, but there was considerable concern about our ultimate research interests. Many discussions were held with the drug abuse prevention program director of the school district in order to share our mutual interests and to develop a relationship on the basis of which the study could proceed. Our discussions culminated, in March 1975, in the writing of a research contract between myself and the school district which addressed major concerns that had been expressed about the work we proposed. The research intentions and obligations we committed ourselves to are set out below:

1. The research we intend to pursue seeks to increase our understanding in regard to how young people relate to substances. It is not the purpose of our work to evaluate any individuals, schools or programs in our research sites. (Obviously, this condition would have to be modified in the case of an evaluation research project.)
2. Any information we collect will be treated with the utmost confidentiality. Every effort will be taken to assure that youngsters who participate in our research cannot be identified. The results of our research will be presented in statistical summary form only.
3. We intend to submit reports of our work for publication in professional journals. In addition to the District Office, schools and individuals participating in our research can, if they wish, receive copies of our published results.

This document went a long way towards eliminating concern over the sincerity of our research interest and the pursuit of our work in a professional manner with due regard to our service and human rights obligations. With this research assurance in hand, the director of the drug abuse prevention programs for the school district began to actively work with us in locating a site for our study.

The district drug prevention program director acted as an intermediary between ourselves and a South Bronx junior high school. This effort culminated in a discussion with school officials and members of the community in the early spring 1975. Our interest in pursuing the research in the school was discouraged, primarily, we later learned, due to school and community anxiety about any reprecussions that might result from publication of the findings of the study. The level of anxiety remained high regardless of our commitment to abide by the terms of the research contract we had written for the school district.

Shortly after this experience, the drug prevention director advised of another school, which served a fairly heterogeneous socio-economic and cultural catchment area in the South Bronx including a number of depressed neighborhoods. The principal of this school was said to be open-minded, enjoyed considerable respect from the teachers and had good relationships with various community interest groups.

Preliminary discussions with the principal, key school officials, and drug and health education staff led to our meeting with community school board and Parent Teacher Association (PTA) members. At the time, the school lacked a well developed drug prevention program – even though it was appreciated that many of the youngsters attending the school were living in high risk neighborhoods. A topic on drug abuse was, in line with state department of education requirements, taught in the health education course each pupil recieved. In addition, small groups run by one drug education teacher serving some 1400 students was the only "organized" drug abuse prevention activity in the school.

The interest expressed by school officials and staff, in our preliminary discussions, in learning more about the students' backgrounds, attitudes, values, social behavior and drug use, so that the school could develop effective and engaging drug prevention programs, was repeated by school board members and PTA officials. The group was told of our ongoing fieldwork, and felt that the experiences we were uncovering were germane to students attending the school. Our research interests converged with the program development concerns of the school. We were invited to pursue our work in the school, with the proviso that approval to proceed would be obtained at each major milestone in the project.

Our first request was for permission to meet informally with students in the school cafeteria, schoolyard, and other gathering places, so that we could begin to relate to one another, and we could gain an understanding of them and assess the degree to which the results of our fieldwork were relevant to the experience of pupils attending the school. Bill and I included this work in with our other fieldwork activities, although most of the school fieldwork effort took place during May and June 1975. We also held a number of detailed discussions with the drug prevention counselor in order to gain insight into the students' needs and learn factors and experiences that were felt important in understanding their drug use.

By July 1975, Bill and I felt sufficiently informed by our fieldwork to put together a very rough draft of the questionnaires we hoped, after refinement and pre-testing, to use in the actual survey, which we planned to administer to two waves, about a month apart, in the winter 1976. Much work remained.

One lesson we learned from our fieldwork was that adults and youngsters often have very different, and usually equally valid, perspectives on various aspects of behavior – such as substance use. Bill and I felt the need to bridge this gap by letting panels of junior high school youths, who attended schools other than the one where we planned to conduct the survey, critique the content, format and organization of the instruments. Painful as this experience was, at times, to our pride, we couldn't have made a wiser decision. We revised the instruments in major ways about three times as a result of the youths' suggestions, each time creating forms with greater clarity, interest and cultural relevance to the youths we intended to study. By late fall 1975, we were ready to put our ideas to test.

Administration of the Winter 1976 Survey

In preparation for the implementation of the survey, Bill and I met with the social studies teachers in the school, in whose classrooms the questionnaires were to be administered, in November 1975. Our discussion covered the purposes of the survey, as well as the procedures of its administration. The staff were quite helpful in our work.

At least part of the reason for staff support rested in the steps we took to ensure the confidentiality of the survey data. The questionnaire instructions specifically asked students not to place their names, or any other identifying information, anywhere on the forms. Further, seals were provided so that the youths' answers would be seen only by the researchers.

Prior to administration of the first wave of the survey in the early winter 1976, the principal placed an article in the PTA Newsletter advising parents of the survey and inviting any comments and suggestions regarding the research effort. A number of questions of clarification of our objectives were received, and they were handled on an individual basis.

The groundwork prepared, the administration of the first survey wave took place without any major difficulty. About six weeks afterwards, the second questionnaire was administered, again without any major problems.

Feedback of the Results

Processing the questionnaire data began at the completion of each survey wave. The N.Y.S. Office of Drug Abuse Services proved to be of great assistance in providing funds for coding, editing and key punching the data. The help of this agency enabled us to fulfill our wish and commitment to feedback to the school and community timely reports of the important results of the survey.

Our first report provided a listing of the youths' responses to all of the questions in the first survey instrument, as well as a number of cross-tabulations regarding the background, attitude and value correlates of the students' drug use. It addressed a primary need of the school in supplying some estimate of the prevalence of the use of various substances by students in the school. We met with key school officials and community representatives in mid-summer 1976 and discussed these preliminary results. Suggestions were invited regarding analyses of the data that would prove helpful to the school and community; and we advised those present of our plans to study the data.

This meeting was quite helpful in formulating our data analysis plans in such a manner that they would produce relevant reports. Another fruitful interaction with school staff took place in December 1976, when a preliminary report of the results of the second survey instrument was provided and discussed.

Although the frequency of our contacts with school officials and community members decreased after administration of the survey, we remained in communication with the school principal. As papers were prepared from our analyses of the survey data, copies were sent to the school for its review and use. By the time our December 1976 meeting was held, the school had received a number of reports of our work. Major implications for drug prevention programming flowing from this work were also considered during this session. As I review some key issues and experiences we uncovered in our research, I hope you will share with me the feeling that our fieldwork and working relationship with the school and community members proved to be invaluable resources in enhancing the quality and relevance of our reports.

Some Key Findings From the South Bronx Survey

The major findings of the South Bronx survey can be grouped into two areas: (1) the factors and processes that are involved in the youths' drug taking and (2) strategies by which drug prevention efforts can be most effectively addressed to the different needs represented by the drug taking of the youths in the school. Since these results are, or will be, available in published form, they will be summarized with particular reference to the thrust of this paper.

Factors and Processes in the Youths' Drug Use – The first and second survey waves probed the youths' use of the following categories of substances:

1. alcohol (beer, wine, hard liquor, etc.);
2. marijuana or hashish (pot, grass, hash, smoke, reefers);
3. L.S.D. or similar drugs (L.S.D., mescaline, peyote, psilocybin, DMT, etc.);
4. depressants (downers, quaalude, seconal, tuinal, barbs, etc.);
5. narcotics (heroin, smack, junk, opium, codeine, paragoric, morphine, etc.);
6. solvents (sniffing glue, gasoline, paint thinner); and
7. stimulants (uppers, methedrine, speed, dexedrine, dexamyl, cocaine, etc.).[1]

Analysis showed that some 40 per cent of the youths claimed to have ever used alcohol and 20 per cent marijuana/hashish, while some 35 per cent and 17 per cent of the students, respectively, indicated they had used these substances during the six months prior to the survey. On the other hand, less than 7 per cent of the youths noted they had used any of the substances in each of the categories of: L.S.D. or similar drugs, depressants, narcotics, solvents and stimulants.

In addition to developing a profile of the youths' drug use, we wished to create an index of involvement with substances. To this end, an illuminating analysis of the ever used data was performed, resulting in a Guttman scale of drug involvement that contained four categories:

1. all use denied;
2. use of alcohol admitted;

[1] Although questions were asked in regard to tobacco use, these data are not reported here.

3. use of marijuana (including hashish) – and usually alcohol – admitted; and
4. use of other drugs – and usually alcohol and marijuana – admitted.

The data on which this scale is based are strongly unidimensional, having high Guttman reproducibility and scalability coefficients. The drug involvement measure is similar to the scale developed by Single, Kandel and Faust [15], and reflects an increased involvement with substances as we go from the no use, through the alcohol and marijuana use categories, to that denoting the taking of other drugs.

The measure has been found to be highly related to the number of substances used, as well as the recency, frequency and concurrency of drug use [16]. Further analysis found the youths' drug involvement to be significantly and positively related to their (1) being drunk or very, very high on alcohol in the year prior to the survey, (2) having missed school or had an accident due to alcohol or drug use in the six months prior to the survey, (3) getting the shakes or depressed unless they used alcohol or other drugs in the last six months, and (4) experiencing trouble with family or friends in the last six months due to alcohol or drug use [7].

We appreciate that the substance use data we collected probably represent conservative estimates of the drug taking behavior among the youths attending the school. For the first survey wave 17 per cent, and for the second wave 22 per cent, of the students enrolled in the school did not participate in the survey. Research has found that youths who do not attend school regularly tend to use substances more frequently than those who do [17, 18]. However, our main interests were less on providing exact estimates of the youths' drug use than in understanding better the correlates of their drug involvement. The convergence of our findings with those obtained by other researchers studying similar groups of youths gives us considerable confidence in our findings.

Ethnicity, Self-concept and Life Style Factors and Drug Involvement – One group of papers emerging from our analyses of the survey data concerned the relationship of the youths' ethnicity, self-images and life style characteristics to their drug use. The results are most interesting.

An analysis of the demographic and attitude/value (peer-social reasons for drug use; escape from problems reasons for using drugs, felt relationships with parents; attitudes to school and machismo) correlates of drug use among the Blacks, Puerto Rican and White youths surveyed was pursued to examine three hypotheses that could explain their substance involvement:

1. *Ethnic subculture* – that the three ethnic groups exhibited different degrees of drug involvement or that their patterns of demographic, attitude/value correlates of drug involvement would differ;
2. *social class* – finding that the youths' socio-economic status (SES)

accounted for the predominant amount of variance in their drug involvement; and

3. *social adjustment* – determining that the students' broken home situation, perceived difficulty in relating to their parents, their disinterest in school, holding machismo views and attitudes supportive of drug use related positively to their involvement with substances – regardless of their SES and ethnic group membership.

The results clearly supported both the ethnic subculture and social adjustment hypotheses. While, in general, the youths' drug involvement can be considered as an alternative to commitment to school and is associated with felt unsatisfactory relationships with significant others, such as one's family, important ethnic group differences were found to exist in the youngsters' drug use. In particular, living in a non-intact household was more strongly associated with drug involvement among the Black youths than among the Puerto Rican students; however, the relationship between felt relationships with one's family and drug involvement was much stronger in the Puerto Rican group than in the Black group. These results suggest that the relationship between family problems and drug involvement varies greatly by ethnic group. While ethnicity was not found to be related directly to the youths' drug involvement, it did interact with other variables to predict their drug use – indicating that the factor of ethnicity cannot be ignored in understanding the students' drug use [19].

Another analysis we pursued involved an examination of the relationship of the youths' self-concepts to their drug use. The boys' and girls' self-images were indexed by clusters derived from varimax factor analyses of the intercorrelations of their replies to questions probing their perceived similarity to fourteen youth types our fieldwork indicated were relevant to their experience. The following factors were developed for further study:

Boys

1. *drug/gang factor:* highly and positively weighted on *Ken*-hustler, knows the ins and outs of the dope scene, *Joe*-gang member and *Frank*-"cool" cat who is into reefers.
2. *male "ideal":* highly and positively weighted on *Andy*-dates a lot, *Jason*-tough and *Charlie*-natural leader.
3. *educational orientation:* highly and positively weighted on *John*-school achiever, and negatively weighted on *Mike*-school rejector and *George*-hangs out with friends.

Girls

1. *leader/gang:* highly and positively weighted on *Gail*-natural leader, *Isabel*-gang member, *Janey*-streetwise, *Sharon*-hangs out with friends and *Cathy*-tough.
2. *drug culture:* highly and positively weighted on *Diana*-"cool" cat who is into reefers and *Fran*-knows the streets, ins and outs of the dope scene.

3. *educational orientation:* highly and positively loaded on *Hilary*-school achiever and negatively weighted on *Sheila*-school rejector.

Our analysis of these data, which involved all ethnic groups combined since the Black, Puerto Rican, White, Other Hispanic and "Other" ethnic groups studied did not differ in their self-concepts, found the youths' self-images to be most strongly associated with their drug involvement. As we would expect, for boys drug/gang and male "ideal" self-images were positively related to their drug involvement, and educational orientation was negatively associated with their drug use – even when their background (age, home composition, head of household educational and occupational levels-measures of socio-economic status) and their attitudes/values (peer-social reasons for drug use, escape from problems reasons for drug use, felt relationships with parents, attitudes to school and machismo views) were controlled for. A similar line of analysis for the girls found that drug culture and leader/gang self-images were strongly and positively associated with drug involvement, and that educational orientation was negatively related to substance use [20]. In showing the boys' and girls' self-images to be significantly related to their involvement with substances, the results raise a number of important issues regarding the relevance of personality and socio-cultural views of drug use to drug prevention strategies for the inner city youths we researched. The findings indicate that the youths' drug use is motivated, adjustive behavior, holding a complex relationship to their personalities and the values in their environment. The youths are best seen as internalizing features of their environment in such a manner that they fit in with their self-conceptions. Hence, focussing on the youngsters as individuals (or psychological entities) or on the cultural values which are prevalent in their neighborhood would provide a limited understanding of them and their substance taking behavior. Cultural values become important when they are incorporated into people's self-perceptions and are reflected in their activities. Drug abuse prevention must, then, be regarded as part of an effort to deal with the larger framework of the lives of the youngsters we studied. Clinically oriented efforts are likely to prove useful with only a minority of youngsters.

Another analysis looked into the relationship of the features of the life styles of the youths to their drug involvement. In particular, our interest centered on the following neighborhood relationship and drug use context features:

1. *view of the neighborhood as tough:* a cluster derived from factor analysis and weighted strongly and positively on items tapping how "tough" it is to get on in one's neighborhood, that it contains a lot of gangs, that young people are into getting high on pot, that it's hard to stay out of trouble growing up in one's neighborhood, and that people tend to get into fights; a question probing how "peaceful" it is to live in one's neighborhood is negatively weighted on this factor.
2. *image of drug using, gang involved persons by peers:* this factor reflects

the esteem the youths' perceived their peers accord to the junkie, pot head, occasional pot smoker and gang member; an item relating to "good student" is negatively weighted on this cluster.

3. *friends' use of alcohol and marijuana*
4. *friends' use of other substances* (depressants, L.S.D. or similar drugs, narcotics, solvents and stimulants)
5. *drug/street culture spare-time activities:* this factor reflects the youths' participation in the following out of school activities: drinking; going to parties, dances, gigs; hanging out; getting high; and fighting; items tapping doing homework for school and being at home with one's family are negatively weighted on this factor.

Analysis strongly suggested that the youths' drug involvement is an environmentally related phenomenon. Their peer held esteem of drug using, gang involved people, friends' use of alcohol and marijuana and the youths' participation in spare-time activities of a drug/street culture nature provide important insights into their drug taking. Drug involved youths, as well as those who are not into substance use, appear to incorporate features of their social and cultural settings in a manner that implicates drug use as a salient or deemphasized behavior. The factors that we determined to be significant in this process should be regarded as elements of a style of life in relation to which the substance use of the youths' we researched can be understood better. In particular, the manner in which the youths studied orient themselves to the tough, streetwise role models in their neighborhoods is a most important factor in their drug use; it is even more important than their friends' taking of alcohol and marijuana [21].

The process of drug involvement – So far, our discussion has focussed on the factors relating to, or predicting the youths' drug use. We were, also, interested in uncovering some indication of the process by which their involvement with various drugs developed. To this end, an enlightening discriminant analysis was performed on the data. In addition to the youths' background characteristics (ethnicity, age, sex and home composition), we were interested in learning how the following neighborhood relationship and context of drug use factors related to their location in one of the four drug involvement groups:

a. *view of the neighborhood as tough*
b. *view of the neighborhood in survival terms:* this factor reflects the youths' felt difficulty in surviving in their neighborhood without being a member of a gang, their perception that people like them don't have much of a chance of making a success in life and their belief that it is hard to get oneself together growing up in his/her neighborhood.
c. *image of drug using, gang involved persons by peers*
d. *friends' use of alcohol and marijuana*

e. *friends' use of other substances* (depressants, L.S.D. or similar drugs, narcotics, solvents and stimulants)
f. *drug/street culture spare time activities*
g. *print media/stay at home spare time activities:* this factor emphasizes the youths' reading of magazines, newspapers, books other than for school, doing homework and being at home with their families.

Preliminary analysis of the data indicated that five of these characteristics provided for the most discrimination of the youths in regard to their location in one of the four drug use groups:

1. view of the neighborhood in survival terms
2. image of drug using, gang involved persons by peers
3. friends' use of alcohol and marijuana
4. friends' use of other drugs
5. drug/street culture spare time activities

Additional analyses found two major dimensions (or functions) to be present in these data. The first function, which is highly and positively weighted on drug/street culture leisure time activities and secondarily weighted on friends' use of alcohol and marijuana reflects a *street scene, social recreational drug use context dimension.* The second function is highly and positively weighted on *friends' use of such "hard" drugs as depressants, L.S.D. or similar drugs, narcotics, solvents and stimulants.* The discriminant analysis results, further, indicates that the movement from drug involved group 1 (all use denied) to drug involved group 4 (use of other drugs) is an orderly progression involving two distinct processes. The first process, involving the movement from group 1 to group 2 (use of alcohol) and from group 2 to group 3 (use of marijuana), is accounted for nicely by the street scene, social recreational drug use function. In the second process, the movement from group 3 to group 4 is strongly associated with friends' being involved in the use of other, "hard" drugs [22].

Some indicated thrusts for drug abuse prevention activities flowing from the results of the survey – The findings just reported suggest a number of ways in which drug prevention activities can be developed to effectively engage the youths we surveyed. Basic to our recommendations to the school and community is the concept that drug prevention needs to involve both community and school resources [7, 23].

Comprehensive studies of specific social and cultural settings can permit the development of a more efficient division of labor in the drug abuse prevention field than exists currently. School and community often provide similar services to a wide range of drug using youths who could profit from more focussed efforts that relate to their specific needs. On the basis of our work, it could be argued that, for the youths we researched, the marijuana and use of "other" drugs groups should be serviced by drug abuse prevention programs in their communities. Such a thrust could capitalize on their street culture involvement by using this important aspect of their lives to reduce the risk of further drug involvement; and attempt to help them develop social sanctions and rituals that could facilitate their relating to substances in a controlled manner [24, 25]. On the other hand, the no use and alcohol taking groups, who, on the basis of our results, appear less at risk of becoming further involved with substances, would be good candidates for school based drug information and values clarification efforts [26]. These program experiences would be designed to deter the development of ties with the life style features which are associated with the drug taking of the marijuana and "other" drug use groups.

Community prevention programs could be developed and run by community based school personnel working in close collaboration with indigeneous individuals and groups. Such a strategy would enable the school to concentrate on what can be best accomplished in an institutional setting: inform young people in regard to the nature and effects of the taking of specific substances in an effort to dissuade non-users or experimental users of drugs from becoming further involved in their use.

How these programs will look in a given neighborhood will depend, among other factors, on the social, cultural and attitude characteristics that are important in understanding the drug use of the various individuals and groups living in it. The development of such an understanding could occur from pursuit of the research process we sought to actualize in our work [6]. An important consideration to keep in mind is that youthful drug use, and the results we obtained reflects this growing appreciation, is to a significant degree an environmentally related phenomenon. Substance taking can, at best, be imperfectly understood and dealt with successfully in a limited manner on an individual level. If they are to be effective, our prevention efforts need to be ethnographically informed, deeper reaching and more extensive in their range of interests than has traditionally been the case – if we are to create prevention programs that relate to important issues in the lives of drug users rather than reflecting adult misunderstandings of them.

CONCLUSIONS

The discussion of our research findings regarding the factors relating to the youths' drug use, as well as suggested prevention program thrusts, met with a very favorable reaction on the part of school officials. The principal indicated that he had for some time felt that the experiences our results captured were important in relation to the drug use of the pupils in the school; and he indicated our results were not only helpful in their own right, but useful in dealing with central office officials in seeking more resources for drug prevention efforts.

The school had a student council, in which youngsters reflecting many different life styles were represented, with which the principal felt he could work to implement some of the ideas our research suggested would be useful in addressing the drug prevention needs of students in the school. Unfortunately, financial problems facing the City of New York resulted in sharp cutbacks in what were called "non-essential services" –including drug prevention activities – so that a number of our ideas were not able to be implemented in program form.

In an ultimate sense, then, our work did not result in the program development efforts we had hoped would occur as one by-product of our work. However, the experience we gained, and the modest contribution we made to increasing school and community awareness of the nature and complexity of the issue of drug use among the youths attending the school, certainly made our work worthwhile. We hope that, by sharing our experiences with researchers and practitioners in the field, our work will become part of the process by which drug prevention work is increasingly grounded theoretically, related to the specific needs of various target groups and involves a close collaboration with research in program development and evaluation.

It certainly is about time that drug prevention work has come to occupy the forefront of interest in the drug field. However, much remains to be accomplished if we are to realize the full promise of the opportunity this interest in our work provides. This objective can be realized, but only if we achieve a greater appreciation of the larger issues that surround our work and seek to develop in such a manner that we grow from a solid and increasingly sophisticated base.

ACKNOWLEDGEMENTS

The successful completion of the South Bronx survey, which is discussed in the present paper, would not have been possible without the help of many people. We are grateful for the assistance given us by the principal, teachers, and parents of the junior high school who must remain anonymous. The reactions of many youngsters to earlier versions of the survey instruments were valuable to our research effort. The support and encouragement of the N.Y.S. Office of Drug Abuse Services, and especially Douglas S. Lipton, Director of the Division of Cost Effectiveness and Evaluation, are appreciated. Ken Marion, Sharon Diamond, Carol Spielman and Phyllis Bergman were helpful in processing the data. However, these persons are not responsible for the views that are expressed in the paper.

REFERENCES

1. Second Report of the National Commission on Marijuana and Drug Abuse, *Drug Use in America: Problem in Perspective,* U.S. Govt. Printing Office, Washington, D.C., 1973.

2. D. J. Lettieri (ed.), *Predicting Adolescent Drug Abuse: A Review of Issues, Methods and Correlates,* U.S. Govt. Printing Office, Washington, D.C., 1975.
3. P. M. Bentler, D. J. Lèttieri and G. A. Austin (eds.), *Data Analysis Strategies and Designs for Substance Abuse Research,* U.S. Govt. Printing Office, Washington, D.C., 1976.
4. R. Dembo, J. Schmeidler, D. V. Babst and D. S. Lipton, Drug Information Source Credibility Among Junior and Senior High School Youths, *American Journal of Drug and Alcohol Abuse, 4,* pp. 43-54, 1977.
5. R. Dembo, J. Schmeidler, D. S. Lipton, D. V. Babst, R. C. Stephens, S. D. Diamond, C. R. Spielman, P. J. Bergman, M. Koval and M. D. Miran, A Survey of Students' Awareness of and Attitudes Toward Drug Abuse Prevention Programs in New York State, Winter 1974/75, *The International Journal of the Addictions,* forthcoming.
6. R. Dembo and W. Burgos, A Framework for Developing Drug Abuse Prevention Strategies for Young People in Ghetto Areas, *Journal of Drug Education, 6,* pp. 313-325, 1976.
7. R. Dembo, W. Burgos, D. V. Babst, J. Schmeidler and L. E. La Grand, Neighborhood Relationships and Drug Involvement Among Inner City Junior High School Youths: Implications for Drug Education and Prevention Programming, *Journal of Drug Education, 8,* pp. 231-252, 1978.
8. E. Schaps, R. DiBartolo, C. S. Palley and S. Churgin, *Primary Prevention Evaluation Research: A Review of 127 Program Evaluations,* Pyramid Project-Pacific Institute for Research and Evaluation, Walnut Creek, California, 1978.
9. C. D. Chambers and J. A. Inciardi, *An Assessment of Drug Use in the General Population: Special Report No. 2,* N.Y.S. Narcotic Addiction Control Commission, Albany, New York, 1971.
10. Response Analysis Corporation, *Nonmedical Use of Psychoactive Substances. Part 1: Main Findings,* Response Analysis Corp., Princeton, New Jersey, 1976.
11. I. Cisin, J. D. Miller and A. V. Harrell, *Highlights from the National Survey on Drug Abuse: 1977,* U.S. Govt. Printing Office, Washington, D.C., 1978.
12. L. D. Johnston, J. G. Bachman, and P. M. O'Malley, *Drug Use Among American High School Students 1975-1977,* National Institute on Drug Abuse, Rockville, Maryland, 1977.
13. D. Randall and M. R. Wong, Drug Education to Date: A Review, *Journal of Drug Education, 6,* pp. 1-21, 1976.
14. J. Rabow, Research and Rehabilitation: The Conflict of Scientific and Treatment Roles in Corrections, In: R. M. Carter and L. T. Wilkins (eds.), *Probation, Parole and Community Corrections* (2nd ed.), 1976.
15. E. Single, D. B. Kandel and R. Faust, Patterns of Multiple Drug Use in High School, *Journal of Health and Social Behavior, 15,* pp. 344-357, 1974.
16. D. V. Babst, R. Dembo and W. Burgos, Measuring Consequences of Drug and Alcohol Abuse Among Junior High School Youths, *Journal of Alcohol and Drug Education,* forthcoming.
17. R. Roth, Student Drug Abuse in Southeastern Michigan and Profiles of the Abusers, In: S. Einstein and S. Allen (eds.), *Proceedings of the First*

International Conference on Student Drug Surveys, Baywood Publishing Co., Inc., Farmingdale, New York, 1972.

18. D. B. Kandel, Reaching the Hard-to-teach: Illicit Drug Use Among High School Absentees, *Addictive Diseases, 1,* pp. 465-480, 1975.
19. R. Dembo, W. Burgos, D. Des Jarlais and J. Schmeidler, Ethnicity and Drug Use Among Urban Junior High School Youths, *The International Journal of the Addictions,* forthcoming.
20. R. Dembo, L. Pilaro, W. Burgos, D. Des Jarlais and J. Schmeidler, Self-concept and Drug Involvement Among Urban Junior High School Youths, *The International Journal of the Addictions,* forthcoming.
21. R. Dembo, J. Schmeidler and W. Burgos, Life Style and Drug Involvement Among Youths in an Inner City Junior High School, *The International Journal of Addictions,* forthcoming.
22. R. Dembo, J. Schmeidler and W. Burgos, Factors in the Drug Involvement of Inner City Junior High School Youths: A Discriminant Analysis, Presented at the Fifth National Drug Abuse Conference, Seattle, April 1978.
23. Office of Drug Abuse Policy, *Drug Use Patterns, Consequences and the Federal Response: A Policy Review,* The Executive Office of the President, Washington, D. C., 1978.
24. N. E. Zinberg, R. C. Jacobson and W. M. Harding, Social Sanctions and Rituals as a Basis of Drug Abuse Prevention, *American Journal of Drug and Alcohol Abuse, 2,* pp. 165-182, 1975.
25. R. Jacobson and N. E. Zinberg, *The Social Basis of Drug Abuse Prevention,* Drug Abuse Council, Washington, D.C., 1975.
26. G. K. Priorkowski, Drug Education at its Best – The Shaping of Values and Anti-drug Attitudes, *Journal of Drug Education, 3,* pp. 31-37, 1973.

suggests that when young adolescents explicitly indicate a plan to use drugs at some time in the future, their intentions are influenced by other factors in addition to their previous drug experiences.

In Chapter 10, Mitic investigates the relationship between adolescent drinking behaviors and different aspects of self-esteem. Among the results, Mitic finds that students characterized as "potential problem drinkers" have lower academic self-esteem than other students. He goes on to suggest that educators should consider activities designed to enhance self-esteem when planning alcohol education programs directed at teenage populations. Such an emphasis may be an important cornerstone in building an approach more responsive to the needs of the individual.

Pederson, Baskerville, and Lefcoe examine adolescent cigarette smoking in the third chapter of this part. The authors attempt to identify variables that reliably predict smoking across a three-year span of time among children in grades six, seven, and eight. Having smoked in the past, being older, having parents and schoolmates who smoke, and repeating grades in school are all predictive of later cigarette smoking. Because of the major importance of earlier smoking experience in determining later smoking status, the authors suggest that educational efforts should begin very early in a child's schooling in order to ensure maximum impact.

The importance of dealing with drug issues early in children's schooling is underscored by Tennant in his chapter on preschoolers' awareness of substance abuse and other health-related behaviors. Tennant reports that many of the five and six year-olds interviewed gave knowledgable answers regarding the consequences of smoking, over-eating, and alcohol consumption. Also, about 26 percent reported having tasted alcohol in the past. These findings indicate substantial awareness of and some direct experience with drugs at very early ages. As a society we must question whether continuous exposure of young children to drug information on television is appropriate.

Bruno and Doscher examine patterns of drug use among Mexican-American students identified as potential high school dropouts. Cigarettes, marijuana, and alcohol are used by a majority of these students, and the levels of use are somewhat higher than those reported in other studies. The authors suggest that drug education programs should attempt to target potential dropouts, a task that is admittedly difficult since these students may be chronically absent or truant.

The last two chapters in this part examine various aspects of drug use among adults. Turner and Willis explored the relationship between self-reported religiosity and drug use among college students. Concluding that although some students who frequently use alcohol and marijuana report themselves to be deeply religious, most students who view themselves this way are not frequent drug users. In addition, non-religious users of drugs tend to discuss drug issues and problems with their peers, while religious non-users tend to bring questions about drugs to the attention of potentially helpful adults, typically their parents. In the Khavari and Douglass chapter, patterns of psychotropic drug use are examined among college students and among industrial workers. The authors suggest that drug users perform an "intuitive" cost-benefit analysis when deciding whether or not to use a particular drug. In other words, users consider such factors as the kind of drug, peer influences, health hazards, monetary costs, and societal sanctions when deciding to try initially a particular drug. Later use is thought to be influenced by these same factors as well as the person's direct drug experiences.

Part II
RESEARCH

Carefully designed empirical research contributes to and advances our basic understanding of the dynamics of drug use and drug abuse. It also provides an essential foundation upon which accurate understanding and effective, practical actions are built. In some cases, research results may have obvious and immediate practical applications to problems of drug abuse prevention, treatment, and rehabilitation. More usually, however, a particular avenue of empirical inquiry may have to be pursued for a long time before enough is uncovered that can be directly applied to the solution of practical problems. This means that the research process is a slow one, and that new findings gradually accumulate in a manner that contributes to the formation of an explanatory theory or model. As we saw in Part I of this book, a valid theory can be a powerful vehicle for generalizing beyond the boundaries of what is currently known to new situations that have yet to be investigated. Indispensible in formulating a useful theory is the conduct of empirical research demonstrating how the specific theory does in fact explain known findings in a logically consistent manner. Only when we are satisfied that a theory accurately explains known research findings can we have confidence about its ability to be extended to new situations.

In this section, we present several chapters that report the results of empirical research on various aspects of the drug use phenomenon: they certainly are not exhaustive ones in that the hundreds of areas of ongoing research are not all represented, but instead have been selected to illustrate typical approaches to acknowledged problems. In the first chapter, Huba, Wingard, and Bentler examine the relationship between adolescents' drug-taking behaviors and their intentions to use drugs in the future. These authors report that experience in using various drugs is reliably related to intentions to use them again in the future. However, intentions do not appear to be perfectly synonymous with actual drug-taking behavior. This

CHAPTER 9
Adolescent Drug Use and Intentions to Use Drugs in the Future: A Concurrent Analysis*

GEORGE J. HUBA
JOSEPH A. WINGARD
PETER M. BENTLER

Drug use among young adolescents has become an increasingly frequent behavior [1]. While numerous investigations have been undertaken to study the causal psychosocial factors of adolescent drug-taking, little attention has been given to the cognitive intentions, as opposed to behaviors, held by youth concerning the ingestion of psychoactive substances [2]. Among some young adolescents the absence of a personal source of supply for various chemicals may inhibit drug-taking whereas the youth is sure that he or she will initiate or escalate drug use when a supply becomes available at some time in the future. Similarly, for the youths who have not begun using drugs, knowledge of their intentions regarding psychoactive substance use may permit successful prediction of which adolescents will be attracted to subcultures that can supply the substance.

While intentions to use drugs are related to drug use among late- and post-adolescent youth [3, 4], there has been no comparable demonstration for much

* This research was partially supported by Grant number DA01070 from the National Institute on Drug Abuse.

younger youth who presumably have less crystalized plans about their futures and less experience with drugs [3, 4]. An examination of the relationship of use and intended use is necessary to ascertain whether intentions about future drug-taking are related to previous experience with drugs. If it can be demonstrated that intentions about general drug use are related to prior levels of drug-taking, it should then be asked if the intentions to use specific drugs are related not only to experience with that particular substance, but more generally with the previous use experience of a large number of psychoactive drugs.

METHOD

Subjects

The participants in the study were 1634 students in the seventh through ninth grades in eleven schools in the greater metropolitan area of Los Angeles. The schools were selected from a larger sample initially contacted through their district offices during the fall of 1975. The parents of each participant provided informed consent. Students and their parents were aware that the U.S. Department of Justice has issued a Grant of Confidentiality legally protecting the anonymity of the responses.

Of the 1634 students providing usable responses, 35.6 per cent were male and 64.4 per cent female. White students comprised 56.4 per cent of the sample with Spanish, Black, and Asian students comprising 14.8, 23.6, and 5.2 per cent respectively. Seventh graders represented 38.7 per cent of the sample, eighth graders 37.2 per cent, and ninth graders 24.1 per cent. More detailed characteristics of the sample are given by Huba, Wingard, and Bentler [5].

Assessment of Drug Use

Each participant completed a questionnaire about the number of times a particular substance had been used. Frequency of use data were collected for cigarettes, beer, wine, liquor, cocaine, tranquilizers, drug store medication used to get "high," heroin and other opiates, marijuana, hashish, inhalants (glue, gasoline), hallucinogenics (LSD, psilocybin, mescaline), and amphetamines. Responses were recorded on an anchored five point scale (never tried, only once, a few times, many times, regularly), using numerical values 1–5.

Assessment of Intentions to Use Drugs

Subjects also completed a questionnaire about their intentions to use twelve drugs in the future. Intentions data were collected for all drugs assessed except hashish which was combined with marijuana. Responses were coded on another five-point anchored scale (never, don't think so, not sure, probably, yes for sure) having the same numerical values.

Average Levels of Drug Use

Since the students were relatively young at the time of testing, it is not surprising that most of their drug use could be roughly categorized as experimental in nature. Table 1 shows the mean level of responding and standard deviation for the drug use and intentions variables.

Data Analysis

In order to determine if drug intentions were significantly related to drug use, canonical correlation analysis was used. The twelve intentions variables formed one set and the thirteen use variables formed the second set. Multivariate

Table 1. Summary Statistics on the Measures

Drug Use	$\overline{X}$	σ
1. Cigarettes	2.32	1.19
2. Beer	2.58	1.09
3. Wine	2.47	1.10
4. Liquor	1.92	1.06
5. Cocaine	1.08	.40
6. Tranquilizers	1.09	.44
7. Drugstore medication	1.23	.74
8. Heroin	1.03	.26
9. Marijuana	1.66	1.17
10. Hashish	1.19	.68
11. Inhalants	1.21	.64
12. Hallucinogenics	1.05	.36
13. Amphetamines	1.14	.55
Drug Intentions		
1. Cigarettes	2.41	1.44
2. Beer	2.99	1.46
3. Wine	3.06	1.46
4. Liquor	2.49	1.48
5. Cocaine	1.43	1.04
6. Tranquilizers	1.42	1.03
7. Drugstore medication	1.46	1.08
8. Heroin	1.35	.98
9. Marijuana-hashish	2.01	1.48
10. Inhalants	1.37	.98
11. Hallucinogenics	1.38	1.02
12. Amphetamines	1.47	1.10

redundancy analysis was used to examine the predictability of the intentions variables from the drug use variables [6].

For each intention variable, setwise hierarchical multiple regression analysis was used to test the hypothesis that predicting the intention to use a specific drug from information about all drug-taking experience yields more accuracy than predicting the intention to use a specific drug only from experience with that particular drug [7, p. 135-6].

RESULTS

It is possible to reject the hypothesis of no significant multivariate association between drug use and intended future use with a large degree of confidence ($\chi^2 = 3113.10$, d.f. = 156, $p < .00001$). Decomposition of the total χ^2 value using Bartlett's method indicates that all twelve dimensions are necessary to explain the covariation of behavior and intentions (with eleven dimensions partialled, $\chi^2 = 6.08$, d.f. = 2, $p < .05$).

Calculation of the standard redundancy index indicated that 19.77 per cent of the variance in the twelve intentions variables can be explained by the thirteen behavior measures when twelve dimensions are assumed to span the domains. Table 2 shows the twelve significant canonical correlations and the percentage of variance that each variate accounts for in the intentions set.

The second hypothesis that the intentions to use a drug are better predicted by all previous drug-taking behavior rather than only that specific behavior was tested using multiple regression analysis. Table 3 shows the correlation between each intention and the corresponding behavior as well as the multiple correlation

Table 2. Canonical Correlations and Redundancy Analysis

Variate	*Canonical Correlation*	*Percentage Redundancy*
1	.70	11.86
2	.51	2.20
3	.47	2.51
4	.44	.66
5	.39	.74
6	.29	.43
7	.27	.32
8	.22	.35
9	.21	.17
10	.19	.34
11	.12	.17
12	.06	.02
Total		19.77

Table 3. Correlations of Intentions with Corresponding Drug Taking and All Drug Taking

Intention	*R with all Behavior*	*R with Corresponding Behavior*	F^a	*Percentage Increment*[b]
Cigarettes	.50	.49	1.99[d]	1.09
Beer	.56	.53	7.79[f]	3.92
Wine	.57	.54	7.88[f]	3.89
Liquor	.54	.51	5.66[f]	2.95
Cocaine	.35	.22	11.28[f]	7.36
Tranquilizers	.37	.28	8.98[f]	5.76
Drugstore medication	.40	.37	3.54[f]	2.17
Heroin	.25	.18	4.37[f]	3.05
Marijuana-hashish[c]	.61	.58	8.53[f]	3.59
Inhalants	.31	.27	3.04[e]	2.03
Hallucinogenics	.26	.15	6.33[f]	4.39
Amphetamines	.40	.36	4.53[f]	2.83

[a] F-ratio of difference between correlations; degrees of freedom for all tests except marijuana-hashish are 12, 1620. Marijuana-hashish test has degrees of freedom 11, 1620.
[b] Percentage of predictable variance gained by predicting the intention for all behaviors rather than just the corresponding one; $100 \times (R^2_{all} - R^2_{specific})$.
[c] Corresponding behavior correlations for marijuana-hashish is the multiple correlation of marijuana-hashish intention with marijuana and hashish use variables.
[d] $p < .05$.
[e] $p < .01$.
[f] $p < .001$.

for each intention and all drug-taking behaviors. For each drug intention studied, significantly more of the variance could be predicted from the total set of drug-taking behaviors than from only the corresponding behavior. Therefore, it is possible to conclude that the individual's intentions to use a drug in the future are more accurately predicted by knowing previous experience with all drugs than by knowing previous experience with just that specific drug.

DISCUSSION

For a large group of young adolescent junior high school students, it was found that the intention to use drugs in the future is associated with current drug-taking behavior. The association between behavior and cognitive plans, while statistically significant, was not of a magnitude large enough to indicate that intentions are entirely synonymous with current drug-taking: only about 20 per cent of the variance in twelve intentions for future use could be explained by the levels of currently using thirteen drugs.

The second hypothesis of the study—that intentions to use a particular drug would be better predicted by all current drug-taking behaviors than by only the level of using that specific drug—was supported for all drugs studied. By considering the total array of drug taking, the accuracy of prediction was increased between 1 and 8 per cent. While the increment is not large in absolute terms, in all cases the increment obtained from the additional information was statistically significant using standard tests.

For the different intentions to use a drug in the future, it was possible to predict between 7 and 37 per cent of the variance. Such levels of predictability would seem to indicate that intentions for future drug use are formed from more than just current levels of drug experience. Future work, then, must seek to determine what additional sources serve to determine the choice to use or not use a particular substance. Such an effort may provide important information for the design of education, prevention, and innoculation programs for adolescent drug use.

REFERENCES

1. L. D. Johnston, J. C. Bachman, and P. M. O'Malley, *Drug Use Among American High School Students 1975-1977.* U.S. Government Printing Office, Washington, D.C., 1977.
2. D. B. Kandel, Convergences in Prospective Longitudinal Surveys of Drug Use in Normal Populations, *Longitudinal Research on Drug Use: Empirical Findings and Methodological Issues,* D. B. Kandel (Ed.), Halsted, New York, 1978.
3. M. L. Brehm, and K. W. Back, Self Image and Attitudes Towards Drugs, *Journal of Personality, 36,* pp. 299-314, 1968.
4. J. W. Goldstein, T. C. Gleason, and J. H. Korn, Whither the Epidemic? Psychoactive Substance Use Patterns of College Students, *Journal of Applied Social Psychology, 5,* pp. 16-33, 1975.
5. G. J. Huba, J. A. Wingard, and P. M. Bentler, Adolescent Drug Use and Peer and Adult Interaction Patterns, *Journal of Consulting and Clinical Psychology, 47,* pp. 124-130, 1979.
6. T. C. Gleason, On Redundancy in Canonical Analysis, *Psychological Bulletin, 83,* pp. 1004-1006, 1976.
7. J. Cohen and P. Cohen, *Applied Multiple Regression/Correlation Analysis for the Behavioral Sciences,* Erlbaum, Hillsdale, N.J., 1975.

CHAPTER 10
Alcohol Use and Self-Esteem of Adolescents

WAYNE R. MITIC

In a society in which the use of alcohol has been symbolically associated with an adult behavior pattern and in which the use of alcohol is legally regulated, surveys have noted that few adolescents wait until they reach "drinking age" to sample alcohol [1–3]. After proclaiming the prevalence of alcohol use among adolescents, researchers, in many cases, fail, however, to extend their analysis further. Singer emphasized that drugs are rarely the abuser's real problem, but were rather only symptomatic of a more deep seated disorder, and added [4]:

> . . . if we treat the symptom (alcohol abuse) and not the underlying problem, the abuser will probably return to drugs, because the problem that originally led him to it still exists.

Following this line of thought investigators have postulated that the underlying problem might be expressed as anomalous levels in a personality trait. Samuels [5] and Warner and Swisher [6] after studying a group of adolescent drug abusers, found that low self-concept was chosen by them (the adolescent) as a major cause of their abusing drugs. Research by Blane et al. examined self-esteem, alienation and attitudes toward irresponsible use of alcohol [7]. The authors proposed that further investigation in the area of self-esteem was necessary to draw suitable conclusions. Samuels proposed that if low self-concept could be positively identified as " . . . a causative factor of drug abuse in most drug abusers, the implications would be extremely important for educators and society in general." [5]

The purpose of this study was therefore not only to investigate the prevalence of drinking among a group of adolescents, but also to examine the personality characteristic of self-esteem and its relations to their drinking behavior.

DEFINITIONS OF TERMS

For purposes of clarity and also categorization of individuals drinking behaviors, the following definitions of terms were used:

1. *abstainer* – a person who never uses alcohol.
2. *occasional drinker* – a person who uses alcohol no more than twice a month, has two or less drinks on each occasion and responds negatively to all questions on the Straus, Bacon Index [8].
3. *regular drinker* – a person who consumes alcohol on a weekly basis (one or more times a week), but less than five drinks a week on each time alcohol is consumed. This individual also responds negatively to all questions on the Straus, Bacon Index.
4. *potential problem drinker (ppd)* – a person who consumes five or more drinks a week or each time alcohol is consumed and/or responds affirmatively to one or more responses on the Straus, Bacon Index.

METHODS

Sample Selection

School board permission was obtained to conduct an alcohol behavior survey within nine schools of a large city (population 200,000) in Southern Ontario. For purposes of this investigation three high schools and three elementary schools were chosen randomly; however, there were only three vocational schools in the area investigated, therefore, random selection was not possible. Individual classes were chosen by the principals in their respective schools on the basis of convenience to the investigator and teachers involved. The public high school group involved one class of students in level one and level three selected from three high schools while the vocational group involved the selection of one class of students enrolled in level one and level three from each of three vocational schools. The elementary group consisted of the grade eight class and opportunity class from three elementary schools.

The Questionnaire

The Coopersmith Self-Esteem Inventory (SEI) was used to assess the self-esteem levels of the participants [9]. The SEI consists of fifty-eight self-report items to which the individual responds either "like me" or "not like me." Overall, self-esteem is reported as the total number of all scores correct. Employing position in the group as an index of relative self-appraisal, the upper third is indicative of high esteem, lower third is indicative of low esteem and middle third is medium esteem.

Within the SEI are four subscales which cycle in sequence. These subscales are self-esteem in the area of: general self, social self, peers, home-parents and school-academic. As with overall self-esteem, position in the group is used to indicate either low or high esteems for that particular subscale. For each subscale the lower one half scores are considered low esteem while the upper-half is indicative of high esteem.

The validity of the SEI was assessed by administering both the SEI and Rosenberg's Self-Esteem Scale [10] to twenty-five subjects. A Pearson Product coefficient of .72 ($p = .001$) was obtained, supporting previous research that the SEI was a valid measure of self-esteem [11–13].

The split-half technique was used to investigate the reliability of the SEI. Eighty questionnaires were randomly selected and the statements in each inventory were divided into equivalent halves. A Pearson Product coefficient of .75 ($p = .001$) was obtained, denoting an acceptable reliability.

RESULTS

Table 1 presents the percentage of students from each academic level by their drinking behavior. Fourteen per cent of the total sample were abstainees, 36 per cent were occasional users, 13 per cent were regular users and 37 per cent were potential problem drinkers.

The Straus, Bacon Index was used to identify the potential problem drinker, in that a student responding affirmatively to any statement in the Index was automatically placed in this category. Table 2 presents the percentage of students responding affirmatively to statements on the Index by their academic levels. Statements which received frequent affirmative responses were:

"Do you ever drink before going to a party?" – 38 per cent
"Have you ever had a blackout?" – 26 per cent
"When drinking, have you ever destoryed things?" – 21 per cent

Table 1. Percentage of Students from Each Academic Level by Drinking Group

Drinking Category	Opp	Grade 8	Voc_1	HS_1	Voc_3	HS_3	Per Cent of Total Sample
Abstainer	19	21	26	9.5	12	3.1	14
Occasional user	56	52	20	44	26	29	36
Regular drinker	14	7.6	9.2	13	9.4	20	13
Potential problem drinker	11	20	45	33	51	48	37

Table 2. Percentage of Students Responding Affirmatively to Statements on Straus, Bacon Index from Individual Academic Levels

Statement from Straus, Bacon Index	Opp	Grade 8	Voc_1	HS_1	Voc_3	HS_3
Drinking affected classwork	0	9.1	14	4.8	7.8	7.3
Lost a friend due to drinking	0	1.5	4.6	1.2	9.4	5.2
Arrest or injury due to drinking	0	4.5	15	7.1	12	16
Sent to principal's office due to drinking	0	0	3.1	0	3.1	3.1
Drank before going to a party	8.3	10	37	31	38	38
Foregone buying things for alcohol	0	1.5	3.1	4.8	12	9.4
Blackout from drinking	8.3	11	32	26	33	32
Drank alone	2.8	15	22	15	20	23
Drank before or instead of breakfast	0	1.5	6.2	2.4	6.3	6.3
Destroyed things while drinking	2.8	12	29	20	30	22

Table 3. Percentage of Students in Each Drinking Cateogry by Level of Self-Esteem

Level of Self-Esteem	Abstainer	Occasional User	Regular User	Potential Problem Drinker
Low	26	36	11	36
Medium	41	35	37	34
High	33	29	52	30

The per cent of students in each drinking category by their level of self-esteem is presented in Table 3. Most abstainers, 41 per cent, possessed medium levels of self-esteem, while 31 per cent had high levels. Conversely, most occasional drinkers, 36 per cent, had low levels of self-esteem and 35 per cent had medium levels. Fifty-two per cent of regular users had high levels of self-esteem, 35 per cent had medium levels and 11 per cent had low levels. Thirty-six per cent of

Table 4. Newman-Keuls' – Mean Differences in Self-Esteem Between Drinking Categories

	ABST 2.07	*OCC* 1.94	*REG* 2.40	*PPD* 1.94
ABST 2.07	–		*a*	
OCC 1.94		–	*a*	
REG 2.40			–	*a*
PPD 1.94				–

[a] Significant difference.

potential problem drinkers had low levels of esteem, while 34 per cent had medium levels.

A Newman-Keuls' procedure was used to investigate significant differences in levels of self-esteem, the dependent variable, between drinking categories, the independent variable (see Table 4). This method allowed pair-wise comparisons of means from the analysis of variance at a .05 level of significance. Mean values of self-esteem did not differ significantly between abstainers, occasional users and potential problem drinkers, however, significantly higher levels of esteem ($p < .05$) were found in regular users when compared to all other categories (see Table 4) (mean values of self-esteem are placed under the drinking category).

The SEI consisted of four sub-scales of self-esteem; home, self, peer and academic, which cycled in sequence throughout the Inventory. The Newman-Keuls' procedure was utilized to investigate significant differences ($p < .05$) in sub-scale levels of self-esteem between drinking categories (see Table 5). In the case of self-esteem in the area of "self," regular users possessed significantly

Table 5. Newman-Keuls' – Difference in Sub-Scale Scores Between Drinking Categories

a. Self

	ABST 1.54	*OCC* 1.48	*REG* 1.70	*PPD* 1.53
ABST 1.54	–			
OCC 1.48		–	[a]	
REG 1.70			–	
PPD 1.53				–

b. Peer

	ABST 1.32	*OCC* 1.36	*REG* 1.54	*PPD* 1.54
ABST 1.32	–		[a]	[a]
OCC 1.36		–	[a]	[a]
REG 1.54			–	
PPD 1.54				–

c. Home

	ABST 1.58	*OCC* 1.57	*REG* 1.66	*PPD* 1.49
ABST 1.58	–			
OCC 1.57		–		
REG 1.66			–	
PPD 1.49				–

d. School

	ABST 1.51	*OCC* 1.46	*REG* 1.54	*PPD* 1.28
ABST 1.51	–			[a]
OCC 1.46		–		[a]
REG 1.54			–	[a]
PPD 1.28				–

[a] Significant difference.

higher mean scores than occasional users (mean values of self-esteem appear under their respective drinking categories). No significant differences occurred between any other drinking categories. For "peer" self-esteem, potential problem drinkers obtained significantly higher mean scores than abstainers and regular users. "Home" self-esteem mean scores did not differ among any drinking categories, however, for "academic" self-esteem, occasional users, abstainers and regular users each obtained higher levels of esteem than potential problem drinkers.

Discussion

Examination of the percentage of students within each drinking category, reveals that few adolescents are able to engage in drinking on a regular basis and avoid the symptoms indicative of problem drinking. Inexperience and having to rely on trial and error tactics may explain the occurrence of this phenomenon. Adolescents, if not taught proper drinking habits, either through parental guidance or alcohol education programs, resort to experimentation and the knowledge (or misconceptions) of their peers to satisfy their curiosity concerning alcohol. This observation, however, is superficial for on further examination of the results an interesting difference is apparent between regular users and all other drinking groups. Adolescents classified as regular drinkers possess higher levels of self-esteem when compared to all other categories. These individuals reflect an "elitist" group who, regardless of the illegality of their behavior, the circumstances under which they consume alcohol, and the potential consequences of alcohol abuse, are able to consume alcohol on a regular basis and avoid problems associated with it. The important factor is not that they drink illegally, but that they are a select group, with high self-esteem, who are able to drink wisely on a regular basis. Individuals with high self-esteem have been found by Hillmer and Stotland to be less likely influenced by others, than those possessing low esteem [14]. Therefore, a person with high self-esteem, if pressured by drinking companions to imbibe excessively, will be less likely influenced to partake in such activities. Individuals who drink alcohol on a regular basis and have low levels of self-esteem, may have been "weeded out" due to peer pressure, to drink excessively and therefore render them in the potential problem drinking category. The regular drinker may be thought of as being insulated from potential problem drinking by possessing a high level of self-esteem.

Within the high school environment, there are a number of goals toward which students strive. Two goals, however, appear to be of major and pervasive importance: academic achievement or recognition and interpersonal socialization [15]. Theoretically, if an individual fails academically, he may seek alternatives to compensate for his unsuccessful behavior. In a more practical sense, the individual may resort to drinking as his "academic" self-esteem decreases. The goal of interpersonal socialization, on the other hand, is achieved through acceptance from the adolescents' peer group. As a prerequisite, however, the individual must acquire certain habits common to the socialization process, in particular drinking.

Inspection of the sub-scales of self-esteem exemplify these two propositions. In "peer" self-esteem, regular and potential problem drinkers attained higher scores than abstainers and occasional users. This is not surprising since Stacey and Davies have labeled the abstainer as a person who stays home most nights and rarely goes to social events [16]. Conversely, Weschler and Thum point out that heavy drinkers relate strongly to the youth subculture [17]. Alcohol use among adolescents has become a symbol of peer group identification and adult status. Farmsworth feels that because alcohol has acquired this symbolic status, it is sometimes considered as a "coming of age" rite [18]. Group identification and the sharing of experiences with friends may be important for young people, especially in a world in which they feel cut off from everyone except peers. Therefore, the circumstances under which the consumption of alcohol occurs (parties) and also the adult status associated with drinking, aids the regular and potential problem drinker in establishing a high level of self-esteem with his peers.

In the case of "academic" self-esteem, the potential problem drinker obtained lower levels of self-esteem as compared to all other categories. Investigations by Smart and Fejer [19], and Kane and Patterson [20], have revealed that the problem drinker often performs poor scholastically. Evidence by Hamachek indicates that low performance in school subjects, as well as misdirected motivation and lack of academic involvement, are characteristic of the under achiever and may be due in part to a negative perception of the self [21]. The individual, upon failing academically, experiences a decrease in "academic" self-esteem and seeks alternatives to compensate for this failure. A social learning theory devised by Rotter states:

> When experience has shown that certain behavior has a relatively low expectation of leading to goals which are valued by the person, alternative behavior which has a relatively higher expectation of leading to these goals or of coping with the failure to attain them, will be adopted [22].

This coping phenomenon is explained by Hamachek as being indirect compensatory reactions which either substitute for the "defect" or draw attention away from it [21]. The function of alcohol, according to Jessor, et al., served as such a retreat from unsuccessful behavior and may represent a way of coping with failure or its anticipation by withdrawal [15]. Alcohol, especially in large quantities, can affect cognitive processes such as memory and recall and thereby enable the individual to avoid or repress thinking about his failure [23]. Drinking can, in short, be used to attain goals for those in which the expectation of success is low and to cope with failure or its anticipation, through forgetting or through inhibiting the relevant thought processes.

An inevitable question remains as to whether self-esteem causes behavior or results from behavior; whether potential problem drinking results from an already existent inadequate "academic" self-esteem or whether low "academic" self-esteem stems from the adolescents drinking behavior. Although the cross-sectional nature of this study does not permit consideration of the causal relationship, the results do indicate that a relationship between self-esteem and drinking behavior do exist. Hamachek describes a phenomenon called the "Bommerang Effect," related to the impact of self-esteem on perception and ultimately behavior [22]. An individual may see himself as being poor academically and projects this into his behavior. By this course of action, it is

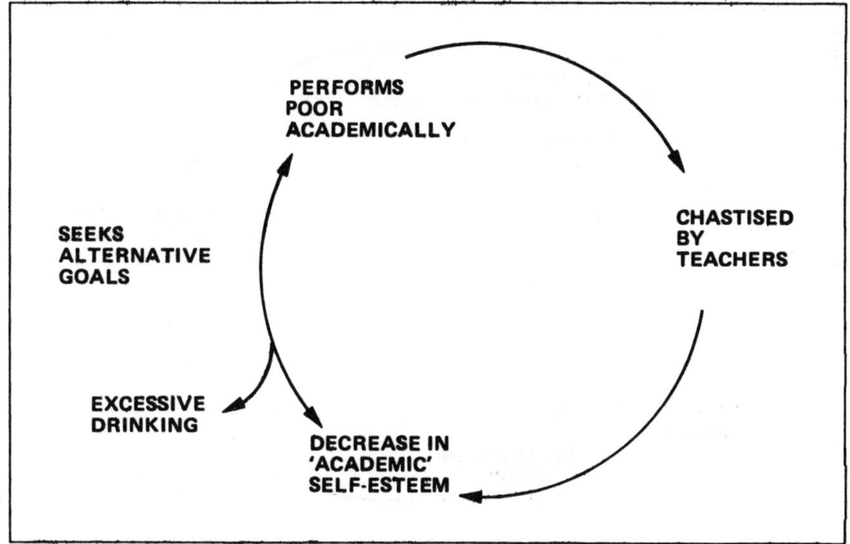

Figure 1. Interacting forces between "Academic" self-esteem and drinking behavior in potential problem drinkers.

possible to perpetuate a negative self-image, necessitating compensatory reactions to take affect. The potential problem drinker may see himself as inadequate in school and acts accordingly by attaining poor grades. In an attempt to seek alternative goals, the individual resorts to drinking excessively. Due to poor academic performance, he is chastised by teachers, which according to Coopersmith results in lowered self-esteem (see Figure 1) [9].

A similar process may occur in "peer" self-esteem in that regular and potential problem drinkers may see themselves as having high self-esteem in relation to their peers. Fitts is of the opinion that the standards and values of a culture must be taken into consideration when examining relationships between self-esteem and behavior [24]. If for instance the individual comes from and identifies with a subculture that expects and, values and rewards drinking, then he may practice such behavior and still maintain a normal or even high level of self-esteem. The individual frequents social gatherings, where because of the availability of alcohol and the peer acceptance of heavy drinking, he is able to drink excessively (see Figure 2). As shown previously, the potential problem drinker associates with those having similar drinking habits. The individual is accepted by the youth subculture, which in turn increases his level of "peer" self-esteem.

The role of the school in the development and change of self-esteem plays an integral part in the basis of the educational system. Within this environment, the student is subjected to the critical evaluations of both peers and teachers and

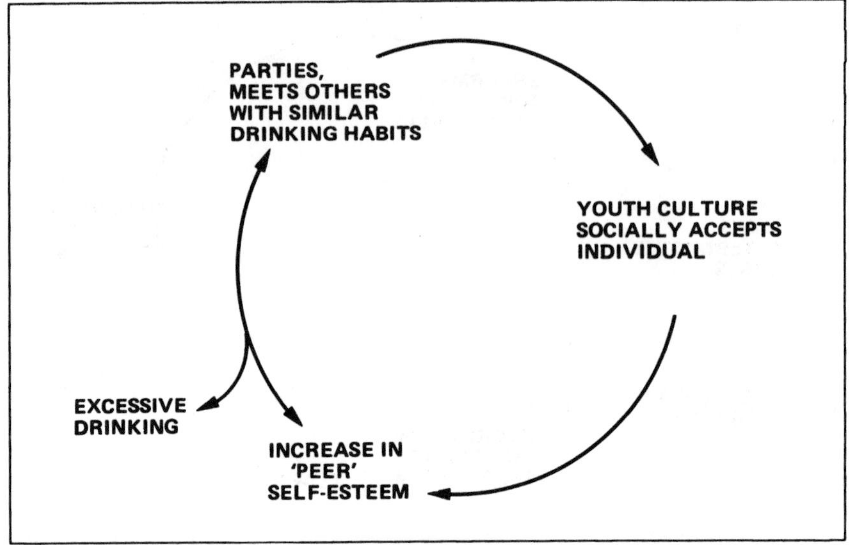

Figure 2. Interactive forces between "Peer" self-esteem and excessive drinking in the potential problem drinker.

is reminded constantly of either his failings or shortcomings or strengths and possibilities. In education there are many writers who have emphasized the importance of self-esteem in regard to personality, learning and counseling. Learning can never be separated from the personality of the learner. Educators, therefore, should consider both variables, self-esteem and drinking behavior when devising and applying alcohol education programs. An atmosphere should be created where students are considered and helped to believe they are of equal worth and value as individuals, regardless of their drinking behavior. However, equally important, is aiding those persons who abuse alcohol to reassess their behavior and take steps toward prevention of future abuse. The school program which emphasized the value of the individual and helps him to make effective adjustments to other people is truly preparing pupils for the future. In effect then, by helping the adolescent gain self-esteem, a likely outcome will be the development of a self that will be less threatened in the future and more adequate in exploring the environment.

REFERENCES

1. R. Hetherington, et al., Attitudes and Knowledge About Alcohol Among Saskatchewan Adolescents, *Canadian Journal of Public Health, 70,* pp. 247-259, 1979.

2. R. Smart, The New Drinkers, Addiction Research Foundation, Toronto, 1976.
3. R. Margulies, R. Kessler, and D. Kandel. A Longitudinal Study of Onset of Drinking Among High School Students, *Journal of Studies Alcohol, 38,* pp. 897-912, 1977.
4. H. Singer, The School Counselor and the Drug Problem, *School Counselor, 19,* pp. 284-288, 1972.
5. D. Samuels, Low Self-Concept As A Cause of Drug Abuse, *Journal of Drug Education, 4,* pp. 421-437, 1974.
6. R. Warner and J. Swisher, Alienation and Drug Abuse: Synonymous?, *National Association of Secondary School Principals Bulletin, 17,* pp. 65-71, October 1971.
7. H. Blane, et al., Alienation, Self-Esteem and Attitudes Toward Drinking in High School Students, *Quarterly Journal of Studies on Alcohol, 29,* pp. 350-354, 1968.
8. R. Straus and S. Bacon, The Problems on Drinking in College, *Society Culture and Drinking Patterns,* J. Wiley and Sons, Inc., New York, 1962.
9. S. Coopersmith, *The Antecedents of Self-Esteem,* McGraw Hill Company, New York, 1975.
10. M. Rosenberg, *Society and the Adolescent Self-Image,* Princeton University Press, Princeton, New Jersey, 1965.
11. T. Morrison, et al., Self-Esteem and Self-Estimates of Academic Performance, *Journal of Consulting and Clinical Psychology, 41,* pp. 412-414, 1973.
12. J. Johnson and C. Spatz, Internal Consistency of Coopersmith's Self-Esteem Inventory, *Educational and Psychological Measurement, 33,* pp. 875-876, 1973.
13. W. Simon, Some Sociometric Evidence for Validity of Coopersmith's Self-Esteem Inventory, *Perceptual and Motor Skills, 34,* pp. 93-94, 1972.
14. M. Hillmer and E. Stotland, Identification, Authoritarianism, Defensiveness and Self-Esteem, *Journal of Abnormal Social Psychology, 62,* pp. 420-425, 1962.
15. R. Jessor, et al., Expectations of Need Satisfaction and Drinking Patterns of College Students, *Quarterly Journal of Studies on Alcohol, 29,* pp. 101-110, 1968.
16. B. Stacey and J. Davies, Teenagers and Alcohol, *Health Bulletin, 30,* pp. 318-319, 1973.
17. H. Wechsler and D. Thum, Teenage Drinking, Drug Use and Social Correlates, *Quarterly Journal of Studies on Alcohol, 34,* pp. 1220-1227, 1973.
18. D. Farnsworth, Drug Use and Young People: Their Reasons, Our Reactions, *Resource Book for Drug Abuse Education, National Clearinghouse for Drug Abuse Information,* U.S. Government Printing Office, Washington, D.C., pp. 3-8, 1975.
19. R. Smart and D. Fejer, High School Drug Use: A Survey with Implications for Education, *Resource Book for Drug Abuse Education,* National Clearinghouse for Drug Abuse Information, United States Government Printing Office, Washington, D.C., 1975.

20. R. Kane and E. Patterson, Drinking Attitudes and Behavior of High School Students in Kentucky, *Quarterly Journal of Studies on Alcohol, 33,* pp. 635-646, 1972.
21. D. Hamachek, *Encounters with the Self,* Holt, Rinehart and Winston, Inc., New York, 1975.
22. J. B. Rotter, *Social Learning and Clinical Psychology,* Prentice Hall, New York, p. 7, 1954.
23. *Alcohol and Alcoholism: Problem, Program, Progress,* National Institute of Mental Health, 5600 Fishers Lane, Rockville, Maryland, 1972.
24. W. Fitts, *The Self-Concept and Delinquency,* Nashville Mental Health Center, Tennessee, 1970.

CHAPTER 11

Multivariate Prediction of Cigarette Smoking Among Children in Grades Six, Seven and Eight*

LINDA L. PEDERSON
JON C. BASKERVILLE
NEVILLE M. LEFCOE

Recent reports present evidence that cigarette smoking among American and Canadian youth is increasing particularly among females [1-3]. While some evidence has been presented which indicates that prevalence of smoking may have been reduced slightly among older teenagers, no change has been observed among the younger ages [4, 5]. One is lead to conclude that youthful cigarette smoking has not declined in a manner similar to that in adults and is, therefore, a cause for concern.

Several studies have demonstrated effective procedures for modification of smoking among junior high [6-9] and high-school aged youth [10]. These programs are based, not so much on the communication of information concerning future disease resulting from smoking, but on positive, current benefits of being a non-smoker. They involve direct instruction in ways to

*This research was supported by a grant from the London and Middlesex Lung Association, London, Ontario, Canada.

combat peer pressures to smoke. These programs have shown short-term effects in terms of reduced prevalence of smoking among exposed groups in comparison to untreated control conditions. Longer-term effects still need to be demonstrated.

It may be that these intense educational efforts are being needlessly directed toward many young people who would not be very likely to become smokers even without the program. In other words, effectiveness of the programs has been evaluated through comparison of group smoking rates without regard to the individual's characteristics associated with success and failure of treatment or no treatment. What is needed are studies which have as their goal identification of variables associated with the initiation of smoking. Identification of children who are at high-risk of becoming smokers provides the basis for the direction and evaluation of intensive educational efforts [11].

A number of investigators have attempted to determine which variables are associated with cigarette smoking by examining bivariate relationships. Relationships have been found with attitudes, knowledge, parental smoking, peer smoking, and school achievement [12-18] among others.

However, investigating one variable at a time is relatively inefficient and does not adequately reflect the complexity of the behavior of interest. Initiation and continuation of cigarette smoking is most likely the result of multiple factors that are not necessarily independent. The use of multivariate statistical procedures offers a mechanism for improving prediction, for assessing relative predictive power of the variables and for examining possible multiple causal mechanisms.

Three studies have applied multivariate techniques to factors related to cigarette smoking in youthful populations. Both Levitt and Edwards [19] and Lanese, Banks and Keller [20] found that peer smoking was the best predictor of current smoking among teenagers. Not surprisingly, Pederson and Lefcoe [21] found the same pattern in children aged nine to eleven. However, these three studies were cross-sectional; measurement of smoking status and the predictor variables were made simultaneously.

One study has attempted to use multivariate prediction of future smoking with the goal of identifying high-risk groups. Allegrante, O'Rourke and Tuncalp [22] found that *pairs* of predictors could be related to smoking two years in the future. By limiting the number of variables which could be considered by two, they may have restricted the extent of prediction possible and may have missed more complex interrelationships.

The purpose of the present study was to relate variables measured concurrently to smoking status three years later using multivariate statistical procedures. Initial measurements were made when the children were in grades four to six (ages 9-11) and smoking behavior determined when these same children were in grades six to nine (ages 11-13). Attitudes toward smoking, knowledge about smoking and health, sociodemographic characteristics and smoking environment were measured. The goal was to identify children, at a young age, who were likely to become regular smokers.

METHOD

Subjects

The subjects in the present study were children from twenty of the sixty-three public schools in London, Ontario, Canada.[1] London is an urban area in southwestern Ontario, with a population of approximately a quarter of a million people. The sixty-three schools were stratified into five parental income levels based on the 1973 Census figures for the district surrounding the school. Four schools were randomly selected from each of the five income levels. Initial testing was done in 1975 on 2,583 children who were in grades four-six. The second testing was carried out in 1978 (approximately 3 years later) on 2,372 children who were in grades six-eight.[2] Results were available for 1,682 children who responded on both occasions. The results presented in this study are for those children who were present for testing both in 1975 and 1978.

Questionnaire

An 83-item questionnaire was adapted from the one developed by the University of Illinois Study Team [23] for use with children in grades seven through twelve. The wording and format of the items was simplified for use with younger-aged children. The questionnaire consisted of the following sections:

1. Items 1-30, attitudes toward smoking,
2. Items 31-46, sociodemographic information,
3. Items 47-57, smoking environment,
4. Items 58-82, knowledge test of the relationship between smoking and health, and
5. Item 83, current smoking status (see Table 1).

Answers were placed on a separate sheet (NCS Trans-Optic P099B-1098). The same questionnaire and answer sheet was used for both testings.

[1]This study was part of a three-year longitudinal follow-up of a smoking awareness curriculum based on that developed by the Chicago Lung Association [27]. Half of the schools that participated in the study were provided with a curriculum guide to be used by the classroom teachers in health education classes while the remainder were given no formal guide for this subject. Topics included were the effects of smoking on the respiratory and circulatory systems, and on fitness. In addition, information was to be presented on initiation of smoking, decision-making and quitting smoking. Follow-ups indicated that teachers were inconsistent in their use of the curriculum material; this resulted in a partial breakdown of the original design of the evaluation.

[2]Two schools were not included in the survey conducted in 1978. One school had been closed in the preceding year and the other was taking part in a national survey on smoking.

Table 1. Questionnaire Item Concerning Current Smoking Status

Which is true for you now?

a. I usually smoke cigarettes just about every day.
b. I now smoke cigarettes once in a while, but not every day.
c. I used to smoke cigarettes just about every day, but I don't smoke them now.
d. I have smoked cigarettes a few times, but I don't smoke them now.
e. I have never smoked cigarettes.

Procedure

Four trained testers were randomly assigned to the classrooms in 1975 and five testers in 1978. Pairs of testers were used in the younger grades, where difficulty in reading ability and comprehension were anticipated, and in classrooms with more than thirty students. Care was taken to ensure that testers were unknown to the children. Classroom teachers were required to be absent during the group testing session.

After the questionnaires, answer sheets, and pencils had been distributed, testers read through the instructions aloud while the children followed silently. Pupils were encouraged to ask questions of the testers, to work speedily and to try to answer all items. The children were told that this was part of a research project, that they would not be receiving a grade and that neither their parents, teachers or principals would be informed of their answers. It was necessary to obtain the children's names in order to match the records from the two surveys. Therefore, an envelope was provided for each answer sheet. The child was asked to seal this envelope before handing it in. Test administration took approximately one hour of classtime.

RESULTS

Stepwise multiple regressions were carried out using the SPSS computer package [24] in order to examine the effects of the predictor variables on the dependent variable (smoking status in 1978). Five levels of smoking status were considered corresponding to the five categories presented in Table 1. Respondents were classified as *regular smokers* if they chose alternative a, *occasional smokers* if they chose alternative b, *ex-smokers* if they chose alternative c, *experimental smokers* if they chose alternative d, and *non-smokers* if they chose alternative e. Table 2 presents the frequencies and percentages

Table 2. Frequencies and Percents for Five Categories of Smoking Status in 1978

	Frequency	*Percent*
Regular smoker	147	6.2
Occasional Smoker	240	10.1
Ex-smoker	154	6.5
Experimental smoker	706	29.8
Non-smoker	1,125	47.4
	2,372	100.0

for each of these response categories in 1978. As can be seen from this table, over half of the sample of children had at least tried cigarettes (52.6%) by the time they were in grades six through eight, with 16.3 per cent being considered as current smokers.

In order to investigate the impact of the predictor variables on smoking status, two sets of analyses were carried out. In the first, the examination of effects of the current status of the variables measured in 1978 on smoking status in 1978 (cross-sectional) was undertaken. The second set of analyses were conducted to examine the effects of variables measured in 1975 on smoking status in 1978 (longitudinal). The first approach can be thought of as a search for explanatory effects in contrast with the second, which is an attempt to predict future smoking status.

The following variables were included in each analysis: Age, sex, grade, SES, exposure to smoking awareness material in school (by design and by report of exposure by the child), repeat of a grade, plans to finish high school, mother's or father's smoking status, peer smoking, knowledge score and attitude scale score. The knowledge score was constructed by summing the number of correct answers given to the twenty-five items which questioned the participants about their knowledge of the relationship between smoking and its effects on the body, health status and distribution of smokers in the population. Only students who responded to all items were included in the analyses. The information was covered by the curriculum described in footnote 1. The attitude scale was constructed using seventeen of the thirty items included on the questionnaire. Thirteen items were eliminated because they measured information rather than attitudes. Preliminary factor analyses indicated that one attitude scale was present, unlike the five scales obtained in the University of Illinois study [23]. It can be described as an attitude toward smoking in general, including feelings about people who smoke and the act of smoking itself. All items were coded so that a high score was indicative of a positive attitude toward smoking.

Cross-Sectional Analysis of Variables Measured in 1978 and Smoking Status in 1978

The correlations between each independent variable and smoking status in 1978 are presented in Table 3. Only those children who responded to all items are included; 29 per cent of the records (687 of 2,372) were eliminated because of missing values.

Neither sex nor the two measures of exposure to the curriculum were significantly related to smoking. Lower smoking status scores (i.e. increasing involvement with smoking) was related to decreasing SES and increasing age and grade. In addition, poorer academic performance, reflected by repetition of a grade and no plans to finish high school, was associated with smoking. The higher the knowledge score and the more negative the attitude toward smoking the lower was the involvement with cigarettes. The amount of smoking in the child's immediate environment also had an effect. Smoking was positively associated with increasing smoking among peer and parents.

The results of the stepwise analysis that was conducted for purposes of explanation are presented in Table 4. Seventy-one per cent of the children tested in 1978 (1,685 of 2,372) provided complete data on the variables and were included in this analysis. The order of entry of the variables, percent of variance explained, and standardized regression coefficients for the final model are presented in this table. Stepwise entry was terminated when no variable could be entered into the model with a coefficient significantly different from 0 ($p \leq .05$).

Table 3. Correlations Between Variables Measured in 1978 and Smoking Status in 1978 (N = 1,685)

Variable	*Y*
SES	-.133[a]
Age	-.179[a]
Sex	.038
Grade	-.179[a]
Repetition of a grade	-.173[a]
Plans to finish high school	-.109[a]
Attitude score	-.462[a]
Knowledge score	.195[a]
Parental smoking	-.235[a]
Peer smoking	-.497[a]
Exposure to curriculum by design	-.056
Reported exposure to curriculum	.022

[a] $p \leq .01$

Table 4. Summary of Stepwise Multiple Regression Analysis for Variables Explaining Smoking Status in 1978 (N = 1,685)

Step	*Variable*	$R2^a$	β^b
1	Peer smoking	.25	- .34
2	Attitude	.34	-.30
3	Knowledge score	.35	.08
4	Parental smoking	.36	-.08
5	Repeat grade	.36	-.06
6	Age	.37	-.05

[a] Cumulative percent of variance explained.
[b] Standardized regression coefficient for the model with six variables.

The first variable to enter was peer smoking which accounted for 25 per cent of the variance in smoking status. Children were more likely to be smokers if all or most of their friends smoked. The second variable to enter was attitude. With peer smoking controlled, the more positive the attitude toward smoking the more likely was the child to be a smoker. These first two variables were the most influential in the model; together they accounted for 34 per cent of the variance. Four additional variables entered; although statistically significant, their addition only accounted for an additional 3 per cent of the variance.

The additional three variables (SES, Grade, Plans to finish HS), showing significant bivariate relationships to smoking status, were not significant when the six variables in Table 4 were controlled. The reason that these variables did not enter in the multivariate analysis is probably related to their correlation with variables which did enter. For example, grade would not enter when age is in the model because of a high correlation between these two ($r = .65$).

Two indicators of exposure to the smoking curriculum were included in this analysis: the child's report of exposure and a measure based on the original design of the study (see footnote 1). These two variables entered last in the stepwise analysis with $p = .57$ and $p = .48$ respectively. Therefore, it can be concluded that smoking program exposure had no direct effect on smoking status. An indirect effect through attitude or knowledge is feasible. There were statistically significant correlations between knowledge and reported exposure ($r = .17$, $p = .000$) and exposure by experimental design ($r = .07$, $p = .01$). These correlations suggest that exposure to the curriculum did have an effect on knowledge; the mean knowledge score was higher in the exposed group than the unexposed group. Since knowledge entered in the stepwise analysis, an indirect effect of exposure is possible.

Longitudinal Analysis of Variables Measured in 1975 and Smoking Status in 1978

Results of analyses examining the bivariate relationships between the predictor variables measured in 1975 and smoking status are presented in Table 5. Increasing involvement in smoking (i.e. a lower smoking status score) was related to increasing age and grade, and parental and peer smoking. Inverse relationships were found with increasing SES, knowledge score and repetition of a grade. The more positive the attitude toward smoking the more involvement with cigarettes. Sex, future plans about school and the two measures of exposure to smoking material did not have significant correlation with smoking status.

The results of the stepwise analysis that was conducted for purposes of prediction are presented in Table 6. Only 44.2 per cent of the children who filled out questionnaires in both 1975 and 1978 (743 of 1,682) were included in this analysis. This was due to the large number of children whose records were lost because of incomplete data in the initial listing.

Smoking status in 1975 was the first variable to enter accounting for 25 per cent of the variance in smoking status in 1978. Children were more likely to be smokers in 1978 if they were smokers in 1975. With this variable controlled, older children were more likely to be smokers than younger ones. Controlling for age and 1975 smoking status, parental smoking was positively related to childhood smoking. With the inclusion of the final two variables (peer smoking and grade in 1975), 32 per cent of the variance in 1978 status was accounted

Table 5. Correlations Between Variables Measured in 1975 and Smoking Status in 1978 (N= 743)

Variable	*r*
SES	–.098[a]
Age	–.265[b]
Sex	–.025
Grade	–.251[b]
Repetition of a grade	–.161[b]
Plans to finish HS	–.046
Attitude score	–.196[b]
Knowledge score	–.097[a]
Parental smoking	–.250[b]
Peer smoking	–.281[b]
Exposure to curriculum by design	–.062
Reported exposure to curriculum	–.029
Smoking status in 1975	–.495[b]

[a] $p \leq .05$
[b] $p \leq .01$

Table 6. Summary of Stepwise Multiple Regression Analysis for Variables Predicting Smoking Status in 1978 (N= 743)

Step	*Variable*	R^2 [a]	B^b
1	Smoking status in 1975	.25	-.41
2	Age	.28	-.11
3	Parental smoking	.30	-.14
4	Peer smoking	.31	-.08
5	Grade	.32	-.10

[a] Cumulative percent of variance explained.
[b] Standardized regression coefficient for the model with five variables.

for in all. The fact that both age and grade entered into this analysis can probably be accounted for by children who repeated grades being older and more likely to be involved with smoking.

Exposure to the smoking awareness curriculum was marginally significant ($p = .09$) when the five variables in Table 6 and repetitition of a grade are controlled. The fact that this variable is more predictive than attitude or knowledge as measured in 1975, in combination with the fact that these latter two variables are important in the analysis of 1978 cross-sectional data, suggests that exposure may be acting through these variables and has, possibly, had its effect on smoking status through them by 1978.

DISCUSSION

The results of the cross-sectional analyses support the findings of other researchers in the area. Current smoking has been found to be related to age, SES, school achievement, attitude, knowledge and parental and peer smoking, as in the present study. The finding of no association with sex supports very recent data which suggests that boys and girls no longer differ with regard to smoking, as studies had shown in the past. In addition, the studies which have used multivariate procedures [19-21], have all found that peer smoking has the strongest relationship to current smoking. The percentage of variance accounted for in this study (37%) was only slightly below those levels reported in the literature (e.g., 45.7% in Levitt and Edwards [19], and 40.7% in Lanese, Banks and Keller [20]).

The set of variables which entered in the stepwise analysis using the predictors measured in 1975 differs from those selected on the basis of the 1978 responses. The first variable to enter is smoking status in 1975 rather than peer smoking. Peer smoking in 1975 was correlated with smoking status in 1975 ($r = .37$, $p < .01$) and, in fact, was the most important predictor at that time [21]. Therefore it was concluded that these results are not inconsistent. Both of these factors must be considered in predicting future smoking status.

The percentage of variance accounted for in 1978 smoking status by the 1975 predictors is 32 per cent. This is fairly high especially in light of the three year time period between the two measurements. However, the question arises as to the practical utility of this level of predictive accuracy for programs in health education. The ability to account for 32 per cent of the variance means that 68 per cent of the variance remains to be explained. However, since the smoking status response is coded from (1) regular smoker to (5) non-smoker, and the standard error for the multiple regression model is 1.02, one would expect less than 5 per cent of those predicted to be smokers would be non-smokers and vice versa (i.e. approximately 95 per cent of the predicted values would fall within ± 2 SE of the actual smoking status code).

The particular variables which were found to predict smoking status offer some clues as to the type of educational programs which might be effectively pursued. The importance of peer and parental smoking in both 1978 and indirectly through smoking status in 1975 suggest that social acceptability or unacceptability may be one of the most important explanatory constructs in initiation to smoking. Educational efforts which focus on this aspect of smoking and attempt to create a social climate hostile to smoking may do more to reduce the prevalance of smoking among the young than any intense effort to communicate material on health and disease. In addition, the importance of peer influences on smoking can explain why programs which use peer leaders and offer instruction in dealing with peer pressure appear to be effective.

Because of the importance of earlier smoking status in determining later status, educational efforts may have an effect if begun very early in the child's schooling. It might be that attempts to prevent any experimenting with cigarettes before grade four could reduce later regular smoking. Programs aimed at adolescents and teens are probably too late to have any significant effect on those children who are fairly likely to become smokers.

Exposure to the particular curriculum used in the present design did not appear to have any direct effect on the smoking behavior of these children. However, there was evidence of an indirect effect through attitudes and knowledge. What is apparent from the results presented here is that any impact of this educational program is relatively weak in comparison to the impact of the child's social environment.

Questions can be raised about the results of this study from two perspectives. First, there was no objective verification of the questionnaire report of smoking status. Pederson, Sidney and Lefcoe [26] present evidence from a subset of this sample which indicates that falsification probably occus in less than 5 per cent of the cases.

Large numbers of cases were lost because the children failed to complete the questionnaire. Even though the questionnaire had been pretested on 100 children with no apparent difficulty, it was found that the form was too long and complex for children in the younger grades. Since school performance is negatively related to smoking, it is likely that children who were unable to complete the form were smokers. Bias may have been introduced into the results which could have ameliorated the effects of the predictor variables on the outcome. However, the distribution of predictor variables were similar for the entire sample and those included in the multiple regression analysis. This supports the conclusion that this factor may not have had an effect on the results.

Attempts to identify additional variables indicative of high-risk should be pursued. While no obvious possibilities are suggested from the literature, one approach might be to focus on the relative importance of health and peers to the child. Studies should continue on smoking awareness programs for both short and long-term effects on behavior. In addition, attempts should be made to identify characteristics of the children for whom these programs appear to be useful. Finally, large scale longitudinal studies need to be carried out on children from point of entry into formal schooling, using multivariate procedures to isolate variables associated with future smoking.

The present study makes a contribution to knowledge in this area for three major reasons. First, the utility of multivariate statistical procedures in identifying high-risk children has been demonstrated. Second, since longitudinal rather than cross-sectional measurement has been used, prediction of future smoking status was possible. Third, the particular age group included in the present investigation has not been the focus of much research prior to this study.

REFERENCES

1. Health and Welfare Canada, *Smoking Habits of Canadians, 1965-1974,* Technical Report Series, No. 1, 1976.
2. J. A. Hanley and J. C. Robinson, Cigarette Smoking and the Young: A National Survey, *Canadian Medical Association Journal, 114,* pp. 511-517, 1976.
3. National Institute of Health, *Teenage Smoking, National Patterns of Cigarette Smoking, Ages 12 through 18, in 1972 and 1974*, U.S. D.H.E.W. Public Health Service, National Institute of Health, DHEW Publication No. (NIH) 76-931, 1976.
4. K. S. Brown, W. H. Cherry and W. F. Forbes, The Smoking Habits of Canadian School Children, paper presented at the 4th World Conference on Smoking and Health, Stockholm, June 1979.
5. Health and Welfare Canada, *Smoking Habits of Canadian School Children: A Summary Report*, January 1980.
6. A. McAlister, C. Perry, J. Killen, L. A. Slinkard and N. Macoby, Pilot Study of Smoking. Alcohol and Drug Abuse Prevention, *American Journal of Public Health, 70:*7, pp. 919-721, 1980.
7. R. I. Evans, W. B. Hansen and M. B. Mittelmark., Increasing the Validity of Self-Reports of Smoking Behavior in Children, *Journal of Applied Psychology, 62,* pp. 521-523, 1977.

8. R. I. Evans, R. M. Rozelle, M. B. Mittelmark, W. B. Hansen, A. L. Bane and J. Havis, Deterring the Onset of Smoking in Children: Knowledge of Immediate Physiological Effects and Coping with Peer Pressure, Media Pressure and Parent Modelling, *Journal of Applied Social Psychology, 8,* pp. 126-135, 1978.
9. D. M. Murray, C. A. Johnson, R. V. Luepker, T. F. Pechacek, D. R. Jacobs and P. D. Hurd, Social Factors in the Prevention of Smoking in Seventh Grade Students: A Follow-Up Experience of 1 Year, paper presented at the annual meeting of the American Psychological Association, New York City, 1979.
10. C. Perry, J. Killen, M. Tilch, L. A. Slinkard and B. G. Danaher, Modifying Smoking Behavior of Teenagers: A School-Based Intervention, *American Journal of Public Health, 70:*7, pp. 722-725, 1980.
11. F. R. Wake, Preventing the Onset of Smoking, paper presented at the 4th World Conference on Smoking and Health, Stockholm, June 1979.
12. V. L. Matthews, *The Saskatoon Smoking Study: Habits and Beliefs of Children in Grades Seven and Eight About Smoking,* Department of Social and Preventive Medicine, College of Medicine, University of Saskatchewan, 1974.
13. A. B. Palmer, Some Variables Contributing to the Onset of Cigarette Smoking Among Junior High School Students, *Social Science and Medicine, 4,* pp. 359-366, 1970.
14. D. J. Merki, The Effects of Two Educational Methods and Message Themes on Rural Youth Smoking Behavior, *Journal of School Health, 38,* pp. 448-454, 1968.
15. J. Revill, Teenage Pressures, *Health Education Journal, 37,* pp. 171-178, 1978.
16. A. O'Farrell and F. R. Wake, *Socio-Psychological Aspects of Cigarette Smoking: August 1969-August 1972,* report to the Department of National Health and Welfare, Canada, 1972.
17. F. W. Schneider and L. A. Vanmastright. Adolescent-Preadolescent Difference in Beliefs and Attitudes About Cigarette Smoking, *The Journal of Psychology, 87,* pp. 71-81, 1974.
18. E. M. Thomas and F. R. Wake, *Effects of Health Education on Smoking Habits in School Children: A Longitudinal Study. Part 1. Smoking Behavior and Attitudes of Grade 7 Ottawa Students-January 1969,* report to the Department of National Health and Welfare, Canada, 1972.
19. E. E. Levitt and J. A. Edwards, A Multivariate Study of Correlative Factors in Youthful Cigarette Smoking, *Development Psychology, 2:*1, pp. 5-11, 1970.
20. R. R. Lanese, F. R. Banks and M. D. Keller, Smoking Behavior in a Teenage Population: A Multivariate Conceptual Approach, *American Journal of Public Health, 62:*6, pp. 807-813, 1972.
21. L. L. Pederson and N. M. Lefcoe, Multivariate Analysis of Variables Related to Cigarette Smoking Among Children in Grades Four to Six, *Canadian Journal of Public Health*, 1980 (in press).

22. J. P. Allegrante, T. W. O'Rourke and S. Tuncalp, A Multivariate Analysis of Selected Psychosocial Variables on the Development of Subsequent Youth Smoking Behavior, *Journal of Drug Education, 7:*3, pp. 237-248, 1977-78.
23. W. H. Cresswell, W. J. Huffman and D. B. Stone, *Youth Smoking Behavior Characteristics and Their Educational Implications: A Report of the University of Illinois Anti-Smoking Education Study*, 1970.
24. N. H. Nie, C. H. Hull, J. C. Jenkins, K. Steinbrenner and D. H. Bent, *Statistical Packages for the Social Sciences*, second edition, McGraw-Hill, Inc., New York, 1975.
25. K. B. Hranchuk, D. Christie, M. Hranchuk and C. Kennedy, *Psycho-Social Aspects of Cigarette Smoking in 1972-1976,* Health and Welfare Canada, 1976.
26. L. L. Pederson, K. Sidney and N. M. Lefcoe, An Objective Measure of the Validity of Children's Responses to a Questionnaire on Health and Smoking, *Canadian Journal of Public Health, 68:*3, pp. 497-498, 1977.
27. Chicago Lung Association, *The Respiratory System and Smoking: A Complete Teaching Curriculum*, 1973.

ACKNOWLEDGEMENTS

The authors are indebted to Dr. R. G. Stennett and Ms. Lorna Earl from the Office of Research and Evaluation, London Board of Education, for their advice and assistance in the design and administration of the questionnaire. The authors wish to thank Marlene Fisher, Marilyn Kilpatrick, Joyce Ruddell and Janet Stewart who serves as testers in 1975, and Mary Lynn Hinton, Ada Meecham, Pat Stibbards, Geraldine Tordiff and Audrey Van Holst who served as testers in 1978 and June Pinkney who served as project director in 1978.

CHAPTER 12
Awareness of Substance Abuse and Other Health-Related Behaviors Among Preschool Children

FOREST S. TENNANT JR.

INTRODUCTION

Over-consumption of alcohol, nicotine, psychoactive drugs, and food has been shown to contribute significantly to most of the leading causes of death in the United States, while certain positive health-related behaviors, including exercise, tooth brushing, and wearing a seat belt have been associated with lowered morbidity and mortality [1–4]. Although the cause of health-related behaviors is poorly understood, studies indicate that health-related attitudes, beliefs, and behavior patterns are formed at a young age; most likely before onset of puberty [5–11]. Pratt interviewed 510 families with children, aged nine to thirteen years, and found that their children's dental, sleep, exercise, hygiene, nutrition, toilet and smoking attitudes and practices were well established [6]. Lewis,

Gochman, Mechanic, and Suchman have reported that grade school children have definite perceptions of health, illness, and attitudes towards health-related behavior [5, 7–9]. Some epidemiologic surveys reveal that over-eating, smoking, drinking, and drug-taking are prevalent among a small percentage of grade-school children [11, 12], and Tennant and Detels have found that use of cigarettes, alcohol and coffee by children in the under-age twelve group is highly correlated with adult abuse of drugs and alcohol [13].

The age at which health-related behaviors emerge in children is of critical interest. Successful primary prevention of certain behaviors may possibly depend upon influencing attitudes and beliefs of children before the critical age is reached, after which time behavior patterns may become unalterably fixed. The study reported here was done to determine awareness of substance abuse and other health-related behaviors among a group of preschool children.

METHODS

A group of forty-six children, ages five and six years, who received a routine, preschool physical examination at a general medical clinic (Community Health Projects, Inc.) in Eastern Los Angeles County was selected for study. Twenty-three (23; 50%) were male and twenty-three (23; 50%) were female. The mean family income of the group was approximately $11,000 per year. One-half (23; 50%) had a Spanish surname.

For approximately ten to fifteen minutes, the children were interviewed by a trained person, and neither parents nor teacher were present. A parent had given prior consent to the interview. The subjects were shown eight pictures from popular, contemporary magazines which depicted drug abuse, alcohol abuse, smoking, over-eating, tooth brushing, exercising, wearing a seat belt, and violence towards others.

Each child was asked the following: identify each health-related behavior, explain its health implication, state whether they had ever practiced the behavior or planned to engage in the behavior, and identify their sources of knowledge about the behavior.

RESULTS

Responses from boys and girls were not significantly different on any question. With the exception of drug abuse, over 85 per cent of the children could identify the depicted health-related behavior (Tables 1–8). Only fifteen (32.6%) could identify the concept of drug consumption for non-medical purposes, depicted by a girl taking oral medication in a psychedelic setting, and another person injecting drugs intravenously (Table 1). The health benefits or hazards associated with each behavior were variously known to the children. Only fifteen (32.6%) identified a hazard of alcohol consumption, while thirty-

Table 1. Drug Abuse

Picture shown to children: a teenage girl in a psychedelic setting, taking pills, and a man injecting a drug intravenously.

	Males *N = 23*	*Females* *N = 23*	*Total* *N = 46*
Could identify drug abuse	7	8	15 (32.6%)
Reported ever using a drug that wasn't prescribed	0	1	1 (2.2%)
Identified one or more health hazards of drug abuse	8	9	17 (37.0%)
Where learned about drug abuse:			
Parents	6	9	15 (32.6%)
Television	2	1	3 (6.5%)
One or more parents abuse drugs	0	2	2 (4.3%)

Selected comments about health hazards:

"If too much, you might die."
"Shots are good if you need them."
"Only if you're not sick."
"Yes, makes you sick."

four (73.9%) knew the benefits or hazards of wearing a seat belt, tooth brushing, or violence against another person. Some comments by the children revealed a rather sophisticated knowledge of health hazards or benefits associated with the behaviors. This knowledge was illustrated by comments concerning smoking ("You might die and get heart disease."); tooth brushing ("So you won't get cavities."); alcohol consumption ("You might get drunk and shoot someone or have a car accident."); and over-eating ("Get fat and your stomach hurts."). In the case of violence towards others, moral or religious comments were frequently elicited: "Never–God doesn't like it"; "It's not nice"; "It's against the rules."

The sources of knowledge concerning these behaviors were reported to be primarily parents, television second, with church, siblings, and teachers ranking third. Parents practiced some of the depicted behaviors with a prevalence close to national surveys of adults [14–19]: smoke cigarettes (20; 43.5%); exercise (1; 2.1%); overeat (10; 21.7%); abuse drugs (2; 4.3%); drink alcohol (29, 63.0%). A high percentage of children reported they had either practiced the depicted behavior one or more times or planned to do so in the future. Three (6.5%) had smoked a cigarette at least one time, and seven (15.2%) planned to smoke in the future; nine (20.0%) stated they currently ate too much; five (10.9%) stated

Table 2. Alcohol Consumption

Picture shown to children: Advertisement showing handsome man drinking bourbon.

	Males *N = 23*	Females *N = 23*	Total *N = 46*
Could identify alcohol consumption	19	21	40 (87.0%)
Reported they had drank alcohol	8	4	12 (26.1%)
Identified one or more health hazards of drinking	8	7	15 (32.6%)
Where learned: Parents	5	5	10 (21.7%)
Television	1	2	3 (6.5%)
Other	2	2	4 (8.7%)
One or more parents drink	17	12	29 (63.0%)
Plan to drink alcohol in the future	4	5	9 (19.6%)

Selected comments about health hazards:

"You might get drunk and shoot someone or have a car accident."

"Get put in jail."

"Bad for teeth. Makes you drunk."

"Can make you drunk—smells."

"You might kill somebody."

Table 3. Cigarette Smoking

Picture shown to children: Advertisement showing handsome man lighting a cigarette.

	Males *N = 23*	Females *N = 23*	Total *N = 46*
Could identify behavior	21	22	43 (93.5%)
Reported smoked a cigarette before	3	0	3 (6.5%)
Identify one or more health hazards	10	10	20 (43.5%)
Where learned about smoking:			
Parents	8	7	15 (32.6%)
Television	3	5	8 (17.4%)
Other	3	3	6 (13.0%)
One or more parents smokes	11	9	20 (43.5%)
Plans to smoke in the future	4	3	7 (15.2%)

Selected comments about health hazards:

"You might die and get heart disease."

"It's a matter of life and death."

"Could have heart attack and die."

"Learned after first puff."

"Father was smoker—died of heart attack."

"Get cancer, cough, and might die."

Table 4. Over-Eating

Picture shown to children: Extremely obese woman in a nightgown who is ravenously devouring a piece of cake with ice cream at an open refrigerator.

	Males *N = 23*	*Females* *N = 23*	*Total* *N = 46*
Could identify over-eating	20	20	40 (87.0%)
Reported they over-ate	5	4	9 (20.0%)
Identified one or more health hazards of over-eating	12	11	23 (50.0%)
Where learned about over-eating:			
Parents	7	8	15 (32.6%)
Television	1	0	1 (2.2%)
Other	2	1	3 (6.5%)
One or more parents are overweight	6	4	10 (21.7%)

Selected comments about health hazards:

"Too fat—get teased."
"Get fat and your stomach hurts."
"You get cavities."
"Trouble walking."

Table 5. Tooth Brushing

Picture shown to children: Young girl brushing her teeth.

	Males *N = 23*	*Females* *N = 23*	*Total* *N = 46*
Could identify tooth brushing	23	22	45 (97.8%)
Reported they brushed teeth	21	22	43 (93.4%)
Identified health benefit of tooth brushing	17	17	34 (73.9%)
Where learned about tooth brushing:			
Parents	13	14	27 (58.7%)
Television	0	1	1 (2.2%)
Other	5	3	8 (17.4%)

Selected comments about health benefit:

"Keeps their teeth clean."
"So you won't get cavities."
"So teeth won't fall out."
"So teeth won't rot out."
"Get teeth white and clean."

Table 6. Exercise

Picture shown to children: Children in athletic suits, running and doing calisthenics.

	Males *N = 23*	*Females* *N = 23*	*Total* *N = 46*
Could identify behavior	20	20	40 (87.0%)
Reported they exercised	8	12	20 (43.5%)
Identified one or more health benefits	12	9	21 (45.7%)
Where learned about exercise:			
Parents	5	6	11 (23.9%)
Television	4	4	8 (17.4%)
Other	2	0	2 (4.3%)
One or more parents exercise	0	1	1 (2.1%)
Plan to exercise in the future	1	1	2 (4.3%)

Selected comments about health benefits:

"So they feel strong."

"Get skinny and it's good for you."

"Good way to be strong."

"Grow good."

Table 7. Wear Seat Belt

Picture shown to children: Mother helping her child fasten a seat belt.

	Males *N = 23*	*Females* *N = 23*	*Total* *N = 46*
Could identify wearing a seat belt	12	16	28 (60.9%)
Reported they wore a seat belt	9	10	19 (41.3%)
Identified health benefits of a seat belt	18	16	34 (73.9%)
Where learned about seat belts:			
Parents	6	12	18 (39.1%)
Television	0	0	0 (0%)
Other	4	1	5 (10.9%)
One or more parents wear a seat belt	9	8	17 (37.0%)

Selected comments about the benefits of seat belts:

"For safety."

"So they can't fall."

"So you can stop fast and won't fall."

"So you won't get hurt when they crash."

"You won't go through the window."

Table 8. Violence Towards Others

Picture shown to children: Man shooting another man, and a fist-fight involving cowboys.

	Males *N* = 23	*Females* *N* = 23	*Total* *N* = 46
Could identify violence	20	21	41 (89.1%)
Reported it is "OK" to harm another person	4	1	5 (10.9%)
Identified health hazards of violence	15	19	34 (73.4%)
Where learned about violence:			
Parents	8	5	13 (28.3%)
Television	2	0	2 (4.3%)
Other	3	6	9 (19.6%)
Reported a plan to hurt someone in the future	3	2	5 (10.9%)

Selected comments about violence:

"Yes, because they hate them."
"Just the bad guys."
"Never—God doesn't like it."
"It's not nice; it's against the rules."

it was "ok" to harm another person and planned to hurt someone in the future; forty-three (93.4%) brushed their teeth; one (2.2%) had taken a drug for non-medical reasons; twelve (26.1%) had previously consumed at least one drink of alcohol, and nine (20.0%) planned to drink in the future; nineteen (41.3%) wore a seat belt in the car; and twenty (43.5%) exercised, but only two (4.3%) planned to do so in the future.

DISCUSSION

All the children interviewed could identify the majority of the health-related behaviors depicted by pictures and were aware of some positive and negative health consequences of the behaviors. In many cases, the children gave knowledgeable answers regarding the consequences of smoking, over-eating, and alcohol consumption. Major sources of knowledge about health-related behaviors were derived from parents and television, which is not surprising, since both parents and television have been reported to influence children's health habits [27–30]. In addition, three (6.5%) of the children stated they had already smoked a cigarette; twelve (26.1%) had tasted alcohol one time; nine (20.0%) stated they over-ate; and one (2.2%) reported consumption of a drug for other than medical purposes. Similar percentages planned to practice these same behaviors in the future, and only two (4.3%) planned to exercise in later life. Five (10.9%) stated it was permissable to harm another person, and an identical percentage (10.9%) stated they planned to harm someone in the future. Responses by the children are believed to be relatively accurate, since they identified health behaviors in their parents that correspond closely to national surveys in adults: cigarette smoking 43.5%; alcohol consumption 63%; obesity 21.7%; drug abuse 4.3% [14–19].

Attempts to prevent alcohol and drug abuse, smoking, and over-eating have not been consistently successful, and a predictable method has not been found to promote positive behaviors of exercise, tooth brushing, wearing a seat belt, and non-violence against others [20–25]. Several studies suggest that prevention programs intended to positively influence health behaviors probably fail because they are targeted at adolescents or adults whose behavior patterns are too fixed to change significantly [23–25]. Tooth brushing, seat-belt use, smoking, and drug-alcohol education appear more effective in changing attitudes when directed toward grade school children [23–25]. Drug abuse behavior among adolescents may apparently even increase as the result of a well-meaning prevention effort [26]. Even though the children studied here represent only a consecutive sample of one general medical clinic and not a general population sample, the results of their interviews indicate that preschool children have considerable awareness of substance abuse and other health-related behaviors. This awareness suggests that preschool children may be a suitable target population for prevention and education efforts. It is unknown, however, if preschool children can be motived to permanently adopt positive health behaviors, because there may be a wide gap between knowledge and behavior.

REFERENCES

1. J. F. Burnum, Outlook For Treating Patients With Self-Destructive Habits, *Ann. Intern. Med., 81*, pp. 387-393, 1974.
2. L. Breslow, Risk Factor Intervention For Health Maintenance, *Science, 200,* pp. 908-912, 1978.
3. N. B. Belloc, and L. Breslow, Relationship of Physical Health Status and Health Practices, *Prev. Med., 1,* pp. 409-421, 1972.
4. G. B. Goir, and B. J. Richter, Macroeconomics of Disease Prevention in the United States, *Science, 200,* pp. 1124-1130, 1978.
5. C. E. Lewis, M. A. Lewis, and A. Lorimer, Child-Initiated Care: The Utilization of School Nursing Services by Children in an Adult-Free System, *Pediatrics* (in press).
6. L. Pratt, Child Rearing Methods and Children's Health Behavior, *J. Health and Social Behavior, 14,* pp. 61-64, 1973.
7. D. S. Gochman, Children's Perceptions of Vulnerability to Illness and Accidents, *Public Health Reports, 85,* pp. 69-73, 1970.

8. D. Mechanic, The Influence of Mothers on Their Children's Health Attitudes and Behaviors, *Pediatrics, 33,* pp. 444-453, 1964.
9. E. A. Suchman, Health Attitudes and Behavior, *Arch. Environ. Health, 20,* pp. 105-110, 1970.
10. F. S. Tennant, Jr., R. Detels, and V. Clark, Some Childhood Antecedents of Drug and Alcohol Abuse, *Amer. J. Epidemiology, 102,* pp. 377-385, 1975.
11. J. R. Hayes, and G. M. Winburn, Drug Abuse Among Elementary School Students in a Suburban School Setting, *J. Drug Education, 2,* pp. 355-361, 1972.
12. M. R. Porter, T. A. Vieria, G. J. Kaplan, et al., Drug Use in Anchorage, Alaska, *JAMA, 223,* pp. 657-664, 1973.
13. F. S. Tennant, Jr., and R. Detels, Relationship of Alcohol, Cigarette, and Drug Abuse in Adulthood With Alcohol, Cigarette, and Coffee Consumption in Childhood, *Prev. Med., 5,* pp. 70-77, 1976.
14. Cigarette Smoking in the United States in *Morbidity and Mortality Weekly Report,* U.S. Department of Health, Education and Welfare, Center for Disease Control, Atlanta, Georgia, Vol. 25, August 6, 1976.
15. H. J. Barry, M. B. Balter, Mellinger, et al., National Patterns of Psychotherapeutic Drug Use, *Arch. Gen. Psychiatry, 28,* pp. 769-783, 1973.
16. D. Calahan, and R. Room, Problem Drinking Among American Men Aged 21-59, *Am. J. Public Health, 62,* pp. 1473-1482, 1973.
17. J. De Lint, and W. Schmidt, Consumption Averages, and Alcoholism Prevalence: A Brief Review of Epidemiologic Investigations, *Br. J. Addict., 66,* pp. 97-107, 1971.
18. M. L. Levinson, Obestiy and Health, *Preventive Medicine, 6,* pp. 172-180, 1977.
19. G. A. Bray, M. B. Davidson, and E. J. Drenick, Obestiy: A Serious Symptom, *Ann. Intern. Med., 77,* pp. 779-795, 1972.
20. E. L. Thompson, Smoking Education Programs 1960-1976, *Am. J. Public Health, 68,* pp. 250-257, 1978.
21. T. J. Coates, and C. E. Thoresen, Treating Obesity in Children and Adolescents: A Review, *Am. J. Public Health, 68,* pp. 143-151, 1978.
22. F. S. Tennant, Jr., P. J. Mohler, D. H. Drachler, et al., Effectiveness of Drug Education Classes, *Am. J. Public Health, 64,* pp. 422-426, 1974.
23. W. T. Wilson, L. P. Lonero, and D. Ish, Increasing Seatbelt Use Through a Program Presented in Elementary Schools, *Proceedings of the 16th Conference of the American Association for Automotive Medicine,* Chapel Hill, North Carolina, pp, 372-387, October 1972.
24. L. U. Martens, P. J. Frazier, K. J. Hirt, et al., Developing Brushing Performance in Second Graders Through Behavior Modification, *Health Services Reports, 88,* pp. 818-823, 1973.
25. F. S. Tennant, Jr., S. C. Weaver, C. E. Lewis, Outcomes of Drug Education: Four Case Studies, *Pediatrics, 52,* pp. 246-251, 1973.
26. S. C. Weaver, and F. S. Tennant, Jr., Effectiveness of Drug Education Programs for Secondary Students, *Am. J. Psychiatry, 130,* pp. 812-814, 1973.

27. C. E. Lewis, and M. A. Lewis, The Impact of Televison Commercials on Children's Health-Related Beliefs and Behaviors of Children, *Pediatrics, 53,* pp. 431-435, 1974.
28. M. E. Chafetz, H. T. Blane, and M. J. Hill, Children of Alcoholics, *Quart. J. Studies Alcoholism, 32,* pp. 687-698, 1971.
29. R. G. Smart, and D. Fejer, Drug Use Among Adolescents and Their Parents: Closing the Generation Gap in Mood Modification, *J. Abnormal Psychology, 79,* pp. 153-160, 1972.
30. F. S. Tennant, Jr., Dependency Traits Among Parents of Drug Abusers, *J. Drug Education, 6,* pp. 83-88, 1976.

CHAPTER 13
Patterns of Drug Use Among Mexican-American Potential School Dropouts

JAMES E. BRUNO
LYNN DOSCHER

INTRODUCTION

Presently, great concern exists among educators concerning problems related to drug use in the schools and concomitant problems of poor school performance and anti-social behavior. This concern is particularly acute in inner-city school situations or at school sites with a high percentage of minority students. This study reports preliminary descriptive results of a research effort directed at examining drug use and related knowledge and attitudes among a group of potential dropouts and low-achieving Mexican-American students.

While the literature is not unanimous in describing levels of adolescent drug use, some trends seem to emerge. Use of "social drugs" (cigarettes and various kinds of alcohol) is fairly high. For example, the percentage of students having used cigarettes is often reported as between 50 and 75 per cent; reported alcohol usage runs between 60 to 80 per cent depending upon the type of alcohol and the characteristics of the sample [1–3]. Reported usage of marijuana varies mainly from about 12 to 30 per cent [1, 3–6]. Most studies report fewer than 20 per cent of students have tried one of the other drugs, such as hallucinogens, amphetamines, opiates, etc. [3, 5].

However, since most studies survey children at school, chronic truants or absentees may be considerably underrepresented in most samples. Kandel found that a sample of "absentees" reported consistently higher drug use than "regular" students surveyed at school [2]; differences were particularly noticeable for hard liquor (58% of regular students, but 71% of absentees had used liquor), marijuana (38% vs. 56%), and barbiturates (16% vs. 28%).

No consistent differences in drug usage by sex are apparent from the literature. Several studies have found lower female usage of all drugs [3, 5]. On the other hand, in Kandel's absentee sample, girls reported higher usage of all substances except marijuana, LSD, beer/wine and opiates other than cocaine [2]. Elinson found similar rates of initiation into drug usage for girls and boys during a two-year study period [1].

Differences among ethnic group drug use is still inconclusive. Among opiate addicts, Blacks are highly overrepresented [7], while marijuana use in adolescent populations seems to show no consistent trends [8]. Johnson has reported more marijuana use among Black than White high school students [9], while at least one study shows higher rates among Whites [8]. Elinson's preliminary finding that Black, Hispanic and White students were equally likely to initiate marijuana use warrants further investigation with a sample composed of a larger percentage of Mexican-Americans, since his sample was only made up of about 1 per cent Hispanic [1].

The purpose of this study is to describe the extent and patterns of drug use and attitudes for a sample of primarily Mexican-American high school students identified as potential dropouts.

SAMPLE

The sample used in this study was a group of potential dropouts participating in a Title III project directed at truant students (mostly Mexican-American) from a medium-sized school district in a metropolitan area. Program participants were ninth to twelfth grade students identified by school officials as being potential dropouts because of truancy and other academic and family background variables. Students in the Title III project in 1975 were asked to complete a written questionnaire on drug use and related attitudes. The seventy-eight students who voluntarily completed this drug questionnaire form the data base for the current analysis.

RESULTS

Table 1 summarizes the extent of drug use for the sample. Notice that marijuana, alcohol and cigarettes are the main drugs used by these students. The proportion of students reporting marijuana usage is higher than that reported by other studies, higher even than Kandel's group of "absentees." The number of students using hard alcohol and cigarettes is similar to that for marijuana and agrees with the extents of use reported by other studies. Notice, however, that a much larger proportion of the sample reported daily usage of cigarettes than daily use of other drugs. About one-quarter to one-third of students in the sample reported having at least tried "sniffing stuff," amphetamines or barbiturates. Reported frequent usage of these and other hard drugs, however, is quite low.

Table 2 summarizes responses given when students were asked if they were using drugs more or less during the past year. There was an observable tendency toward "more" use of the "social" drug substances listed. Students showed a marked increase in their use of Alcohol–Beer/Wine, in Cigarette Smoking, and in Alcohol–Hard Liquor. Marijuana (or Hashish) had also been used more often during the preceding year by the survey group of students. Students reported less usage of "hard" or other drugs; this may suggest that many students "experiment" with such drugs but do not become regular or frequent users.

Responses to selected drug attitude questions are given in Table 3. It appears that many of these students think that drug usage may cause school problems, such as poor grades or dropping out, but many students do not connect drugs and social problems. In addition, there may be a distinction made by students between "drug usage" and *heavy* drug usage. Many students do not think that drug usage in general causes particular social problems; but *heavy* drug usage may cause problems.

Discriminant analysis was used to explore differences in drug use and attitudes between girls and boys. The SPSS stepwise discriminant analysis procedure was used on a subset of variables. The means, standard deviations, discriminant function, and classification functions are given in Table 4. The function results in significant discrimination between girls and boys ($F = 5.97$, $df = 19{,}58$) with a canonical correlation of .81. The classification matrix is the following, with 94 per cent of the sample correctly classified:

		Classified into	
		Girls	Boys
Actual group:	Girls	30	2
	Boys	3	43

A histogram of discriminant scores is given in Figure 1, emphasizing the discrimination.

Table 1. Extent of Drug Use Percent of Students Who Use Drugs at Various Frequencies (n = 78)

	Do not use	*Use less than once a month*	*Use about once a month*	*Use about once a week*	*Several times a week*	*Use daily*	*Total percent that use*
Marijuana/Hashish	33%	9	14	21	19	4	67
LSD	89	6	4		1		11
Other Hallucinogens	96	3		1			4
Amphetamines	68	14	9	3	5	1	32
Barbiturates	78	12	5	5			22
Opiates	96	3		1			4
Sniffing Stuff	79	13	5	1	1		20
Cocaine	88	6	4		1		11
Cigarette Smoking	33	4		5	8	50	67
Alcohol (beer/wine)	22	14	5	31	17	12	79
Alcohol (hard liquor)	37	14	17	21	9	3	64

Table 2. Changes in Drug Use Over Previous Year

	% of students		
		Use	
	Do not use	*Less*	*More*
Marijuana or Hashish	33	29	37
LSD	88	8	4
Other Hallucinogens	96	3	1
Amphetamines	68	21	12
Barbiturates	78	12	10
Opiates	96	3	1
Sniffing Stuff	79	12	9
Cocaine	88	9	3
Cigarette Smoking	33	10	56
Alcohol (beer/wine)	22	21	58
Alcohol (hard liquor)	37	22	41

Table 3. Responses to Selected School-Related Drug Attitude Questions by Percent of Students (n = 78)

	Response		
Question	*True*	*No opinion*	*False*
Students who take drugs regularly can't get along with others	29%	27	44
Taking drugs a lot causes students to drop out of school	64	21	15
Students respected by teachers don't use drugs	19	35	46
Heavy drug users are not the most well-liked	38	35	27
Drugs can make you more creative	32	37	31
Taking drugs doesn't hurt school grades	23	27	50

Table 4. Results of Discriminant Analysis of Girls and Boys by Selected Drug Use and Attitude Variables (n = 78, 32 girls and 46 boys)

	Mean		*Standard deviation*		*Discriminant function (canonical correlations)*	*Classification function*	
	Girls	*Boys*	*Girls*	*Boys*		*Girls*	*Boys*
I fear drugs because of getting disapproval from relatives.	.25	.37	.44	.49	.24	3.11	4.55
I fear drugs because of getting a drug other than what I expected.	.50	.28	.51	.46	-.47	2.95	.21
Frequency of use of marijuana	1.81	2.04	1.73	1.63	.55	-.03	.90
Frequency of use of LSD	.38	.07	.87	.33	-.54	.75	-1.77
Frequency of use of amphetamines	.91	.50	1.53	.89	-.28	-.21	-.86
Frequency of use of alcohol (beer/wine)	2.16	2.59	1.78	1.64	.47	.04	.82
One way of taking marijuana is to eat it.	1.03	1.22	.93	.89	.32	.46	1.44
Most adults would try marijuana if they knew where to get it.	.50	.89	.76	.77	.50	.83	2.68
If you don't take it too often, marijuana can give you a healthy outlook on life.	.91	1.24	.73	.74	.51	1.55	3.49
Barbiturates are also called "ups."	.91	.63	.82	.68	-.55	-.81	-2.90
Most of the students who are respected by their teachers don't use drugs.	1.47	1.13	.67	.81	-.20	1.33	.57

Table 4. Cont'd.

	Mean		*Standard deviation*		*Discriminant function (canonical correlations)*	*Classification function*	
	Girls	*Boys*	*Girls*	*Boys*		*Girls*	*Boys*
Using drugs can increase your awareness of the world and the people around you.	.84	1.24	.63	.71	.47	1.40	3.36
The present marijuana laws should be strictly enforced.	1.38	1.11	.66	.82	-.52	3.68	1.77
Heavy drug users are not usually the most well-liked students at school.	1.09	.74	.86	.74	-.24	2.13	1.29
Marijuana and hash come from the same plant.	.88	1.07	.79	.80	.35	.99	2.21
Tranquilizers are sometimes called "downs."	.41	.65	.56	.60	.24	.86	2.02
Barbiturates are called "downs."	.59	.91	.67	.63	.29	2.07	3.32
When you're high on drugs, you see things as they really are.	1.22	1.02	.91	.68	-.47	4.30	2.62
Heavy marijuana smokers usually get hooked on stronger stuff.	1.19	.85	.82	.79	-.25	1.50	.64
Constant						-11.96	-14.71

[a] High scores on "fear of drug use" questions indicate agreement with the statement or fear of drugs. Higher scores on "frequency of drug use" questions indicate more frequent use. High scores on other questions indicate *dis*agreement with the statement.

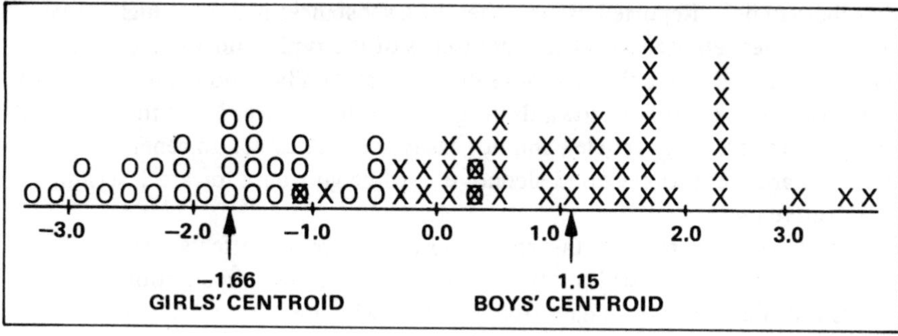

Figure 1. Histogram of Discriminant Scores (Girls = O, Boys = X)

The items which were most important relative to other variables in discriminating boys and girls include usage of marijuana and LSD and knowledge about whether barbiturates are called "ups." In addition, several other questions about marijuana were also important ("most adults would try it," "it can give you a healthy outlook" and "marijuana laws should be strictly enforced").

From the classification functions, we see that boys more than girls are apt to think that adults would not try marijuana, that marijuana does not give one a healthy outlook, that using drugs does not increase one's awareness. In addition, boys are particularly apt to think that barbiturates are called "ups." Fearing drugs because of getting unexpected drugs, thinking that marijuana laws should not be strictly enforced, and thinking that one does not see things as they are when high on drugs characterize girls. In terms of drug usage, boys are characterized by higher usage of marijuana and alcohol than girls and less usage of LSD and amphetamines.

SUMMARY

We can see from the above descriptive analysis of this potential dropout sample of Mexican-American students that:

1. Drug use is widespread;
2. Marijuana is used by about the same number of students as cigarettes and hard alcohol (but cigarettes are used more frequently);
3. More students are using more "social" drugs more often; and
4. That students do not think that general drug usage causes social problems, but heavy drug use may cause school problems.

The results show substantially higher social drug and marijuana usage for this sample of Mexican-American student potential dropouts than has been reported in other studies. Reported use of other drug substances is slightly higher than drug use rates reported in other drug studies of the typical high school environment. Finally, girls and boys differ substantially in both the patterns of drug use and the attitudes towards drugs. These differences in attitudes and patterns are very complex and not easily summarizable. In general, boys tend toward marijuana use and alcohol use, while girls tend toward LSD and barbiturate use.

No attempt was made in this study to isolate potential effects due to minority status as opposed to "potential dropout" status. In addition, it remains difficult to obtain data from students who are often absent and/or uninterested in participating in any school-related activity. The sample used in this study was based upon voluntary participation. The results, therefore, should not be generalized to the Mexican-American community nor to all potential dropouts. Most likely, drug use is higher among those potential dropouts who chose not to participate in the study.

A follow-up ethnographic study by Haro of the same population of students included some questions on drug use and corroborated both the findings and the speculation that drug use was higher among those not participating in the study [10]. More research work is needed in the areas of drug use of minority students and its relation to school performance.

Results of this study tentatively suggest the possibility that particular emphasis on drug education programs should be directed in trying to include or reach the potential dropout who may be chronically absent or truant. Possibly drug education programs may require different content emphases for girls and boys.

REFERENCES

1. J. Elinson, Changes in Drug Use Behavior Among High School Students: Some Antecedents and Consequences, D. Kandel (ed.), *Strategies of Longitudinal Research on Drug Use,* in press, 1976.
2. D. Kandel, Reaching the Hard-to-Reach: Illicit Drug Use Among High School Absentees, *Addictive Diseases, 4,* pp. 465-480, 1975.
3. J. Hays, The Incidence of Drug Abuse Among Secondary School Students in Houston, 1971, *St. Joseph Hospital Medical Surgical Journal, 7:*4, Fall 1972.
4. *Report of the National Commission on Marijuana and Drug Use,* Appendix I, U.S. Government Printing Office, Washington, D.C., 1972.
5. D. Hager, A. Verner, and C. Stewart, Patterns of Adolescent Drug Use in Middle America, *Journal of Counseling Psychology, 18:*4, pp. 292-297, 1971.
6. R. Jessor, S. Jessor, and J. Finney, A Social Psychology of Marijuana Use: Longitudinal Studies of High School and College Youth, *Journal of Personality and Social Psychology, 26:*1, pp. 1-15, 1973.

7. J. C. Ball and C. Chambers (eds.), *The Epidemiology of Opiate Addiction in the United States,* Charles C. Thomas, Springfield, Illinois, 1970.
8. W. A. Glenn and L. G. Richards, *Recent Surveys of Non-Medical Drug Use: A Compedium of Abstracts,* National Institute on Drug Abuse, Rockville, Maryland, 1974.
9. B. D. Johnson, *Marijuana Users and Drug Subcultures,* John Wiley & Sons, New York, 1973.
10. C. Haro, An Ethnographic Study of Truant and Low Achieving Chicano Barrio Youth in the High School Setting, unpublished doctoral dissertation, UCLA, 1976.

CHAPTER 14
The Relationship Between Self-Reported Religiosity and Drug Use by College Students

CAROL J. TURNER
ROBERT J. WILLIS

INTRODUCTION

Many studies address the question of religion and drug taking among college students. A review of the literature from 1968–1973 indicates in eighteen investigations that students who report themselves as "having no religion," being Jewish, or signifying "other religion" had a higher rate of drug usage than Catholic or Protestant self-reporters. Eleven studies during this same period report an inverse relationship between drug usage and formal religious participation [1].

Since 1973 many studies confirm and expand upon the earlier work.

Frequent drug users tend to shy away from formal religious practices [2–8]. They moreover move toward disaffiliation with the major religious denominations [4, 9–11].

The relationship between frequent drug usage and decreases in formal religious practices and affiliation was not suggestive of the relationship between frequent drug usage and self-reported religiosity, however. Thorpe reported that frequent drug users said that their religious feelings have deepened while taking drugs [11].

The present study sought to refine and extend understanding of the relationship between self-reported religiosity and drug use by students as part of an extensive survey of drug use patterns at a small, private college. Specifically, the purpose of this study was to explore the following questions:

1. Is there any relationship between self-reported religiosity and current drug usage?
2. Is there any relationship between self-reported religiosity and reasons for abstaining from particular drugs?
3. Is there any relationship between self-reported religiosity and acceptable sources for referral in case of drug problems?
4. Is there any relationship between self-reported religiosity and the persons with whom students discuss their attitudes toward drugs.

METHOD

Subjects

A sample of 1000 college students was randomly selected from a population of 3541 full-time day students at a private school in suburban New Jersey to receive drug questionnaires. The 379 students in the random sample who completed and returned the anonymous surveys were the subject in this study. Of these, 53 per cent were females and 47 per cent were males. With respect to age, 34 per cent were between eighteen and nineteen; 52 per cent were between twenty and twenty-one; and 14 per cent were twenty-two or more. The present religious affiliation of subjects was reported as follows: 41 per cent were Catholic; 20 per cent were Protestant; 19 per cent were Jewish and 20 per cent said "other" or "no religion."

The response rate of 37.9 per cent from the random sample was accepted because student participation in the study was completely voluntary: questionnaires were delivered and returned by campus mail so there was no direct contact with subjects; there was no financial compensation for completion of the survey; and there was no follow-up to determine reasons for non-participation.

Materials

The anonymous, self-report questionnaire which was used in this study was composed of 147 questions with associated multiple choice response alternatives. It explored selected demographic characteristics of subjects, the nature and incidence of drug use, the causes and effects of drug usage and attitudes toward drugs.

With respect to demographic characteristics, subjects were asked to describe themselves as persons (age, sex, etc.); to describe themselves as students (class, major, grade point average, etc.); to describe themselves as family members (parents' education, marital status, income, etc.); and to describe themselves as religious persons (upbringing, present affiliation and self-reported religiosity).

The nature and incidence of drug usage was assessed for each of ten drug categories (alcohol, marijuana, amphetamines, etc.) as follows: ever used these drugs; current use of same; person(s) who suggested first use, and age at time first used.

The causes and effects of drug usage were assessed for each of the ten groups of drugs as follows: perception of short-term effects of drugs and reasons for abstaining from these drugs; parents' attitudes toward drugs and parents' experience with drugs; friends' usage of drugs and attitudes toward drug use.

Attitudes toward drug usage included perceptions of student drug use in general (agreement with liberal or conservative statements about drug use); stated willingness to refer friends with drug problems to various agencies (doctor, other friends, etc.) and stated comfort in discussion of drugs with others (students, parents, doctor, etc.).

There was no investigation of reliability and validity of this study because the questionnaire was based on a comprehensive survey developed and administered by the Inter-University Drug Survey Council of Metropolitan New York in 1968–1969. All items on the Inter-University questionnaire were maintained without change as they were originally drawn from a pool of 800 items and were field tested at six metropolitan area schools [12]. In some cases, multiple choice response alternatives on the Inter-University questionnaire were rewritten so that no item in this study had more than six response alternatives. In addition, simultaneous ratings of related items on the Inter-University questionnaire were reformulated so that each question in this study was rated separately. Whenever a change was initiated, however, every effort was made to maintain the significant response alternatives provided by the Inter-University questionnaire.

Procedures

All students in the random sample received the following materials through campus mail during November 1975: a cover letter from the Counseling Center

Director which informed students of the study's purpose, assured anonymity and urged participation; a copy of the self-report questionnaire described prior; an addressed return envelope for the completed questionnaire; and a postcard addressed to the Counseling Center which could be signed as an indication of having returned the questionnaire under separate cover. Students in the random sample who did not return a signed postcard by January 1976, received a reminder letter in February 1976.

For the purpose of this study, all subjects who completed and returned questionnaires were assigned to a group based on their response to demographic item 12 on the drug questionnaire, "How religious are you now?": 7 per cent of all subjects responded "very" religious; 43 per cent of all subjects responded "moderately" religious; 33 per cent of all subjects responded "somewhat" religious; and 17 per cent of all students said "not at all" religious.

Group responses on religiosity were then crosstabulated with selected non-demographic items so that multiple choice response alternatives for each group defined a cell in the contingency table. A chi-square test of association was computed for selected cases in which the minimum expected frequency for each cell in the contingency table was greater than or equal to five. The level of significance was set as $p = 0.01$ because the large number of analyses might lead to spurious results. In those cases in which a significant association obtained, the strength of the association was estimated by a Pearson product-moment correlation coefficient for the two variables comprising the contingency table: correlations greater than $r = 0.14$ were significantly different from zero for $N = 379$.

RESULTS

The demographic variable self-reported religiosity was significantly related to the current incidence of alcohol and marijuana use; to reasons for abstaining from marijuana, amphetamines, barbiturates and hallucinogens; to referral of drug problems to drug-wise friends; and to discussing drug attitudes with parents and college counselors.

Nature and Incidence of Drug Use

The results of self-reported religiosity and current use of alcohol and marijuana by students in a small, private college are reported in Table 1.

There was a significant relationship between religiosity and current use of alcohol and marijuana: With respect to alcohol, $\text{chi}_X{}^2$ (3) = 13.68, $p < .01$; in the case of marijuana, $\text{chi}_X{}^2$ (3) = 19.62, $p < .01$. In both cases, subjects who described themselves as more religious tended to be infrequent users and subjects who defined themselves as less religious tended to be more frequent users. The

Table 1. Self-Reported Religiosity and Current Use of Drugs

Religiosity	*Drug* / *Current drug use* *Frequent*	*Infrequent*	chi_X^2	*df*	*r*	*N*
	Alcohol					
Very religious	16	12				
Moderately religious	72	88	13.68[a]	3	0.15[a]	374
Somewhat religious	77	47				
Not at all religious	42	20				
	Marijuana					
Very religious	3	25				
Moderately religious	38	123	19.62[a]	3	0.28[a]	374
Somewhat religious	36	88				
Not at all religious	31	30				

[a] $p < 0.01$.

strength of the relationship as estimated by the correlation coefficients was different from zero for both: for alcohol, $r = 0.15$ and for marijuana, $r = 0.28$.

Reasons for Abstaining from Drug Use

The results of self-reported religiosity and students' reasons for abstaining from amphetamines, barbiturates, marijuana, LSD and other psychedelics are reported in Table 2.

There was a significant relationship between religiosity and abstaining from marijuana because "not interested or curious," chi_X^2 (3) = 17.99, $p < .01$. Subjects who described themselves as more religious used this as a reason for abstaining while subjects who were less religious did not. The strength of the relationship as estimated by the correlation coefficient was $r = -0.22$.

On the other hand, there was no significant relationship between religiosity and abstaining from the following drugs because "not interested or curious": amphetamines, chi_X^2 (3) = 10.40, *ns;* barbiturates, chi_X^2 (3) = 9.16, *ns;* LSD and other psychedelics, chi_X^2 (3) = 9.44, *ns.*

There was a signficant association between religiosity and abstaining from the following drugs because of the "influence of parents or friends": amphetamines, chi_X^2 (3) = 13.69, $p < .01$; barbiturates, chi_X^2 (3) = 12.94, $p < .01$; marijuana, chi_X^2 (3) = 11.95, $p < .01$; and LSD and other psychedelics,

Table 2. Self-Reported Religiosity and Reasons for Abstaining from Drugs

Religiosity	*Drug* *Reasons for abstaining* *Yes*	*No*	chi_{χ}^2	*df*	*r*	*N*
	Amphetamines not interested					
Very religious	20	8	10.40	3	-0.14	375
Moderately religious	119	42				
Somewhat religious	83	41				
Not at all religious	32	30				
	Barbiturates not interested					
Very religious	21	7	9.16	3	-0.13	375
Moderately religious	118	43				
Somewhat religious	87	37				
Not at all religious	33	29				
	Marijuana not interested					
Very religious	18	10	17.99[a]	3	-0.22	375
Moderately religious	68	93				
Somewhat religious	39	85				
Not at all religious	14	48				
	LSD and other psychedelics not interested					
Very religious	22	6	9.44	3	-0.14	375
Moderately religious	120	41				
Somewhat religious	88	36				
Not at all religious	34	28				
	Amphetamines parental influence					
Very religious	6	22	13.69[a]	3	-0.16[a]	375
Moderately religious	44	117				
Somewhat religious	25	99				
Not at all religious	3	59				
	Barbiturates parental influence					
Very religious	6	22	12.94[a]	3	-0.14[a]	375
Moderately religious	43	118				
Somewhat religious	28	96				
Not at all religious	3	59				

[a] $p < 0.01$.

Table 2. (Cont'd.)

Religiosity	*Drug* — *Reasons for abstaining* *Yes*	*No*	chi_X^2	*df*	*r*	*N*
	Marijuana parental influence					
Very religious	6	22	11.95[a]	3	−0.15[a]	375
Moderately religious	41	120				
Somewhat religious	25	99				
Not at all religious	3	59				
	LSD and other psychedelics parental influence					
Very religious	7	21	13.56[a]	3	−0.15[a]	375
Moderately religious	48	113				
Somewhat religious	30	94				
Not at all religious	4	58				

[a] $p < 0.01$.

chi_X^2 (3) = 13.56, $p < .01$. In all cases, more religious subjects used this reason for abstaining from drugs and less religious subjects did not.

In all cases, the strength of the relationship between religiosity and abstaining from drugs because of parental influence was significantly different from zero: r = −0.16 for amphetamines; r = −0.14 for barbiturates; r = −0.15 for marijuana, LSD and other psychedelics.

Sources of Referral for Drug Problems

The results of self-reported religiosity and acceptable sources for referral in case of drug problems are reported in Table 3. A significant relationship obtained between religiosity and referral to "drug-wise friends," chi_X^2 (3) = 12.86, $p < .01$. More religious students would not use this referral source while less religious students would. However, the degree of the relationship, r = −0.13, was not significant for $p = 0.01$. On the other hand, there was no significant relationship between referral of friends with drug problems to the following resources: to health service, chi_X^2 (3) = 5.10, *ns;* to the counseling center, chi_X^2 (3) = 9.83, *ns;* to the resident assistants (student staff in dormitories) chi_X^2 (3) = 1.02, *ns;* and to particular faculty members, chi_X^2 (3) = 7.83, *ns.*

Table 3. Self-Reported Religiosity and Referral Sources for Drug Problems

Religiosity	Acceptable referral source: Yes	No	chi_X^2	df	r	N
	Drug-wise friends					
Very religious	13	14	12.86[a]	3	−0.13	360
Moderately religious	69	84				
Somewhat religious	67	53				
Not at all religious	43	17				
	Health service					
Very religious	14	14	5.10	3	0.01	362
Moderately religious	104	50				
Somewhat religious	77	43				
Not at all religious	33	27				
	Counseling service					
Very religious	25	3	9.83	3	0.12	362
Moderately religious	134	20				
Somewhat religious	96	24				
Not at all religious	42	18				
	Resident assistants					
Very religious	17	10	1.02	3	0.02	356
Moderately religious	84	69				
Somewhat religious	69	49				
Not at all religious	31	27				
	Particular faculty					
Very religious	11	17	7.83	3	−0.07	358
Moderately religious	79	75				
Somewhat religious	48	68				
Not at all religious	37	23				

[a] $p < 0.01$.

Comfort Discussing Drugs

The results for self-reported religiosity and comfort discussing drugs with others are reported in Table 4.

There was a significant relationship between religiosity and comfort discussing drugs with parents and comfort discussing drugs with a college counselor. Specifically, with respect to parents, $chi_X^2\ (6) = 17.31, p < .01$ and with respect to the college counselor, $chi_X^2\ (6) = 17.75, p < .01$. The more

Table 4. Self-Reported Religiosity and Comfort Discussing Drugs with Significant Others

	Person						
Religiosity	*Very comfortable*	*Somewhat comfortable*	*Not at all comfortable*	*chi* χ^2	*df*	*r*	*N*
	Any student						
Very religious	11	10	7	14.79	6	−0.10	361
Moderately religious	34	84	37				
Somewhat religious	27	75	16				
Not at all religious	21	32	7				
	Any faculty member						
Very religious	11	12	5	12.16	6	0.02	361
Moderately religious	41	75	38				
Somewhat religious	19	69	31				
Not at all religious	16	36	8				
	Deans or assistant deans						
Very religious	11	9	8	13.62	6	0.08	362
Moderately religious	39	57	59				
Somewhat religious	16	41	62				
Not at all religious	15	22	23				
	Your doctor						
Very religious	12	12	4	7.02	6	0.06	362
Moderately religious	58	63	34				
Somewhat religious	31	52	36				
Not at all religious	19	27	14				
	Your parents						
Very religious	15	5	8	17.31[a]	6	0.14[a]	362
Moderately religious	69	46	40				
Somewhat religious	33	42	44				
Not at all religious	14	22	24				
	College counselor						
Very religious	15	13	0	17.75[a]	6	0.04	356
Moderately religious	59	69	26				
Somewhat religious	28	58	29				
Not at all religious	26	22	11				

[a] $p < 0.01$

religious subjects were comfortable discussing drugs with parents and college counselors while less religious subjects were not. The strength of the relationship, as expressed by the correlation coefficient, was significant with respect to discussing drugs with parents, $r = 0.14$, but it was not significant with respect to discussing drugs with a college counselor, $r = 0.04$. Finally, there was no significant relationship between religiosity and comfort discussing drugs with any student, chi$_X^2$ (6) = 14.79, *ns;* faculty members, chi$_X^2$ (6) = 12.16, *ns;* deans or assistant deans, chi$_X^2$ (6) = 13.62, *ns;* or a doctor, chi$_X^2$ (6) = 7.02, *ns.*

DISCUSSION

Because of statistical requirements the current study is not able to report on the relationship between self-reported religiosity and specific drugs other than alcohol and marijuana. Such, in general, would be helpful.

The present study does provide a refinement and extension of Thorne's finding that frequent drug users report a deepening of religious feeling, however. While some frequent drug users in this study saw themselves as deeply religious, most students who saw themselves in this way were not frequent users of drugs.

This relationship between self-reported religiosity and drug usage is further clarified in the reasons frequent and infrequent users give for abstaining from drugs. Parental influence was significantly related to religious students abstinence from marijuana, barbiturates, amphetamines, and the hallucinogens. Parental influence was inversely related to reasons for abstaining among non-religious peers. At the same time religious students were significantly less interested in smoking marijuana while non-religious students were.

One may speculate on this significant "interest" difference. As indicated earlier frequent users may attach religious experiences and deepened religious feeling to marijuana use. Their getting high by their own report may be seen as an alternative way to religious experience. Paradoxically, these "non-religious" students may be turning to drugs for "religious experience" while their "religious" peers condemn such use as militating against such "religious experience."

A larger question presents itself here; namely, does frequent formal religious practice by students correlate directly or inversely with the depth and meaningfulness of one's personal religious values? The "straight" religious world would undoubtedly hold for directly, while the "stoned" alternative may be proclaiming just the opposite.

Faced with parental disapproval, legal sanctions, and a general lack of adult experience with the realities of the youth drug culture, non-religious, frequent drug-users would tend to steer drug-related problems to drug-wise friends. Moreover they would shy away from talking about their own drug world with those possibly most concerned (their parents) and most knowledgeable about drugs and health (college counselors). Inversely, their religious, non-using fellow students would tend to bring drug-related questions and problems to the attention of potentially helpful adults.

If the adult world is to have a positive influence upon the student who *will* take drugs in the face of general societal disapproval, these findings would point generally in two directions: generalized drug education for students, so that "drug-wise" friends may add the best of scientific knowledge to personal experience; and steps by adult society both to lessen a student's fear of bringing his drug questions and problems to adults, and to increase the understanding of responsible adults about the realities of the students' world of drugs.

REFERENCES

1. L. Bowker, College Student Drug Use: An Examination and Application of the Epidemiological Literature, *Journal of College Student Personnel, 16:*2, pp. 137-144, 1975.
2. J. L. Strimbu and L. F. Schoenfeldt, Life History Subgroups in the Prediction of Drug Usage, *Catalog of Selected Documents in Psychology, 3,* p. 83, 1973.
3. J. L. Strimbu and O. S. Sims, A University System Drug Profile, *The International Journal of the Addictions, 9:*4, pp. 569-583, 1974.
4. E. R. Martino and C. V. Truss, Drug Use and Attitudes Toward Social and Legal Aspects of Marijuana in a Large Metropolitan University, *Journal of Counseling Psychology, 20:*2, pp. 120-126, 1973.
5. D. A. Biggs, J. B. Orcutt, and N. Bakkenist, Correlates of Marijuana and Alcohol Use Among College Students, *Journal of College Student Personnel, 15:*1, pp. 22-30, 1974.
6. D. Wardell and N. Mehra, Prediction of Marijuana Usage Among Students in a University Residence, *Journal of College Student Personnel, 15:*1, pp. 31-33, 1974.
7. L. F. Henze and J. W. Hudson, Personal and Family Characteristics of Cohabitating and Noncohabitating College Students, *Journal of Marriage and the Family, 36:*4, pp. 722-726, 1974.
8. M. L. Fischler, Drug Usage in Rural, Small Town New England, *The Journal of Altered States of Consciousness, 2:*2, pp. 171-183, 1975–76.
9. R. A. Steffenhagen, C. P. McGree, and H. L. Nixon, Drug Use Among College Females: Socio-Demographic and Social Psychological Correlates, *The International Journal of the Addictions, 7:*2, pp. 285-303, 1972.
10. W. H. Cunningham, I. C. M. Cunningham, and W. D. English, Sociopsychological Characteristics of Undergraduate Marijuana Users, *The Journal of Genetic Psychology, 125:*1, pp. 3-12, 1974.
11. C. B. Thorpe, Marijuana Smoking and Value Change Among College Students, *College Student Journal, 9:*1, pp. 9-16, 1975.
12. S. Pearlman, Myths and Realities of the College Drug Scene: Adventures in Epidemiology, *Management of Adolescent Drug Use,* Stash Press, Beloit, Wisconsin, 1973.

CHAPTER 15
Empirically-Derived Hierarchy of Use for Psychotropics: A Cost Benefit Index*

KHALIL A. KHAVARI
FRAZIER M. DOUGLASS

INTRODUCTION

Considerable concern and controversy has appeared, in recent years, with respect to use of psychoactive drugs. Medical experts, scientists, parents, politicians, and others have expressed their opinions with respect to potential benefits/hazards of these drugs. The only commonly shared view is that the issue deserves careful study and attention.

Various positions espoused by different people vis-a-vis a given drug are often highly emotional in tone and relatively lacking in scientific evidence. Additionally, a great deal of this debate is carried out, by and large, by people who are not themselves directly and deeply involved with the use of drugs.

*Supported by NIDA research grant DA01080 and funds from the College of Letters and Science and the Graduate School of the University of Wisconsin-Milwaukee, to K. A. Khavari.

Drug use is a form of behavior where general laws and principles of instrumental learning are likely to apply. To a large extent, the processes involved in the decision to use a drug are the same as those which lead the individual to engage in other kinds of behavior. That is, drug use is rational, goal-directed behavior aimed at achievement of specific results [1]. Thus, little is gained with respect to understanding of this behavior by labelling it as pathological, sick, deviant, immoral, and the like.

A COST-BENEFIT APPROACH

It is proposed here that the individual's decision to use drug(s) is reached through a rational, yet complex process of cost-benefit analysis. That is, numerous considerations (e.g., the kind of drug, peer influences, health hazards, monetary costs, societal sanctions, personal values, etc.) influence his decision regarding the initial trying of the substance. Subsequent continuation of use is also influenced by the above factors and the individual's personal experience with the drug. Consequently, these dynamic factors will eventually determine the extent of the person's involvement with drug usage.

The present study provides actual data, rather than opinions, regarding use of fifteen drugs or classes of drugs. The findings reveal a hierarchial order of use for these psychotropics which can be viewed as indexes of cost-benefit. That is, the data from 1121 adult respondents of this study reflect some sort of rank-order for these substances along a use continuum.

THE PARTICIPANTS

The data reported here were obtained from two different groups, during a period from January through July 1975. One group consisted of 310 industrial workers whose participation in the research was obtained through the cooperation and encouragement of labor unions. This group, primarily male (80.3%), included a broad range of occupations (e.g., welders, fork-life operators, inspectors, handymen, assembly workers, etc.) in industrial settings. Age ranged from eighteen to fifty-three years (mean = 25.9); the range for formal education was from none to university degree; and, annual income ranged from less than $2,500 to over $25,000.

The second group consisted of 811 college students enrolled at a university during the summer of 1975. Approximately 67 per cent were female and 86 per cent were white. This group included many professionals (e.g., teachers) who were taking summer courses. Thus, 32 per cent were seniors or graduate students; nearly 25 per cent were over twenty-five years of age, and nearly 34 per cent had a grade point average of "B" or higher.

The total sample was composed of 517 males and 604 females. The racial composition was: 954 white, 124 black, and 33 "other."

PROCEDURE AND RESULTS

Each respondent was given a battery of tests which included a self-administered drug use questionnaire. "Ever tried," "currently using," and "frequency of current use" information were obtained on fifteen psychoactive drugs or classes of drugs.

We employed the standard statistical procedure for transformation of the data into standardized scores [2]:

$$T = 50 + 10\frac{X - \overline{X}}{SD}$$

This T distribution provides for a population mean = 50 and standard deviation = 10.

Data from the drug questionnaire were converted into T scores by first assigning a value from 0 to 7 to each of the eight response categories related to drug use.

Tried		*Currently Using*					
Never Tried	Tried But Currently Not Using	Less Than Monthly	Once A Month	Once A Week	Several Times A Week	Daily	Several Times A Day
0	1	2	3	4	5	6	7

T values for each level of use, for each drug, were then calculated by treating its respective assigned value as the X in the equation.

Regardless of the underlying dynamics of drug use behavior, the present data provide an empirically-derived hierarchy of psychotropics usage. Means, standard deviations, and dispersion units for the fifteen drugs are given in Table 1. These dispersion units are in T values and they reflect the distance, in terms of T units, between two adjacent usage levels for a given drug. For example, the T score associated with "never tried" for tobacco is 39.65. The T score for the next level of use, i.e., "tried but currently not using" is 43.17. Thus, the difference between the two use levels is 3.52 which we have chosen to call the dispersion unit for tobacco. These dispersion units can be interpreted to represent cost-benefit indexes. Therefore, a numerically small dispersion unit represents a low cost-high benefit ratio, as determined by actual use. A numerically large dispersion unit, on the other hand, represents a high cost-low benefit ratio.

Employing this analytic approach results in derivation of the drug use hierarchy of Table 1. Furthermore, the dispersion units (cost-benefit indexes) provide quantitative measures of drug use "deviance." By deviance, in this context, we mean the statistical distance from the mean, in terms of T score

Table 1. Fifteen Psychotropic Drugs or Classes of Drugs, Mean and Standard Deviation for Frequency of Usage, and the Dispersion Units Reflecting the Cost-Benefit Index Associated with Each Drug

Substance	*Mean*	*S.D.*	*Dispersion Unit*
Tobacco (Cigarettes, Cigars, Pipe, Chewing Tobacco, etc.)	2.94	2.84	3.52
Marijuana	1.67	1.90	5.27
Alcohol (Beer, Wine, Hard Liquor, Brandy, Whiskey)	3.79	1.40	7.11
Relaxants (Librium, Valium, Equanil, Serax, Solacen, etc.)	.64	1.30	7.69
Amphetamines (Benzedrine, Dexedrine, Methedrine, Ritalin, etc.)	.54	1.10	9.10
Hashish	.75	1.08	9.25
Tranquilizers (Thorazine, Mellaril, Stelazine, Compazine, Serentil, etc.)	.39	.99	10.10
Barbiturates (Amytal, Nembutal, Phenobarbital, Seconal, Tuinal, etc.)	.35	.87	11.51
Sedatives (Placidyl, Valmid, Doriden, Quaalude, Dormison, Bromides, etc.)	.28	.73	13.70
Cocaine	.30	.72	13.89
Anti-Depressants (Elavil, Tofranil, Marplan, Surmontil, etc.)	.12	.60	16.67
Other Psychedelics (DET, DMT, Peyote, Mescaline, STP, Psilocybin, etc.)	.25	.60	16.75
LSD	.24	.58	17.22
Opiates (Heroin, Morphine, Opium)	.16	.52	19.38
Methadone	.04	.33	30.14

units associated with a specific usage level of a given drug. For instance, an individual who is a consumer of tobacco products at the usage level of several times a day is not statistically deviant (T = 64.29) from the population norm, with regard to this use. In contrast, even having only tried methadone constitutes statistically significant deviation (T = 79.01) from the population norm, since the T score is nearly two standard deviations above the population mean. With respect to a substance such as alcohol, on the other hand, not having tried alcohol is highly deviant (T = 23.05), nearly three standard deviations below the mean.

Another area of concern is with respect to incidence and frequency of drug use. Clearly, trying a substance is a necessary but not sufficient condition for further use. Moreover, different drugs appear to have different probabilities of use and usage levels associated with them. It is constructive to examine, briefly, certain use parameters associated with alcoholic beverages, tobacco, and marijuana.

RESULTS

Alcohol was reportedly tried by nearly 99 per cent of this population. Of those who had tried alcohol less than 6 per cent considered themselves to be non-users of alcoholic beverages, at the time of the test, while 7 per cent reported consumption of alcohol at a frequency of daily or more. Thus, the conclusion that nearly everyone had tried alcohol and that the overwhelming majority (94%) continue to drink past the initial trying.

Tobacco products were reportedly tried by 77 per cent of this population. Thirty-five per cent of those who had tried tobacco products did not continue with their consumption of tobacco, while 39 per cent reported consuming tobacco products with a frequency of daily or more. Thus, considerably fewer people seem to try tobacco products, as compared to alcohol. Moreover, use of tobacco products beyond the initial trying is less likely, as compared to alcohol.

Marijuana was reportedly tried by 62 per cent of the respondents. Twenty-eight per cent of those who had tried marijuana did not continue to use it, while 6 per cent reported heavy use of marijuana (daily or more).

Precise exposition of the factors which influence drug-trying in the first place and continuation/abandonment of use requires considerable research. The present data suggest several research possibilities. We have proposed, here, a set of notions regarding drug use behavior which can be put to empirical tests. The behavior itself is viewed as, by and large, rational, goal-directed instance of instrumental behavior. The data seems to justify the proposition that an individual's use of a given drug is determined by his assessment of the drug's risk-benefit characteristics. All kinds of considerations may contribute, to various degrees, to use of a particular drug. These considerations may be based upon actual/perceived attributes of the substance. In a sense, use of a drug is assumed to be determined by performance of a complex cost-benefit analysis. If costs (psychological, physiological, social, economic, etc.) associated with use are judged to be higher than benefits (euphoria, pleasure, relaxation, etc.), then usage is reduced or terminated. But, when actual/perceived benefits are judged to warrant the costs, usage is maintained or even intensified. Thus, when a cigarette smoker judges the cost of smoking (e.g., current respiratory difficulties and being subject to higher risk of incurring lung cancer) to be greater than the benefits, he is likely to discontinue smoking. By the same token, a marijuana smoker may find smoking marijuana to be justifiable when subjected to cost-benefit analysis.

It should be pointed out that the position of a given drug in the hierarchy of Table 1 may change when a different population is considered or assessment of use is made in the future. In this event, the findings may be significant in pointing out important differences in drug use practices among groups/cultures or shift of usage within a group/culture over time.

Numerous issues deserve careful study and research to help further our understanding of drug use behavior. Detailed analysis of motivational variables involved in drug use should prove to be highly informative. For example, we should learn about the critical factors which lead to the individual's initial trying of a substance. What are the major determinants of choosing a drug or a class of drugs. What subsequent conditions lead to maintenance/intensification or abandonment of use. It is this sort of research which should ultimately provide the needed data for effective prevention and treatment of abusive drug use.

ACKNOWLEDGEMENT

The authors would like to thank Mae Humes for her contribution to portions of this work.

REFERENCES

1. R. Jessor, S. L. Jessor, and J. Finney, A Social Psychology of Marijuana Use: Longitudinal Studies of High School and College Youth, *Journal of Personality and Social Psychology, 26,* pp. 1-15, 1973.
2. R. P. Runyon and A. Haber, *Fundamentals of Behavioral Statistics,* Addison-Wesley, Reading, Massachusetts, 1971.

Part III
PRACTICE

The last section of this book is concerned with the experimental and clinical settings where specific approaches to drug education and rehabilitation are implemented, evaluated, assessed, and adopted. The practice or utilization of specific programs can be considered as the implementation of theoretical constructs in a realistic milieu. To be sure not *all* education or rehabilitative modes are included in this section of the book. Yet we have selected those which, in our judgment, represent practical models for providing us with more information about educational fundamentalities and rehabilitative constructs. If nothing else, these readings should excite your creative and imaginative processes in order to seek more and better approaches to the educational and rehabilitative success we all wish to achieve. Of course, success is often limited by practical issues of setting, funding, and staffing, and we also seek programs which in fact can be implemented with resources now available.

Specifically, Sheppard discusses sources of informational credibility in drug education and those who one learns to trust most. Decision-making about drug use and the advice one seeks are also sources of information which are considered, evaluated, and implemented in programs. Furthermore, Sheppard provides a better understanding of those individuals perceived as credible and trustworthy as sources for advice and decision-making. Obviously, any drug education must make maximum use of credible sources of information.

Greenberg and his associates provide information pertaining to the impact of TV on young viewers. He suggested that "Social learning theory suggests that exposure to content stimuli which are consistent on theme and of considerable frequency can impact a young viewer." Greenberg took a holistic view of TV programming during two TV seasons 1976-77, and 1977-78. It was during this period that there was significant reference to the use of alcohol, tobacco and both licit and illicit drugs in entertainment programs. However, in a subsequent study of "Smoking, Drugging and Drinking" in top TV rated programs, he concluded that drinking alcohol is "conspicuously present in all top ten TV rated shows. Additional data revealed that during the 1979-80 TV season, smoking was out, drugging was out, but continued use of alcohol in TV programs indicated that alcohol is still a socially acceptable drug in this country. To further explore the effect of media, Sheppard and Goodstadt reports that films are a good educational mode. They report that notwithstanding the value of films, some teachers use film as one approach to avoiding direct student contact in the classroom setting. Teachers, they suggest, use films which are old and frequently outdated. New and more responsive audio-visual materials are being developed daily.

Monismith, Shute, St. Pierre, and Alles tested the opinions of seventh to twelfth grade students regarding the effectiveness of pro- and anti-smoking messages. Generally, the nonsmokers saw value in the message while the smokers found specific messages to be dull and boring. We must strive to improve our communication skills so as to make our messages more meaningful.

In the area of rehabilitation, Mann and Wingard reviewed three treatment modalities at Synanon in the United States, and the Hassela Collective and Valmortorp Foundation of Sweden. Synanon employed the "Game"—a self-help approach to rebuild one's character. The game, according to Diederick of Synanon is "not designed to solve problems but to demolish them." The Hassela Collective operates a spartan-like approach to drug rehabilitation. They retrain the individual to function in a perceived permissive environment. Rather than therapy, the Hassela Collective refers to their approaches as an alternative pedagogy. The Valmortorp Foundation operates its program on Gestalt-like philosophy employing Transactional Analysis as its foundation. This modality is a noncoercive and nonmanipulative form of modern therapy. Alternate therapies should not be dismissed casually.

Sideroff claims that Gestalt Therapy assists to develop a trusting relationship between the client and the counselor. The Gestaltist avoids interpretation but relies on the client to express his inner feelings and interpret them. Sideroff presents the general principles of the approach as they would be applied to drug abusers.

Notwithstanding modalities for drug rehabilitation programs, and for that matter alcoholism, Skuja describes the issues attendant on training the alcoholism counselor. If the personal stress levels of the counselor can be attended to then it can serve as a basis for effective counselor training.

Lastly, Murphy indicates that the current mode of evaluating federally funded programs; i.e., client oriented data acquisition (CODAP) does not allow for specific treatment philosophies as objectives and argues that additional program data from clients in the outpatient setting be employed, so that a more clear evaluating of specific behavior changes can be recorded. It will then be possible to more accurately determine the important results brought about by different drug programs.

CHAPTER 16
Sources of Information About "Drugs"

MARGARET A. SHEPPARD

INTRODUCTION

An important component in any "drug" education program is information. "Drug" education program in this context is any concentrated effort to deter, reduce or eliminate consumption of any chemical (that is not for medical purposes), by the target audience. Some programs focus on decision-making, lifestyle, or values, yet all have some informational component.

The first step is to decide what information is needed and relevant to the target audience; then how best to get the information to the target in a way that will be accepted, believed and acted upon. For this process, one must take into account not only the message and the target but the communicator and the medium of communication.

For the continuum of target audiences – the very young to older adults; non-users, experimenters, users to heavy users and abusers – is there a continuum of messages, communicators and media?

In an effort to develop such a continuum, studies of sources of drug information were collected and their results examined.

METHOD

In all there were sixteen separate studies identified that contained some reference to source of drug information. These studies were categorized by kind of question asked in the interview or questionnaire along with date, sample and results.

RESULTS

The number of studies and the type of question asked are summarized in Table 1. There was a wide variety of questions asked, however a smaller grouping shows that fifteen (68%) deal directly with drug information – the others being adjuncts or peripheral to the main issue. I will deal with each of these groupings separately first.

Where One Would Go to Get Information About Drugs [1–3]

Each study dealt with a different population:

1. professional adults in several Ontario communities;
2. elementary and secondary school students in California; and
3. elementary and secondary school students in Ontario.

Only study 3 differentiated between drug users and non-users.

The professional adults reported that they would first go to other professionals for information on drugs, then the mass media – magazines, periodicals, etc. The students in California indicated parents, television, friends, in that order. In the Ontario study drug users said they would ask friends, non-users, a physician.

Who Is Perceived as Being Most Credible? [4–7]

Again, these studies questioned different populations:

1. secondary school students in Ontario county;
2. adults in the largest city in Ontario;
3. university students in Ontario;
4. university students in Connecticut; and
5. secondary school students in Kansas plus a selection of drug clinic clients.

Each of these studies divided their population into drug users and non-users and reported these separately. In general, youthful users reported that other users or ex-users were the most credible when it came to drug information while the youthful non-users referred to scientists, doctors or the media. The adult users said that professionals were most credible and adult non-users quoted the media.

Table 1. Questions Asked in Studies of Source of Information by Year

Type of Question	*Years*	*N*	*%*
1. To whom would one listen for advice about drugs?	1972, 1976	2	9
2. Who is most credible in giving drug information?	1971, 1971, 1972, 1973, 1975	5	23
3. Who is most trusted in giving information?	1970, 1971	4	18
4. Where would one seek help for a drug problem?	1971, 1973	3	14
5. Who is most influential in helping one make drug use decisions?	1970, 1973	2	9
6. From whom does one learn the most?	1970, 1971	3	14
7. Where would one go for information?	1973, 1975, 1977	3	14
TOTALS:		22[a]	100

[a] This is more than sixteen because some studies addressed multiple questions.

Who Is Most Trusted? [4, 5, 8, 9]

Three of these studies [4, 5, 8] divided their sample by user – non-user; all were young people.

The users generally reported that they trusted the information from friends or doctors; while the non-users said that they trusted the media or health professionals.

From Whom Does One Learn the Most? [9–11]

Fejer et al. [9], divided the sample into users, non-users; Smart [11] divided his sample by age. Again, the mass media scored highest for learning information while friends and personal experience were often quoted especially by users or older students.

Table 2. Population Samples by Results

Population	*Where To Get Information*	*Credible Sources*	*Trusted Sources*	*Learn Most From Whom*	*Influential*	*Advice*	*Help*
Under 18 years	friends, media, doctors	users, doctors	friends, media	media, friends, experience	parents, media, friends		friends
University		users				older silbing	friends
Adult	professionals, media	doctors, media	doctors			doctor	

Most Influential in Helping Making Drug Use Decisions [12, 13]

In making a decision to use a specific drug, Smart [12] found that depending upon the drug in question, either friends or mass media influenced the decision, while Streit [13] found that parents most often deterred drug taking behavior.

To Whom Would One Listen for Advice? [14, 15]

Pascale and Streit [14] asked school students who generally replied – an older sibling.

Gallup asked adults and they said a doctor or researcher.

The Final Question Deals With Getting Help for a Problem Related to Drugs [6, 13, 16]

Roth [16] found that the majority of students both users (80%) and non-users (96%) had never sought help. However, if they had sought help or would feel the necessity to seek help, most would go to a friend. Both Hanneman [6] and Streit [13] had the same result.

Taking the sample populations and grouping them produces the results shown in Table 2.

There are some consistencies: friends, mass media, professionals rank highly for most of the population as credible, trusted sources of information.

DISCUSSION

What are the implications for anyone who would attempt to impart knowledge in the context of a drug education program?

Unfortunately, there does not seem to be any follow-up of questions and target groups in this area. Each study that has been quoted was a once only study. Generally, the respondents were given a selection of sources from which to choose, which naturally limited the choices and gave a predisposition to certain choices.

There does not appear to have been any attempt to check if the sources cited had been used and how effective they were. It seems that the premise was – if one wanted information where would one go. Experience has taught that people do not seek out such information until a need arises – perhaps a school project for students or a problem in the family for adults.

Also, no effort has been made to ascertain the kinds of information the sources are perceived to have, how any information would be used, and if it was obtained how much was remembered, or used.

In most cases, if the mass media was given as a choice that ranked high for everyone. Yet, it is clear that much information given by the mass media is inaccurate either by commission or omission. There has been little attempt to systematically find out which aspect of the media has been used or is perceived to be of most value.

Professionals, especially doctors, are perceived to be good sources for drug information. Yet, many doctors will readily admit to their lack of expertise when it comes to areas of non-prescription drugs and this is the presumed area of inquiry for the people questioned in these surveys.

The other major source for information given by the respondents was friends, peers, users of the drugs in question. While studies have shown that drug users often have more and more accurate information than non-users, their opinions and information should not be taken as definitive. Friends who do not use drugs may simply pass on misinformation that they have picked up from other friends or equally questionable sources.

While it is obviously important that the target audience perceive that the sender of any message is credible, knowledgeable, trustworthy, etc., it is really capable of making such decisions?

Perhaps the most qualified senders of information should take the time to establish their credibility and trustworthiness before giving information.

Media messages should be carefully assessed as to which target responds best to which medium and then establish trustworthiness, etc.

Much needs to be done in this most important area if drug information processes are to be optimized. We need systematic messages to be tested using different media and senders reaching different audiences.

REFERENCES

1. *A Study of Drug Information Needs of Professionals in Five Ontario Communities,* Info Results, Toronto, Ontario, 1973.
2. R. Clark, et al., The Influence of Information Sources and Grade Level on the Diffusion and Adoption of Marijuana, *Journal of Drug Issues,* pp. 177-188, Spring 1975.

3. M. S. Goodstadt, et al., *The Status of Drug Education in Ontario, 1977,* Addiction Research Foundation, 1977.
4. R. Smart, Sources of Drug Information for High School Students: Their Relative Influence and Credibility, *Journal of Alcohol Education, 17,* pp. 1-15, 1971.
5. R. Smart and D. Fejer, *Most Influential and Credible Sources of Drug Information for Adults: Differences Between Marijuana Users and Non-Users,* Addiction Research Foundation Substudy, 1971.
6. G. J. Hanneman, Communicating Drug Abuse Information Among College Students, *Public Opinion Quarterly,* pp. 171-191, 1973.
7. R. E. Sennett, et al., Credibility of Sources of Information About Drugs, *Psychological Reports, 36,* pp. 299-309, 1975.
8. M. Lassey and J. Carlson, *Drinking Among Teenagers. Rural-Urban Comparison in Peer Influence.*
9. D. Fejer, et al., Sources of Information About Drugs Among High School Students, *Public Opinion Quarterly, 31,* pp. 235-241, Summer 1971.
10. R. Smart, *Sources of Drug Information for High School Students: Changes Between 1967-1970,* Addiction Research Foundation Substudy, 1970.
11. ———, *Age and Sex Differences in the Most Influential Sources of Drug Information,* Addiction Research Foundation Substudy, 1971.
12. ———, *Most Influential Sources of Drug Information and Extent of Drug Use,* Addiction Research Foundation Substudy, 1971.
13. F. Streit, The Importance of Significant Others in Youth's Decision-Making About Drug Use and Other Deviant Acts, *Journal of Drug Education, 4:*4, pp. 409-419, Winter 1974.
14. P. Pascale and F. Streit, A Study of the Credibility Factor in Drug Education Program, *Journal of Drug Education, 2:*4, pp. 391-394, Winter 1972.
15. The Canadian Gallup Poll, February 1976.
16. R. Roth, *Student Drug Abuse in Southeastern Michigan and Profiles of Abusers,* S. Einstein (ed.), Proceedings of the First International Conference on Student Drug Surveys, pp. 55-66, 1971.

CHAPTER 17
Trends in Use of Alcohol and Other Substances on Television*

BRADLEY S. GREENBERG
CARLOS FERNANDEZ-COLLADO
DAVID GRAEF
FELIPE KORZENNY
CHARLES K. ATKIN

INTRODUCTION

Concern about the portrayal of alcohol and other drugs on television shows is tied to the expectation that these portrayals are frequent and typically favorable. If that is so, then the further expectation is that viewers will respond to such displays of alcohol in terms of their attitudes and possibly their drinking habits as well.

More specific concern about television's depiction of alcohol and other drugs focuses on the potential social learning which might occur among young viewers. Young viewers are expected to be particularly vulnerable because childhood and

* This project was funded by Grant 90-C-635 from the Office of Child Development, HEW. All authors are associated with the Department of Communication, Michigan State University, where Profs. Greenberg, Korzenny and Atkin are faculty members, Mr. Fernandez-Collado is a graduate student and Mr. Graef is an undergraduate. This paper was written while Dr. Greenberg was a Fellow in the Communication Institute of the East-West Center, Honolulu.

adolescence are periods of information-seeking during which the child learns what to expect from the world and what the world expects from the child. Children derive information from many sources, but television in particular provides graphic and dramatic exposure to wordly behaviors which go substantially beyond the child's immediate experiences. And television presents attitudes and values which may differ from those of family and peers [1–2]. There also is substantial evidence that the observation of social models specifically including television models, may account for a significant segment of information that is communicated to young people [3–5].

Lyle and Hoffman found that the first graders spent about twenty-four hours each week watching television, sixth graders about thirty hours and tenth graders about twenty-eight hours [6]. More current national audience data from Nielsen rating, indicate that all age groups have expanded their viewing time since the early 1970's. Thus the potential for learning from television exists in terms of time spent with the medium, and the young viewer's use of TV for social information.

This rationale is built on the premise that alcohol at least is available on a widespread basis during television's prime hours, inside the programs, exclusive of commercials. Yet, the evidence on this issue is scanty and less than systematic. This paper reports on a content analysis of the usage of alcohol, tobacco and illicit drugs during two recent television seasons, 1976-1977 and 1977-1978.

In a lengthy review of mass media content dealing with alcohol and other drugs, Winick and Winick asserted, "During the last few years, there has been a decline in the presentation of casual social drinking on television, along with the larger culture's growing sensitivity to the problems posed by alcoholism." [7] They provide no data to support either of those assertions and the present review of the few empirical studies available on television-alcohol content, does not support the first proposition.

In 1973, Hanneman and McEwen analyzed television content for eighty program hours in March and for twenty-one hours in November [8, 9]. The hours were "essentially prime time." They recorded references to and the use of alcohol, tobacco and both licit and illicit drugs in entertainment programs. They found 105 alcohol instances in the first time period and thirty-two in the second, or an average depiction of 1.3 to 1.5 incidents per program hour; all other substances analyzed were neglible by comparison. The incidents were fairly evenly divided between situation comedy/variety shows and dramatic shows, and actual usage exceeded references.

In 1975, Garlington coded alcohol use in five episodes of each of fourteen different soap operas [10]. He found alcohol being used an average of three times in each segment, with the segments running about twenty-one minutes for each half hour show, given commercial inclusions. Drinking took place in drinking scenes, rather than as background or by references to drinking; the home setting predominated, and the modal drink was straight liquor.

In the spring of 1975 and again that December, the *Christian Science Monitor* reported its own study findings [11]. The December study analyzed sixty-six hours between eight and eleven p.m. and said that little difference had been found between this study and the one the prior spring. One incident of alcohol usage was found for each seventeen minutes of program time, or about three incidents per hour in the evening.

The sparse data available belie the Winick and Winick contention. But the several studies represent different sampling frames for programs and airtimes, as well as different seasons. And the Winicks may have believed that these reported levels were lower than what was available before 1973, the first season for which some empirical evidence was reported. The present study up-dates the available data on this issue, and provides the first set of data which is comparable for more than a single television season. While focusing on alcohol, it also presents information on tobacco and illicit drug portrayals.

METHODS

In each of two seasons – 1976-1977 and 1977-1978 – a composite week of the three commercial networks' programming was videotaped off-the-air. The week included one episode of each prime time and Saturday morning fictional series. It excluded variety shows, public affairs, movies, sports and miscellaneous non-fiction programs. Each season, approximately sixty hours were taped, representing about eighty different shows. The taping was normally completed over a three-week period, to accommodate pre-emptions and other alterations of the regularly-scheduled series.

Content Analysis

As part of a more comprehensive coding of specific behaviors and character interactions during the shows, a special effort was made to identify and code all instances of specific substance use. Substance use was defined as that set of behaviors which included each incident of the consumption of, attempt to consume, inducement to consume, and making laudatory remarks about the consumption of alcohol, tobacco and illegal drugs. It also included the sale of illegal drugs, such as marijuana, heroin and LSD. In addition, demographic information was collected for each TV character who participated in these behavior, e.g., sex, age and race, enabling a portion of this analysis to identify selected characteristics of television's substance users.

Coders underwent about forty hours of training, a portion of which was devoted to the sub-set of behaviors analyzed here. Given the manifest nature of the substance usage behaviors, reliability in identifying substance usage was consistently high. Coders had the videotapes available and could examine the material as often as necessary to make their coding judgments.

RESULTS

The first analysis will describe the overall substance usage rates for the two seasons; the second will break down the usage rates by time and type of programming and by network; the final analysis will describe attributes of substance users on commercial television.

Table 1 presents the overall incidence of substance acts for each of the sample weeks, for alcohol, tobacco and illegal drugs. In both seasons, alcohol predominated, accounting for more than two-thirds of all the coded substance acts. More than two acts of alcohol use were found per hour in each season, with the 1977-78 sample week averaging 2.66 alcohol acts per hour of fictional television programming. This was an increase of nearly one more alcohol act every two hours. Tobacco usage averages under an incident per hour; illicit drug use is also at that level.[1]

Whereas a viewer had to watch television for two hours to observe someone smoke a cigar, cigarette or pipe, and about as long for illegal usage to occur, that same viewer could observe alcohol being offered and/or consumed every twenty-one minutes in the second year's sample of shows, exactly the rate Garlington (1977) identified in his study of soap operas. The trend between seasons suggests an increase in alcohol use portrayals.

Table 2 extends the analysis of alcohol use on television by examining its use by time period, by program type and by network. There were clear and consistent differences in the analysis by time period. The three time periods used represent Saturday morning programming of cartoons and non-cartoons, especially for child audiences; 8-9 p.m., formerly known as the family hour, but now a period during which the networks claim to be providing programs for a

Table 1. Frequency and Rate of Substance Use in Fictional Television Series

	1976-77			*1977-78*		
	f	*%*	*Hourly*	*f*	*%*	*Hourly*
Alcohol	128	70	2.19	168	67	2.66
Tobacco	41	23	.70	31	12	.48
Illegal Drugs	13	7	.22	52	21	.83

[1] In the 1977-78 data, one episode of "All in the Family" accounted for eighteen of the drug acts.

Table 2. Usage Rate of Alcohol in Fictional TV Series

	1976-77	*1977-78*
Overall per hour rate	2.19	2.66
Rate by time period		
Saturday a.m.	–0–	.08
8-9 p.m.	1.78	1.64
9-11 p.m.	3.36	4.92
Rate by program type		
Family drama	2.50	2.00
Situation/Comedy	1.40	4.72
Crime	3.78	4.60
Action/Adventure	2.74	1.20
Saturday non-cartoons	–0–	–0–
Saturday cartoons	.12	.08
Rate by network		
ABC	1.80	3.22
CBS	2.70	2.98
NBC	2.04	1.86

general family audience; and 9-11 p.m., the key prime time designated for more mature programming. In each of the two season's samples, significant differences ($p < .001$) occurred across these three time periods. Alcohol use on Saturday morning programs was nil; it occurred somewhat more than one and one-half times per hour during the 8-9 p.m. time slot; from 9-11 p.m., it exceeded three instances per hour in the first season analyzed, and bordered on five instances per hour in the second season. Whatever trend appears for an increase in alcohol display in fictional television programming was entirely accounted for during the 9-11 time period, a jump of more than one and one-half instances per hour in the 1977-78 data.

The program type data were consistent across seasons for some types and not for others. Significant differences occurred across program types within each season ($p < .001$). Both types of Saturday shows – the cartoons and the live character programs – contained trivial incidences. Crime shows in both seasons displayed about four instances of alcohol use per hour and family dramas contained about two per hour. Situation comedies, relatively low in incidence during the first season analyzed, showed a striking rise to first position during the second season, with 4.72 acts per hour, making it equivalent to crime shows – which had the highest incidence during the first season.

By network, CBS shows typically contained somewhat more frequent instances during the first season, but ABC reached the CBS level during the second year analyzed. If anything, NBC was the least frequent purveyor of alcohol acts during the 1977-78 season, based on this sample of programs. However, the differences among networks with a season, or for the same network between seasons were not statistically significant.

Similar analyses were performed for the tobacco and drug acts. However, the low frequencies involved do not warrant full presentation of those two substances. Rather, Table 3 combines all three substances into a single index to permit an examination of trends for the substances as a group.[2] The overall substance use rate increased from just over three instances per hour during the 1976-77 shows to virtually four instances per hour in the 1977-78 shows analyzed. The sharp distinction among time periods identified in the alcohol usage table is even more apparent in Table 3. The Saturday shows did not average one act among these substances in an hour; from 8-9 p.m., the viewer could anticipate two to three acts per hour; and from 9-11 p.m., the viewer could receive five to six acts per hour.

Table 3. Usage Rate of Three Substances in Fictional TV Series[a]

	1976-77	*1977-78*
Overall per hour rate	3.11	3.97
Rate by time period		
Saturday a.m.	.32	.42
8-9 p.m.	2.00	3.62
9-11 p.m.	4.98	6.18
Rate by program type		
Family drama	3.50	2.16
Situation/Comedy	1.52	7.86
Crime	5.84	6.32
Action/Adventure	3.50	1.50
Saturday non-cartoons	–0–	.32
Saturday cartoons	.62	.44
Rate by network		
ABC	2.42	3.82
CBS	3.86	5.40
NBC	3.06	2.56

[a] The three substances were alcohol, tobacco and illegal drugs.

[2] Tables presenting tobacco and drugs data separately are available from senior author.

By program type, both types of Saturday shows remain quite sterile in terms of showing drinking, smoking or drug acts. Crime shows were the most frequently consistent purveyor of all three categories of acts, with situation comedies showing the most inconsistency. Family dramas and action-adventure shows were likely to be in the one to two acts per hour range. Again the differences among program types were statistically significant in each season ($p < .001$).

The network differences are not consistent, although the trend was for NBC to display the fewest of all three substance acts.

The frequency of occurrence of alcohol acts was sufficiently large to permit an analysis of the demographic attributes of the television characters who engaged in those acts. The original analysis separated agents or offerors of alcohol from targets or recipients of alcohol. The results were identical, regardless of whom was being analyzed. Table 4 presents the information for user-agents. The data reflect proportions who were users, the proportions of acts each user group committed, and the average number of instances for each user category. For example, 65 per cent of the users were males (they constituted 71% of the television character population), who committed 68 per cent of the alcohol acts, with an average number of acts quite similar to that of females. Thus, one can conclude that males and females participated in alcohol acts in proportions and quantities similar to their representation in the population of television characters.

By race, blacks (who were 9% of the TV population) were 6 per cent of the users, committed 6 per cent of the acts, and did not differ substantially in total average acts of alcohol usage from white characters.

By age groupings, those under twenty (20% of the TV population) were less likely to be users, and committed fewer acts both proportionately and on the average than any of the other age groupings. Of course, this age group included substantial numbers of children. Those twenty to thirty-four were likelier to be heavier drinkers, and those over fifty (16% of the TV characters) were more likely to be part of the user group.

In terms of the socio-economic-status of the characters, as categorized from their occupations, the lower SES characters (15% of the characters) were less likely to be users and even the users in that SES group did less using. The middle class characters did heavier drinking, and the upper-middle and upper class characters (29% of the TV characters) were more likely to be users.

The coders also made a general judgment about each character, in terms of whether the character was portraying essentially a serious or comic role in the TV show. Although the serious characters outnumbered the less serious ones, the latter were more likely to be heavier drinkers.

Finally, it should be noted that the alcohol user group comprised slightly more than 6 per cent of all the TV characters.

Table 4. Attributes of Alcohol Users on Fictional Television Series

	% of Users (n = 78)	% of Acts (n = 154)	$\overline{x}$ Acts
Sex:			
Males	65	68	2.04
Females	35	32	1.85
Race:			
Black	6	6	1.80
White	94	94	1.99
Age:			
20	9	6	1.29
20-34	33	39	2.35
35-49	32	30	1.88
50+	26	25	1.90
SES:			
Lower	10	8	1.20
Middle	45	54	2.11
Upper	44	38	1.50
Role:			
Serious	71	62	1.75
Comic	29	38	2.52

DISCUSSION

Before drawing any implications from these data, it is necessary to identify certain omissions in the analysis. Important descriptors relevant to the consumption of alcohol on television shows, as well as the other substances, remain to be determined. For one, any subsequent analysis should collect data with regard to the *effects* of consumption on the TV users. Knowing whether there are negative or positive social consequences is critical if one is interested in projecting possible impact on the viewer. If, for example, the typical drinking scene results in greater joy, or as a possible prelude to victory for the hero, then one would expect a positive impression from those scenes on viewers.

Second, one should examine the *context* of drinking scenes. Are such episodes typically carried out in a social, rather than private, context, among convivial folk? If so, one could anticipate that drinking would be associated with happy events and situations in the minds of viewers. Third, one might determine the *motives* which precede substance usage. How much drinking occurs for no apparent reason, or no necessary reason other than to give the characters something to do as they deal with the story situation? How much is done at the time that the serious characters set about solving this episode's problem? Such information would further identify viewers just what the principal reasons seem to be for substance usage.

In contrast, if the consumption of illicit drugs is accompanied by suffering, or by legal punishment, or other negative consequences, one would posit a possible aversion toward such behavior by the viewer. For some substances, the consequences depicted typically may be positive and others negative. Thus, a more comprehensive analysis of substance use on television would provide more than conjecture about this issue.

One problem peculiar to descriptive content analyses is the temptation to label identified acts or occurrences as "a lot" or "too much" or "two few." Such statements attach values that are not inherent in the data, but are superimposed by the researcher. Here, at least, we have been able to compare two seasons, and say there is more or less; we have been able to compare three substances, and can say one is found more or less often than the others. But how much is enough, or too much, is indeterminate. The lesser-found substances of tobacco and illegal drugs have not received the emphasis in this presentation accorded alcohol. Their incidence is much less. Yet, if one averages the two seasons of data and concludes that smoking and drugging are occurring about once every two hours of television, then one can begin to examine that incidence relative to other factors. For example, national surveys indicate that the typical elementary school age youngster watches television about four hours each day. So, that child sees two acts of smoking and drugging each day, or about 700 instances of each across a year's period of time. Thus, as one moves from a small figure of one-half act per hour, to reflect on how many acts that is in a year of viewing, there may be cause not to slough off the low incidence rates of the lesser used substances as inconsequential. We don't know how many times something has to be seen to be liked, or imitated, or for certain types of beliefs to develop. Further, when one begins to deal with exposures of that magnitude, it perhaps becomes clearer why additional information about consequences, motives, etc., for these acts is imperative.

Even with that caveat, it is difficult to pass through the data presented on alcohol portrayals and not conclude that the incidence rate is a high one. During no hour of the evening does the alcohol usage rate on fictional television series average less than one and one-half acts per program hour. And during the primer hours of prime time – 9 to 11 p.m. – no hour goes by with an average of less than three instances of usage. One can find no program type, save on Saturday mornings, with less than one or two instances per hour. And the more heavily-watched types of situation comedies and crime shows exceeded four acts per hour during the most recent season analyzed. Conservatively, a youngster, too young to drink, will be exposed to ten drinking acts on television during a day's viewing; perhaps it is excessive to indicate that this will be extended to more than 3,000 in a year's period.

This analysis was done in the context of a research project examining social learning among young people from television content. Social learning theory suggests that exposure to content stimuli which are consistent in theme and of considerable frequency can impact on a young viewer. Actually the theory does not delimit the age of the viewer, in terms of impact, but most tests of the theory have chosen young people as study groups. To the extent that social behaviors on television, such as acts of drinking, are performed by liked characters, in a positive context, without negative consequences, or with positive rewards, social learning is more likely to occur. Such learning can take several forms. It can affect the viewer's aspirations and expectations about the observed behaviors; it can impinge on the viewer's beliefs with regard to the acceptability or appropriateness of the behavior, it can teach the behavior, and it can induce either imitation or a desire for imitation. To the extent that the behavior is a common one, with the implements easily accessible, then the likelihood of such learning is further enhanced.

In addition to examining some content attributes of substance usage not yet analyzed, it would be appropriate to begin to determine what, if any, social learning accrues from the display of alcohol in fictional television programs. Coupling that question to the advertising of alcohol on television would also be in order.

REFERENCES

1. D. Roberts and W. Schramm, Children's Learning from the Mass Media, W. Schramm and D. Roberts (eds.), *The Process and Effects of Mass Communication,* University of Illinois Press, pp. 596-611, 1971.
2. D. Roberts, Communication and Children: A Developmental Approach, I. de Sola Pool, et al. (eds.), *Handbook of Communication,* Rand McNally, Chicago, pp. 174-215, 1973.
3. A. Bandura and R. H. Walters, *Social Learning and Personality Development,* Holt, New York, 1963.
4. J. Flanders, A Review of Research on Imitative Behavior, *Psychological Bulletin,* pp. 31-337, 1968.
5. W. Hartup and B. Coates, The Role of Imitation in Childhood Socialization, G. A. Hoppe, R. A. Milton, and E. C. Simmel (eds.), *Early Experiences and the Process of Socialization,* Academic Press, pp. 109-142, 1970.
6. J. Lyle and H. R. Hoffman, Children's Use of Television and Other Media, Rubinstein, Comstock, and Murray (eds.), *Television and Social Behavior,* Government Printing Office, Washington, D. C., pp. 129-256, 1972.
7. C. Winick and M. Winick, Drug Education and the Content of Mass Media Dealing with Dangerous Drugs and Alcohol, R. Ostman (ed.), *Communication Research and Drug Education,* Sage Publications, Beverly Hills, pp. 15-37, 1976.
8. W. McEwen and G. Hanneman, The Depiction of Drug Use in Television Programming, *Journal of Drug Education,* pp. 281-293, 1974.

9. G. Hanneman and W. McEwen, The Use and Abuse of Drugs: An Analysis of Mass Media Content, R. Ostman (ed.), *Communication Research and Drug Education,* Sage Publications, Beverly Hills, pp. 65-88, 1976.
10. W. Garlington, Drinking on Television: A Preliminary Study with Emphasis on Method, *Journal on Alcohol,* pp. 2199-2205, 1977.
11. J. Dillin, TV Continues to Emphasize Liquor, *Christian Science Monitor,* December 26, 1975.

CHAPTER 18
Smoking, Drugging and Drinking in Top Rated TV Series*

BRADLEY S. GREENBERG

In the 1979 volume of this journal, we published a first analysis of television trends in the use of alcohol, tobacco and illegal drugs [1]. The purpose of that study was to provide systematic evidence as to the general portrayal of all of these substances on commercial television series. Using sample weeks of prime time and Saturday morning television series for the 1976-77 and 1977-78 seasons, we demonstrated that the overall incidence of alcohol consumption averaged three acts per hour in prime time of the first season studied and four acts per hour in prime time of the second season. That same study found that both tobacco use and situations involving illegal drugs were very infrequent by comparison, averaging about one incident for every two hours of television programming for each of those substance categories. Those same studies showed that these substances were absent or negligible from Saturday morning programs

*This project was undertaken as part of the Conference on Health Promotion and the Mass Media, held on September 9, 1980, by the Institute of Medicine, National Academy of Sciences in Washington, D.C. The conference was made possible by a gift from the Irving Harris family of Chicago, awarded in 1979 for the Institute's general support.

targeted for children, much less apparent in the first hour, 8 to 9 p.m., of prime time, and that the hours of 9 to 11 p.m. contained pervasive portrayals of social drinking.

Subsequent interest in television's depiction of alcohol and other drugs focuses on the potential for its impact on young viewers. Television provides dramatic experiences with a variety of behaviors not directly available to many children. Social learning theory posits that the presentation of these experiences in positive social circumstances would tend to increase the favorability of viewers' attitudes toward these social behaviors. That first study took a holistic examination of television content as its context. The method provided for analysis of one episode of every fictional series telecast by each of the commercial networks. A more sophisticated examination of social learning theory would make more precise hypotheses about the impact of television content based on programs and on program characters most preferred by the viewers. It is one thing to know what the base line or normative portrayal of these types of behaviors is across all television; it is another thing to know what these behaviors look like within the programs that have the largest audiences. It is more reasonable to base expectations about general and specific effects from that subset of programs to which the viewers orient themselves with the greatest regularity. Thus we chose to follow up our earlier studies in a newer television season, not by a global portrayal of substance use and abuse, but by a more intensive examination of television programs which top the rating charts.

METHODS

At the conclusion of the 1979-80 television season, we contacted the Nielson rating organization at its home office in Chicago, Illinois, and asked a representative to identify the ten top-rated prime time fictional television series for the 1979-80 season. This group of programs was supplemented by the identification of the two top rated soap operas for the same season.

The top-ten prime time fictional series in the United States last season were (in order) *Three's Company*, *Alice*, *M*A*S*H*, *The Jeffersons*, *One Day at a Time*, *Dallas*, *Eight is Enough*, *Taxi*, *Archie's Place*, and *WKRP in Cincinatti*. Eight of these are half hour and two (*Dallas* and *Eight is Enough*) are one hour. The two top-rated soaps were *General Hospital* and *All My Children*, both one hour shows.

During the early summer of 1980, three episodes of each of the top ten prime time series were videotaped. A fourth episode was drawn from a sample created earlier that same season. Eight episodes of each of the two top rated soaps were also videotaped for subsequent analysis.

A coding form was created in which all instances of all speaking characters who smoked, drank, or used illegal drugs were itemized. Drinking could be alcoholic or non-alcoholic; drugging was identified only if it were non-medical.

Two trained coders analyzed each episode in this sample of programs. The overtness of the behavior minimized coder error; occasional discrepancies occurred when some beverage was not clearly identifiable as alcoholic or not. What is reported in this paper consists only of those instances that were unambiguous to the coders. Given the videotapes as the basis of this content analysis and the opportunity to re-examine the same program material as often as necessary to make coding judgments, reliability remained consistently high.

RESULTS

This analysis will primarily itemize the incidents of substance usage across this special subset of television programs.

Smoking

In the sixteen hours of two soap operas, the total tobacco use consisted of a single cigar. It was carelessly thrown by a workman into materials which exploded. The explosion incapacitated a doctor from shooting his wife (another doctor) during a romantic interlude with her lover (another doctor). Five of the ten prime time series had absolutely no smoking incidents in the twenty episodes analyzed. Two others had a single cigarette in eight episodes, including one series whose setting in a bar would presumably have been quite susceptible to frequent smoking. Two other series had characters who smoked a pipe, one on one episode of the series, and one on three episodes of a second series. Only one episode of any series in this entire analysis contained multiple cigarette smokers. Even that one involved a character smoking in bed, a resultant fire and considerable subsequent chaos from that.

Interestingly, one central character on the series *One Day at a Time* typically had a package of cigarettes bulging from the sleeve of his t-shirt, but he never smoked them in the four episodes analyzed.

Smoking on prime time television in the top rated series contained two critical smoking incidents, both distinctly negative in their consequences for the smokers and as any kind of modeling source for viewers. A violent explosion and a bedroom fire are not portrayals likely to induce acceptance of the behavior by the viewers, either smokers or non smokers.

Overall, the coders identified five incidents of cigarette smoking, four with pipes, and two cigars in forty hours of the top rated commercial shows. Somebody smoked something once every four hours of programming–a miniscule rate by anyone's standard.

Drugging

If the small amount of smoking on these programs is surprising, drug consumption is even more of a content void on these shows. No one smoked pot, used cocaine or heroin, smoked hash, etc. In one episode of one soap, a father suggested to his daughter that she take a sedative to calm down. In one episode of one prime time series, a mother cautioned her daughter not to associate with some characters who "shoot stuff in kids' arms." That was the sum of instances on all these shows that could be reliably identified as related to illicit, non-prescribed drug consumption, and the former example was not coded as illicit. In the 1979-80 television season, drugging just did not occur for this set of major shows, within the sampled episodes.

Drinking

The results in this analysis of drinking in top-rated shows are startling, both in terms of absolute occurrence and certainly by contrast to the results for smoking and drugging.

Table 1 presents the rates of alcohol consumption, inducements to consume, and laudatory remarks about the consumption of alcohol for the top ten prime time fictional series. *Archie's Place*, set in a bar, tops the list with 16.5 incidents per hour of programming or an average of eight for each of its half hour episodes. Two other series, *Dallas* and *Taxi*, presented alcohol incidents more than thirteen times per hour. The middle range of shows contained six to eight incidents per hour, and in the low range, the average dropped to three incidents per hour. It is noteworthy that the shows at the bottom of this distribution contained alcohol incidents at a rate equivalent to the average for all television programs from the 1979 report. Among the top rated shows, no series fell below the overall average of the prior seasons studied.

The ten series yielded a total of 195 alcohol incidents among 380 total drinks, or 8.13 separate incidents of alcohol consumption per program hour. Half of all the beverage consumption was alcoholic. For the first five programs listed in Table 1, alcohol incidents exceeded the rate of consumption of non-alcoholic

Table 1. Drinking Rates on Top-Rated Television Series

	Hourly
Archie's Place	16.5
Dallas	13.3
Taxi	13.0
WKRP	8.0
The Jeffersons	8.0
M*A*S*H	7.0
One Day at a Time	5.5
Eight is Enough	3.5
Alice	3.0
Three's Company	3.0

beverages. It is to be noted that for a drinking incident to be counted, it had to occur with a character who had some speaking role in the scene; the drinking rates identified occurred among major and minor characters in the shows with speaking parts, ignoring background silent characters who might also be drinking.

Programs varied systematically in their choices of beverages, within a breakdown of alcohol types. Beer was the primary drink on *Taxi*, *Alice*, and *Archie's Place*; wine was primary on *Three's Company* and *One Day at a Time*; only *The Jeffersons* featured hard liquor as its primary beverage. These drinks correspond to both the social class and ethnic emphases of these series. Beer was featured on series focusing on working class characters, wine with more middle-class characterizations, and hard liquor with the only Black situation comedy in the top ten.

The coders were questioned as to the context of drinking in the nighttime programs. They did not systematically code the extent to which the context was positive or negative; prior analyses have demonstrated a quite positive presentation of alcohol incidents and the purpose of the debriefing was largely to determine whether coders unfamiliar with prior research had judgments which were different. These coders reported that the contexts of drinking were distinctly positive and social; there was primarily camaraderie and fun, with little indication of potential or actual risks.

The two soap operas yielded thirty-six incidents of alcohol use among 110 total drinks, or 2.25 per program hour with no substantial difference between the two soaps. The top-rated soaps don't approximate the rate of alcohol consumption of the top-rated nighttime shows. However, on the soaps, some of the drinking incidents were associated with negative consequences. The coders reported that several characters in the soaps had professional or personal problems that were directly and explicitly linked to over-consumption of alcohol.

In summary, drinking alcohol is conspicuously present in all these shows, although there is substantial variance among the ten shows. More importantly, the rates of consumption for these top-rated series in 1979-80 far exceed the rates identified in earlier seasons. In 1976-77, the rate of alcohol consumption for all series broadcast between 8 and 9 p.m. was 1.78 per hour; in 1977-78, it was 1.64 per hour; for the four shows in this analysis broadcast between 8 and 9 p.m., it was 7.40. In the first year studied, the rate for all fictional series broadcast between 9 and 11 p.m. was 3.36 per hour; in the second season it was 4.92 per hour; here, for the six shows broadcast between 9 and 11 p.m., it was 9.36. We cannot definitively state whether these sharp differences are a function of the different seasons, or a function of comparing top-rated showed with all shows, or both. We would posit that it is primarily a function of the shows which emerge at the top of the ratings, because so large a difference between seasons has never been identified across a myriad of content analyses of social behavior on television [2]. It seems that alcohol drinking is just a more frequent pasttime for actors and actresses in this subset of programs.

DISCUSSION

To make the top ten ratings for an entire season, a series has to draw from 25 to 35 million viewers per episode. Included will be several million young viewers, those for whom the consumption of alcohol and/or cigarettes is not even yet likely to be a legal act. Regardless of the legality, there is a bombardment of alcohol-related incidents in the shows they prefer to watch, they watch the most, and with the characters with whom they most identify. One aspect of identification is a desire to emulate or imitate the behavior of the character with whom one identifies. These results show that there is no reason to anticipate modeling or even a more favorable valence toward smoking or using drugs, from TV exposure. One might believe that smoking has almost been formally banned from fictional series, although no network's code does that. It is also possible to suggest that the removal of smoking from TV series coincides closely in time to the banning of cigarette commercials from the networks. Smoking is out and drugging is out and one can find little reason to expect them to reappear.

At the same time the presentation of alcohol is pervasive. The occurrence of any single category of human behavior at a rate of nearly ten incidents per hour from 9-11 each night has to rank high on the set of things that one could reasonably expect to be occurring frequently. Physical violence, the most commonly analyzed portion of television content, rarely reaches such a level. Let us exemplify how much of a concentration there is on Sunday evening, when the four CBS situation comedies making the top-ten list are telecast. The four are *Archie's Place*, *The Jeffersons*, *One Day at a Time* and *Alice*. If one watched this lineup with any regularity, and 30+ millions did every Sunday night last season, there would be fifteen to twenty alcohol incidents in their two hour time period. No other night of the week and no other network could claim such a bloc of successful programming time.

This research has not yet been taken to the point of examining whether these portrayals affect TV users. It is clear that there is a sufficient number of incidents, typically presented in very positive social circumstances, to posit potential impacts on the viewer. For example, it is anticipated that regular viewers of such television series would be more likely to believe that:

1. everyone does it;
2. it's fun to do it;
3. nothing bad happens to you if you do it; and
4. it's readily available.

Some of these belief items may conform to reality. The argument is that all such statements would more likely be accepted among those viewers who are particularly young and inexperienced in real life with the content area described.

It is curious to find very sharp differences between earlier years which analyzed all series and the present analysis which focused only on the top-rated series. What was characterized earlier as a high incidence rate pales by comparison with these data. The first report makes a conservative estimate that a youngster, too young to be of legal drinking age, would be exposed to approximately ten drinking acts during an evening's viewing. Now dealing with programs that viewers are far more likely to be watching, it is possible to double the estimate of exposure to television drinking during an average evening's viewing.

If one moves to consideration of the impact of these television incidents on values, aspirations, expectations, or behaviors regarding alcohol, there should be a coupling of this phenomenon to the parallel activity of alcohol advertising. The advertising of hard liquor is prohibited from network television but the featuring of beer and wine ads is not a rare occurrence. Whether there are independent and/or interactive effects of featuring alcohol within programs and the assemblage of alcohol ads around programs is a question of some importance.

A final note, perhaps offered as a caveat, is to warn against overdoing the sheer incidence of any behavior. This study focuses on a quantitative presentation, supplemented by an examination of some program and contextual attributes. It does not differentiate along some dimensions that would appear to be important in subsequent investigations. For example, consuming a drink in a three or four second sequence is treated here as nominally equivalent to a four or five minute scene of steady drinking by a single character. These are different in quality, perhaps in something which might be called the intensity of the portrayed act. Also, one might wish to compare reactions to a single character drinking four or five times during a given episode with those characters who drink but once. We would wish to examine the content of the conversation accompanying the drinking incidents, e.g. is what is being said about alcohol or not, does the consumption of alcohol relate to certain topics of conversation or to certain problem situations in the story more than to others? Further what are the whys for drinking, the social functions, the motivations, as presented within the plot line? Is the drinking gratuitous, secondary, or primary? All these additional characteristics would enhance our portraiture of the consumption of alcohol in prime time television. More important, these would be the bases for making more precise hypotheses as to potential effects of such program content on viewers.

REFERENCES

1. B. S. Greenberg, C. Fernandez-Collado, D. Graef, F. Korzenny and C. K. Atkin, Trends in Use of Alcohol and Other Substances on Television, *Journal of Drug Education, 9:*3, pp. 243-253, 1979.
2. B.S. Greenberg, et al., *Life on Television*, Ablex, Norwood, New Jersey, 204 pp., 1980.

CHAPTER 19
Films and Drug Education

MARGARET A. SHEPPARD
MICHAEL S. GOODSTADT

INTRODUCTION

Several studies have recently been conducted examining the uses of drug education films [1–3]. The first study, as part of a promotion for a film review service, asked elementary and secondary school teachers about their use of drug education films and their expectations of such films. The second study was to make an inventory of drug education materials, including films, in public and school libraries. The third study reported on students' perceptions of use and their evaluation of drug education films.

Many similarities emerged from these three studies having implications for drug education in general and drug education films in particular.

RESULTS AND DISCUSSION

In most jurisdictions in North America drug education is prescribed for elementary and secondary schools.

Guidelines for its teaching are set out by local boards of education, and curricula are developed to facilitate teaching. Films and printed material are produced as resource, back-up and information packages. Studies are done on drug education programs; evaluations of drug education films are circulated; promotion campaigns are launched to sell packaged materials. Someone obviously assumes that drug education is alive and kicking. Yet, 31 per cent of students surveyed by Goodstadt reported never having had any drug education in their entire school career [3], and 20 per cent of teachers reported that drug education was never taught in their schools [1]. Therefore, to assume that drug education is being universally taught is erroneous.

There are many different guises of drug education. It can be didactic, substance oriented. It can be affective, non-substance oriented. Yet, since it was perception of drug education that was being reported, type plays no significant part in this discussion.

Many studies report that teachers do not feel comfortable teaching drug education. Moreover, so many other priority topics compete within health education that it is understandable why in-depth teaching may not be the norm.

Films are frequently thought to be the solution to this dilemma: a thirty minute drug education film could be used to fill the class period and still transmi much needed information.

The Audio-Visual Assessment Group of the Ontario Addiction Research Foundation has reviewed over 350 drug education films during the past seven years and never manages to exhaust producers' and distributors' catalogues. Even with this abundance of material from which to choose, 65 per cent of teachers reported that they seldom used drug education films [1] and 49 per cent of students reported not having seen a drug education film during their last school year [3].

Some people *are* teaching drug education and some are using drug education films. The preferred type of film is one that deals with physical effects of drug use, utilizing a case history approach, with the objective of reducing abuse of drugs [1]. Such films would include: "The Secret Love of Sandra Blain," "A Slight Drinking Problem," "Gail is Dead," "Go Ask Alice," which could be used with secondary school classes.

With alcohol and cigarettes being the drugs most used by students, and having the more serious consequences for society, it would be expected that films on these two topics would be most used. However, when teachers listed the films they used and liked, as well as their judgement as to what their students liked, the three most used and highly regarded films dealt with illegal drugs [1], while alcohol films appeared in fourth, fifth and eight place and smoking films ranked sixth and seventh. It is also instructive to realize that the most popular films were also relatively old; the three most popular "drug" films being produced in 1967, 1968, 1970; even the most popular alcohol and tobacco films were all made before 1975.

When sources for films were examined, teachers generally replied that they obtained their films from their school board or public library. This fact clarifies the previously reported popularity of the older films, teachers are able to obtain their films free of charge from these two preferred sources. Classroom teachers do not have access to enough money to rent films from distributors at a minimum of $24.00, and school boards or public libraries may be the only source available in relatively small or isolated centres. These problems are compounded since school boards and public libraries also do not have access to enough funds to be able to purchase even the best new drug education films, particularly when there is apparently little use being made of such resources. The circle is therefore complete: teachers do not use films because they are difficult to obtain; the films teachers use are old and frequently out-dated; students do not give good ratings to the films they see [3]; 54 per cent rated the films they had seen as "fair-to-good"; teachers tend not to use drug education films; libraries and school boards do not pruchase drug education films as they get few requests for them.

But films can have an important place in a drug education program, as long as they do not constitute the entire program. Drug education films can be tools to start discussion, deliver facts in an interesting manner, be a mirror of society. If such films are to be a part of a total drug education program a new perspective needs to be taken. Film producers and consumers should be more in touch with each other so that needs can be better identified. Teachers and education decision-makers should be kept informed as to new films that are good; but steps should also be taken to see that these films are readily available. Information on poor and outdated films is also important: those who distribute films from school boards and public libraries should not allow such films to be taken for showing within a school setting.

Since cost is a large factor in use of films, perhaps social, or community organizations could be persuaded to help finance rental or purchase of good, new films. Closed-circuit and community/educational television systems may, in the long run, prove to be a good way to utilize filmed material. A teacher could request a film be shown and it would be beamed from a central location. Time in transportation and circulation would be saved so that films could be more widely used. As films become out-dated, it would be advantageous if they could be traded in on newer models, as one would a car or appliance.

Film distributors could also be encouraged to put their films on video-tape—a much cheaper medium than film.

It is unfortunate that our young people are denied the use of good audio visual resources. The situation could be remedied by more efficient marketing, distribution and utilization of the better drug education films constantly coming onto the market. This would, however, require ongoing leadership by those responsible for these areas in school and public settings. Given the economic climate, resources are not likely to become more plentiful, but they could be used more effectively.

REFERENCES

1. M. Sheppard, G. Chan and M. S. Goodstadt, The Marketing of Drug Education Film Reviews ("Projection") in Ontario Schools. ARF Substudy #1059.
2. C. Muir, The Availability of Alcohol and Drug Information in Four Selected Ontario Library Populations. ARF (Unpublished).
3. M. S. Goodstadt, M. Sheppard, K. Kijewski, The Status of Drug Education in Ontario, 1977. ARF Working Paper.

CHAPTER 20

Opinions of Seventh to Twelfth Graders Regarding the Effectiveness of Pro- and Anti-Smoking Messages*

SAMUEL W. MONISMITH
ROBERT E. SHUTE
RICHARD W. ST. PIERRE
WESLEY F. ALLES

Cigarette smoking is the single most important behavioral factor contributing to premature mortality in the United States today [1]. This preventable, premature mortality is related to increased death rates from ischemic heart disease, cancers of the respiratory tract, and the chronic obstructive pulmonary diseases; emphysema and bronchitis.

The association between cigarette smoking and increased mortality and morbidity has important implications when teenage smoking is considered. Survey data suggest that teen and early youth smoking habits are major determinants of life long cigarette consumption [1]. In addition, evidence is accumulating that the negative health effects of smoking evolve and intensify over a lifetime [2, 3]. The mortality rates from ischemic heart disease and cancers of the respiratory tract are significantly higher among those who initiate smoking earlier in life [4].

Clinical, experimental, pathological, and epidemiological studies in humans and animals demonstrate that cigarette smoking produces measurable damage, even in very young age groups [5, 6]. In a survey of 12,595 high school students in Rochester, New York, Rush found that reported respiratory symptoms (regular cough, phlegm production, and/or wheezing) were strongly correlated with smoking [6]. The connection between pediatric respiratory illness and adult chronic respiratory physical effects associated with cigarette smoking have even greater implications for teachers when one considers the incidence of smoking among teenagers, especially females.

The impact of both the short and long term health consequences of smoking on teenagers is intensified when the frequency of exposure to smoking messages is considered. Smoking messages are conveyed through advertisements in newspapers, magazines, and on billboards, which often show people smoking and may influence an individual's decision to purchase cigarettes.

To counteract these pro-smoking messages there are advertisements, films, pamphlets, posters, and other printed materials presented in schools and various community settings which attempt to discourage smoking behavior. Communication and educational research has long reflected a preoccupation with the persuasive power of these mass communication messages [7]. Rarely, however has such research focused directly on the impact of mass communication on teenagers. The persuasive effects of mass communication are particularly relevant in the areas of teenage smoking behavior. The prevalence of both pro- and anti-smoking messages in the school and community setting warrants further examination of how teenagers perceive the effectiveness of such messages.

SIGNIFICANCE OF THE STUDY

Although television and radio advertising of cigarettes was banned in 1971, tobacco companies still spend 800 million dollars each year promoting and advertising their products in newspapers, magazines, and billboards [8]. The tobacco companies deny that their advertisements are designed to influence young people's decisions on whether or not to smoke. Occurring simultaneously, educators and numerous voluntary and public health agencies have initiated a wide variety of anti-smoking campaigns in both school and community settings. Because of the concurrent existence of both types of smoking messages it is imperative that adolescent opinions regarding the effectiveness of these messages be examined. Mendelsohn has emphasized that the effects of smoking messages presented via such vehicles as billboards, magazines, and displays be studied more precisely [9]. Despite the variety of educational approaches being used around the country and attempts by researchers to evaluate their impact, the majority of educators know little about the kinds of learning experiences that are most effective in *preventing* young people from becoming habitual smokers.

This study was an attempt to examine how teenagers *perceive* the effectiveness of both pro-smoking and anti-smoking messages. Previous studies in this area have centered primarily on the measurement of smoking message effectiveness by examining cigarette per capita consumption. Thus, a drop in consumption indicated success. In contrast, this project examined the actual responses of teenagers concerning several aspects of smoking messages in order to obtain some practical insight for educators, health professionals, and volunteers who are attempting to structure preventive educational smoking and health programs.

SUMMARY OF PROCEDURES

The instrument used in this study was a questionnaire developed in 1978 by Dr. Robert E. Shute for the Pennsylvania Division of the American Cancer Society. All questions were objective in nature, and the responses examined in this study included the following:

1. Demographic measures of class standing, sex, age, race, and school name.
2. Opinions concerning exposure to anti-smoking messages, i.e., motion pictures, books, magazines, pamphlets, posters, signs, drawings, homework assignments, and class activities or projects.
3. Opinions concerning exposure to pro-smoking messages, i.e., billboards, magazines, television programs, and advertisements.

For each major area examined (i.e., motion pictures, pamphlet, etc.), students were asked to indicate whether or not they had been exposed to the particular message/medium in question over the past school year. If they had been exposed, they were asked their opinions about such matters as whether or not the message/medium was interesting, easily understood, boring, etc., as well as whether it made them worry about their health, helped people to quit smoking, affected their choice regarding smoking, and so on. Opinions about pro-smoking messages included such areas a whether or not these messages encouraged other people to smoke, helped people choose brands, and encouraged the respondents to smoke.

The data were analyzed using the *Statistical Package for the Social Sciences* (SPSS) program. The first level of analysis was a cross-tabulation of subject responses (Yes/No) with the smoker/non-smoker categories, a procedure which yielded forty-eight 2 X 2 frequency tables. Subjects who "did not remember" or who did not answer the questions were deleted from the analysis. The χ^2 statistic was determined for each frequency table and the .001 level of significance was used to control for familywise error over the forty-eight comparisons. Tables 2 through 8 portray the outcome of this analysis and include the computer-generated levels of significance to permit the reader to judge the relative "importance" of the outcomes. Standard chi-square tables were used to verify the significance levels since SPSS may generate inaccurate values at low probability levels.

The data were further examined by multivariate tabular analysis, using grade level and sex as control variables, to reveal if the observed relationships for the aggregate data remained stable at deeper levels of examination. Since there were nearly four hundred tables generated, the .0001 level of significance was used to maintain the overall error rate at approximately .05. Significant results at the .001 level of significance were considered to be suggestive of a trend. With these conservative statistical controls, there were very few instances in which the conclusions from the first level of analysis were altered. A global and very subjective impression gleaned from the multivariate analysis is that females seemed to be more likely to endorse smoking education and its positive consequences that did males. The analysis by grade level did not suggest any systematic trends. It was concluded, therefore, that the aggregate data presented herein represents the most clearly interpretable portrait of the reaction of smokers and non-smokers to pro and anti-smoking messages.

SUMMARY OF FINDINGS

Profile of Subjects

The subjects in this study were junior and senior high school students attending twenty-eight schools located throughout the Commonwealth of Pennsylvania. The cooperation of the schools and the students was arranged by local units of the American Cancer Society under the auspices of the Pennsylvania Division. Standard human subjects procedures were implemented to assure informed consent of respondents, confidentiality, and the right to refuse to answer any of the questions.

The subjects ranged in age from eleven to nineteen years, and the sample was predominantly white (96.2%). Of the 3,100 junior and senior high school students in the study, 3,092 (99.7%) were identifiable by grade level. Participant representation by grade was balanced, with seventh grade including the largest number of subjects (647 or 20.9%) and twelfth grade including the least number of subjects (234 or 7.5%). Within the 3,092 seventh through twelfth graders, 2880 (93.1%) were categorizable as smokers or non-smokers based on specific questionnaire responses. Including all grade levels, the majority of subjects were non-smokers (78.7%). The seventh grade included the smallest percentage of smokers (13.4%) and twelfth grade included the largest percentage of smokers (26.6%). In fact, a direct increase in smoker percentage occurred with ascending grade levels. Based on subject response, it was impossible to identify 212 (6.9%) subjects as either a smoker or non-smoker.

The sample included 1,470 (47.4%) males and 1,603 (51.7%) females. Of the 3,072 identifiable males and females, 2,862 (93%) were categorizable as smokers or non-smokers. Females represented a greater percentage of smokers than males (23.2% vs. 19.1%). Twenty-eight (0.9%) of the subjects could not be identified as male or female (see Table 1).

Table 1. Breakdown of Study Population by Grade, Sex, and Smoker vs. Non-Smoker

	Total Respondents N (% of Total)	Non-Categorizable Data N (%)	Total Study[a] Population N (% of Total)	Smoker N (%)	Non-Smoker N (%)
Grade					
7	647 (20.9)	59 (9.1)	588 (19.0)	79 (13.4)	509 (86.6)
8	547 (17.6)	57 (10.4)	490 (15.8)	97 (19.8)	393 (80.2)
9	588 (19.0)	33 (5.6)	555 (17.9)	123 (22.0)	432 (78.0)
10	508 (16.4)	18 (3.5)	490 (15.8)	117 (23.9)	373 (76.1)
11	568 (18.3)	29 (5.1)	539 (17.4)	140 (26.0)	399 (74.0)
12	234 (7.5)	16 (6.8)	218 (7.0)	58 (26.6)	160 (73.4)
N.I.[b]	8 (0.3)	— —	220 (7.1)	— —	— —
Total	3100 (100.0)	212 (6.9)	3100 (100.0)	614 (21.3)	2266 (78.7)
Sex					
Male	1470 (47.4)	127 (8.6)	1343 (43.3)	256 (19.1)	1087 (80.9)
Female	1602 (51.7)	83 (5.2)	1519 (49.0)	353 (23.2)	1166 (76.8)
N.I.[b]	28 (0.9)	— —	238 (7.7)	— —	— —
Total	3100 (100.0)	210 (6.8)	3100 (100.0)	609 (21.3)	2253 (78.7)

[a]This column reflects the number and percentage of respondents who could be identified on the basis of the questionnaire as smoker or non-smoker from the total respondents.

[b]This row reflects the number and percentage of respondents who were "not identifiable" by grade level or sex.

Opinions Toward Anti-Smoking Films

Exposure to films related to the negative effects of smoking during the past year was similar for both smokers (54.2%) and non-smokers (53.3%). Non-smokers found films to be more interesting (77.0% vs. 63.8%) and was easily understood (91.4% vs. 84.1%) than smokers. Non-smokers (59.1%) were much more willing than smokers (36.1%) to state that films did affect their choice to smoke or not. Exposure to films resulted in a nonstatistical difference between smokers and non-smokers (56.9% vs. 61.7%) regarding concern for their health (See Table 2.)

Table 2. Frequency and Percentage of "Yes" Responses with χ^2 Comparisons of Smokers vs. Non-Smokers for the Question "Have You Seen Any Motion Pictures About Smoking in Any of Your Classes?"

	Smoker *N (%)*		*Non-Smoker* *N (%)*		χ^2	*p*
Exposure to films?	273	(54.2)	1014	(53.3)	0.1	.7705
If exposed:						
Interesting?	166	(63.8)	720	(77.0)	17.7	.0001
Easily understood?	228	(84.1)	886	(91.4)	11.6	.0007
Boring?	112	(41.9)	245	(26.3)	23.5	.0001
Want to know more?	108	(40.8)	493	(51.6)	9.4	.0022
Affected your choice to smoke or not?	97	(36.1)	572	(59.1)	44.0	.0001
Worry about health?	153	(56.9)	597	(61.7)	1.8	.1758
Help others to quit?	111	(42.7)	607	(63.1)	34.3	.0001
Useless?	85	(33.3)	117	(12.3)	62.8	.0001

Opinions Toward Anti-Smoking Books, Magazines, and Pamphlets

About 75 per cent of the sample reported having seen books, magazines, and pamphlets which warned about the health problems associated with smoking. Non-smokers found these materials to be interesting (76.8% vs. 67.9%) and easily understood, (82.8% vs. 76.2%) while smokers more frequently reported these materials to be boring (42.5% vs. 24.7%) and useless (30.3% vs. 13.4%). Almost twice as many non-smokers as smokers indicated that books, etc., affected their choice to smoke or not (62.0% vs. 33.6%). (See Table 3.)

Table 3. Frequency and Percentage of "Yes" Responses with χ^2 Comparisons of Smokers vs. Non-Smokers for the Question "Have You Read Any Books, Magazines, or Pamphlets Which Told You About the Health Problems Caused by Smoking?"

	Smoker *N (%)*		*Non-Smoker* *N (%)*		χ^2	*p*
Exposure to books, magazines, pamphlets?	445	(77.3)	1568	(74.7)	1.5	.2220
If exposed:						
Interesting?	288	(67.9)	1123	(76.8)	13.3	.0003
Easily understood?	320	(76.2)	1228	(82.8)	9.0	.0027
Boring?	180	(42.5)	401	(27.4)	34.2	.0001
Want to know more?	188	(44.2)	843	(57.7)	23.7	.0001
Affected your choice to smoke or not?	145	(33.6)	944	(62.0)	109.0	.0001
Worry about health?	250	(59.1)	939	(62.7)	1.7	.1941
Help others to quit?	152	(36.2)	897	(61.4)	82.7	.0001
Useless?	127	(30.3)	197	(13.4)	64.8	.0001

Opinions Toward Anti-Smoking Posters, Signs, and Drawings

Exposure to posters, signs, and drawings was similar for smokers (68.5%) and non-smokers (70.0%). Approximately 90 per cent of smokers and non-smokers found posters, etc., to be easily understood, but non-smokers (68.5%) found them to be much more interesting than did smokers (47.2%). As far as their personal smoking behavior was concerned, 47.7 per cent of non-smokers and 30.6 per cent of smokers reported that posters, etc., influenced their choice to smoke or not. (See Table 4.)

Table 4. Frequency and Percentage of "Yes" Responses with χ^2 Comparisons of Smokers vs. Non-Smokers for the Question "Have You Seen Any Posters, Signs, or Drawings on the School Walls or Bulletin Boards Which Warned You About Dangers of Smoking?"

	Smoker *N (%)*		*Non-Smoker* *N (%)*		χ^2	*p*
Exposure to posters, signs or drawings?	383	(68.5)	1409	(70.0)	0.7	.4063
If exposed:						
Interesting?	168	(47.2)	901	(68.5)	54.4	.0001
Easily understood?	319	(87.6)	1266	(93.1)	10.8	.0010
Silly?	160	(44.4)	338	(25.6)	47.5	.0001
Want to know more?	110	(30.1)	530	(40.0)	11.4	.0007
Affected your choice to smoke or not?	112	(30.6)	645	(47.7)	33.7	.0001
Worry about health?	156	(42.7)	659	(49.4)	4.8	.0280
Help others to quit?	119	(33.4)	678	(51.6)	36.5	.0001
Useless?	151	(41.9)	294	(22.1)	56.8	.0001

Opinions Towards Anti-Smoking Messages on Television

Over 80 per cent of smokers and non-smokers reported seeing advertisements or programs on television which addressed the health problems caused by smoking, and more than 90 per cent of both groups felt that the programs made people aware that smoking is dangerous. Both groups felt that anti-smoking messages made people worry about their health. Related to this, 55.9 per cent of the smokers and 61.6 per cent of the non-smokers indicated that these messages made people want to stop smoking. As far as assertiveness is concerned, 71.6 per cent of smokers and 80.6 per cent of non-smokers reported that anti-smoking messages made non-smokers tell smokers not to smoke. (See Table 5.)

Table 5. Frequency and Percentage of "Yes" Responses with χ^2 Comparisons of Smokers vs. Non-Smokers for the Question "Have You Ever Seen Advertisements (or Other Programs) on TV Which Showed You About the Health Problems Caused by Smoking?"

	Smoker *N (%)*		*Non-Smoker* *N (%)*		χ^2	*p*
Seen anti-smoking advertisements or TV programs?	465	(81.3)	1831	(86.2)	8.4	.0038
If exposed:						
Make people aware that smoking is dangerous?	429	(92.9)	1683	(94.4)	1.3	.2566
Make people want to stop smoking?	219	(55.9)	889	(61.6)	4.0	.0452
Make people worry about their health?	311	(72.8)	1162	(76.0)	1.7	.1941
Make non-smokers tell smokers not to smoke?	302	(71.6)	1299	(80.6)	15.7	.0001

Opinions Toward Smoking Education Homework, Class Activities, or Projects

Approximately 25.4 per cent of smokers and 30 per cent of non-smokers reported doing homework and class activities or projects which investigated the dangers of smoking. Both smokers and non-smokers found homework and class activities or projects easy to understand. However, 67.6 per cent of smokers, as opposed to 79.9 per cent of non-smokers, reported homework and class activities to be interesting. Regarding the choice to smoke or not, there was a significant difference between smokers and non-smokers. Among smokers, 39.6 per cent indicated these activities affected their choice, while 62.5 per cent of the non-smokers indicated an affect. (See Table 6.)

Opinions Toward Pro-Smoking Advertisements on Billboards or in Magazines

Approximately 93.2 per cent of smokers, as compared to 89.1 per cent of non-smokers, reported having seen advertisements on billboards and in magazines which made smoking look enjoyable or pleasant. Among smokers, 50.4 per cent reported that these advertisements made them want to smoke, while among non-smokers it was only 13.6 per cent. However, non-smokers more frequently reported that such advertisements make others want to smoke (84.1% to 70.4%). (See Table 7.)

Opinions Toward Smoking Behavior in Television Programs

Almost all smokers (97.8%) and non-smokers (97.8%) reported having seen television programs in which people were smoking. Although exposure was the same for smokers and non-smokers, the impact on smoking behavior was significantly different. Among smokers, 33.9 per cent indicated that smokers on television made them want to smoke, while only 5.1 per cent of the non-smokers reported this. Slightly less than half of the smokers (48.1%) and 66.1 per cent of the non-smokers indicated that smokers in television programs made other people want to smoke. (See Table 8.)

Table 6. Frequency and Percentage of "Yes" Responses with χ^2 Comparisons of Smokers vs. Non-Smokers for the Question "Have You Done Any Homework, Class Activities, or Projects Which Helped You Investigate the Dangers of Smoking?"

	Smoker *N (%)*		*Non-Smoker* *N (%)*		χ^2	*p*
Exposure to homework, class activities, projects?	144	(25.4)	625	(30.3)	5.0	.0250
If exposed:						
Interesting?	94	(67.6)	482	(79.9)	9.2	.0025
Easily understood?	116	(81.7)	508	(85.5)	1.0	.3115
Boring?	52	(37.1)	105	(25.5)	7.1	.0079
Want to know more?	72	(50.4)	393	(65.4)	10.3	.0014
Affected your choice to smoke or not?	57	(39.6)	383	(62.5)	24.2	.0001
Worry about health?	77	(54.6)	394	(64.6)	4.5	.0347
Help others to quit?	62	(44.9)	393	(65.9)	20.1	.0001
Useless?	51	(36.4)	83	(13.7)	38.4	.0001

Table 7. Frequency and Percentage of "Yes" Responses with χ^2 Comparisons of Smokers vs. Non-Smokers for the Question "Have You Ever Seen Advertisements on Billboards or in Magazines Which Made Smoking Look Enjoyable or Pleasant?"

	Smoker *N (%)*		*Non-Smoker* *N (%)*		χ^2	*p*
See billboards or magazines which made smoking look enjoyable or pleasant?	563	(93.2)	1980	(89.1)	8.4	.0037
If exposed:						
Make people want to smoke?	347	(70.4)	1424	(84.1)	45.9	.0001
Help people choose brands?	439	(81.1)	1601	(86.4)	8.6	.0034
Make you want to smoke?	245	(50.4)	251	(13.6)	307.6	.0001

Table 8. Frequency and Percentage of "Yes" Responses with χ^2 Comparisons of Smokers vs. Non-Smokers for the Question "Have You Ever Seen TV Programs in Which People Were Smoking?"

	Smoker *N (%)*		*Non-Smoker* *N (%)*		χ^2	*p*
Seen TV programs in which people smoked?	587	(97.8)	2181	(97.8)	.0	.9632
If exposed:						
Make other people want to smoke?	239	(48.1)	1186	(66.1)	53.2	.0001
Make you want to smoke?	177	(33.9)	106	(5.1)	354.0	.0001

CONCLUSIONS AND IMPLICATIONS

Based on the findings, and within the limitations of this study, the following conclusions are offered:

- A large majority of teenagers in grades seven through twelve are exposed to anti-smoking messages through various media in schools. Clearly, teenagers remember these messages and are made aware of the dangers of smoking.
- Anti-smoking messages presented in schools are received more positively by non-smokers, and smokers are frequently bored by anti-smoking messages.
- Non-smokers are more likely than smokers to believe that anti-smoking messages help people to quit smoking.
- Anti-smoking messages presented in schools alone are not sufficient to impact upon the smoking behavior of teenage smokers.

- Insufficient follow-up, i.e., homework, class activities or projects, exists after anti-smoking messages are presented or displayed in schools.
- Promotional smoking advertisements on billboards or in magazines are very effective in depicting smoking as enjoyable or pleasant to teenagers, and teenage smokers' desire to smoke is reinforced by these advertisements.
- A large majority of teenagers feel that pro-smoking advertisements help people to choose cigarette brands.
- The vast majority of teenagers (97.8%) are exposed to smokers in television programs, and feel that the people smoking in television programs make other people want to smoke.
- Teenagers are highly-exposed to anti-smoking messages on television, and the anti-smoking messages are very effective in making teenagers aware of the dangers of smoking.

These data indicate that the majority of teenagers surveyed are exposed to anti-smoking education information and materials in schools. Films, books. magazines, pamphlets, posters and signs which emphasize the dangers of smoking are all being presented to the junior and senior high students in this sample. The students perceive these materials to be of good quality, and students notice and understand the information which is being presented. However, as indicated by Bradshaw and supported by this study, smoking education must not rely on the presentation of factual information about smoking as sufficient for the desired behavioral outcomes to occur [10]. For the purpose of imparting information, anti-smoking messages are very effective, and make students aware of the dangers and negative consequences of smoking, but of themselves cannot be expected to significantly deter or modify smoking behavior.

Teenagers in this study frequently indicated that anti-smoking messages made them worry about their health, but were more hesitant to indicate that anti-smoking messages affected their personal smoking behavior. Anti-smoking messages do appear to be supportive in helping non-smokers maintain their abstinence, but only about one-third of the smokers reported that anti-smoking messages influenced their choice to smoke or not to smoke. Clearly, smoking education must go beyond merely the dissemination of anti-smoking information and materials if it is to be effective in preventing teenage smoking.

This point is of particular importance because this study revealed that insufficient follow-up exists after anti-smoking messages are presented or displayed in schools. Less than one-third of all respondents indicated that they had done homework or class activities or projects concerning smoking. This supports James' finding that smoking education programs have typically assumed that, since smoking has been found harmful, preventive education can be successful merely by presenting the harmful effects associated with smoking as a means to deter or modify smoking behavior [11]. However, there is very little research evidence to support this contention. Because smokers and non-smokers were most often in agreement about their interest in and perceived effectiveness of homework and class activities or projects in this study, the investigators strongly recommend the inclusion of a variety of in-class and out-of-class learning activities and projects.

In addition, the classroom instructor must recognize that there are statistically significant differences between teenage smokers and non-smokers in their receptivity to anti-smoking education messages. Non-smokers find anti-smoking messages to be more interesting and are more likely to be encouraged to want to know more about smoking, while smokers often find anti-smoking messages to be boring and useless. Because of these findings, it may be productive in some instances to separate smokers and non-smokers into different groups for discussion and clarification purposes. Also, teachers should consider more careful evaluation of materials used for specific target populations.

As reported by McAlister et al., and supported by this research, there is little evidence to indicate that promotional smoking advertising exerts a direct influence on the adoption of smoking during adolescence [12]. In this study, only 13.6 per cent of non-smokers reported that smoking advertisements on billboards or in magazines made them want to smoke. However, promotional smoking advertisements are very effective in depicting smoking as enjoyable or pleasant to teenage smokers' desire to smoke. Therefore, it is strongly recommended that smoking education programs include activities and projects to examine and counteract the technique which smoking manufacturers employ in their advertisements to make smoking seem appealing.

Anti-smoking messages which appear on television have been seen by over 80 per cent of the respondents in this study. Both teenage smokers and non-smokers feel that these public messages are very effective in making people aware of the dangers of smoking, and over half of all respondents indicated that these messages do make people want to stop smoking. Based on this finding, it is recommended that anti-smoking public service messages include a contact or referral telephone number or address for those individuals who desire more information or need additional support for altering their smoking behavior.

REFERENCES

1. United States Surgeon General's Report, Smoking and Health, US Department of Health, Education and Welfare, DHEW Publication No. (PHS) 70-50066, 1979.
2. E. C. Hammond, Smoking in Relation to the Death Rates of One Million Men and Women, W. Haenszel (ed.), *Epidemiological Approaches to the Study of Cancer and Other Chronic Disease*, National Cancer Institute Monograph 19, US Department of Health, Education, and Welfare, US Public Health Service, National Cancer Institute, 1966.
3. E. Rogot, Smoking and Life Expectancy Among US Veterans, *American Journal of Public Health, 68,* pp. 1023-1025, 1978.

4. O. Averbach, E. Hammond, L. Garfinkel, and D. Kirman, Thickness of Walls of Myocardial Arterioles in Relation to Smoking and Age, *Archives of Environmental Health, 22,* pp. 20-27, 1971.
5. B. Bewley, and J. M. Bland, Smoking and Respiratory Symptoms in Two Groups of School Children, *Preventive Medicine, 5,* pp. 63-69, 1976.
6. D. Rush, Respiratory Symptoms in a Group of American Secondary School Students: The Overwhelming Association with Cigarette Smoking, *International Journal of Epidemiology, 3,* pp. 153-156, 1974.
7. M. T. O'Keefe, The Anti-Smoking Commercials: A Study of Television's Impact on Behavior, *Public Opinion Quarterly, 35,* pp. 242-248, 1971.
8. J. Califano, Remarks to the Youth Conference: National Interagency Council on Smoking and Health, San Francisco, California, 1979.
9. H. Mendelsohn, Mass Communications and Cancer Control, J. W. Cullen, B. H. Fox, R. N. Isom, (eds.), *Cancer: The Behavioral Dimensions*, Raven Press, New York, 1976.
10. P. W. Bradshaw, The Problem of Cigarette Smoking and Control, *International Journal of Addiction, 8,* pp. 353-371, 1973.
11. W. G. James, Smoking and Youth Education, R. G. Richardson (ed.), The Second World Conference on Smoking and Health: Proceedings of a Conference Organized by the Health Education Council, Imperial College of London, 1971.
12. A. L. McAlister, C. Perry and N. Maccoby, Adolescent Smoking: Onset and Prevention, *Pediatrics*, in press, 1979.

CHAPTER 21

A Cross-Cultural Field Study of Drug Rehabilitation Methodologies in Sweden and the United States* **

ROBERT D. MANN
JOSEPH WINGARD

This research represents a cross-cultural field study of rehabilitation methodologies comparing a selected American trend with two contrasting trends in another country that is also experiencing substance abuse problems. Sweden was selected for the cross-cultural comparison for several reasons. First, there has been a marked increase in drug abuse in Sweden in the past ten years [1]. In addition, the highly socialized welfare system is actively promoting a variety of treatment plans for drug abusers, and since the country

*This article has been presented in part at the Western Psychological Association's annual convention, Honolulu, Hawaii, May 6, 1980.

**This research was supported by a UCLA President's Undergraduate Research Award to the author, and by the UCLA Center for the study of Adolescent Drug Abuse Etiologies, Department of Psychology, University of California, Los Angeles. This center is supported by Grant DA1070 from the National Institute on Drug Abuse.

is geographically small, it is relatively easy to review treatment facilities. Finally, because of the governmentally subsidized welfare system, treatment programs are bureaucratically centralized providing access to information and visitation permission.

Sweden's political philosophy and structure was also an important factor in determining its suitability for cross-cultural comparison. Sweden represents perhaps the most modern and successful example of the "social democratic state." It has also been cited as a model of what the United States may become in the future, as well as an example of political egalitarianism [2]. Thus, one objective of this study was to examine the type of rehabilitation methodology that is generated from our examples of an egalitarian socialist philosophy.

For comparative purposes, American treatment modalities can be generally divided into two opposing viewpoints, chemical "blockades" such as methadone maintenance and residential therapeutic communities [3]. While it is recognized that many other forms of counseling are available to drug users, such as crisis counseling, open ward hospital treatment, private psychotherapy, streetside and day clinics, the limits of this study encompass only one kind of residential treatment community. Synanon was chosen as the representative of American drug rehabilitation because it was one of the earliest residential treatment communities in the United States, and because its unique therapy has provided the inspiration for many rehabilitation programs throughout the country, including Daytop Village (New York), Phoenix House (Arizona), Delancey Street (California), Tuum Est (California), and Cedu (California).

Several dimensions of program organization and operation will be used to compare the American and Swedish therapeutic communities. These dimensions include age of the residents, types of drugs misused, specific services provided, theoretical framework, administrative structure, staff qualifications, treatment period, and political affiliation. A description of the Synanon organization and its treatment methodology is first presented,[1] and then two Swedish organizations are reviewed. The Swedish programs are diverse but representative examples of the range of Swedish rehabilitative theory, and include the Vallmotorp Foundation and the Hassela Collective.

SYNANON

The Synanon Foundation, now more than twenty years old, began as few members without a clear, systematic approach to rehabilitation. The current membership numbers over one thousand, and the age of residents spans sixty years. The types of drugs misused by its members include all available, although

[1] The discussion of Synanon is intended to highlight those aspects of the organization which are most relevant in its treatment of drug addiction. It is conceded that the organization now views itself as a social movement. This study focuses on Synanon as a drug rehabilitation center.

Synanon has been most noted for its treatment of heroin addiction. Recently it has been reported that the number of heroin addicts entering the organization is decreasing.

Simply described, Synanon is a residential community in which all members participate in the activities involved in maintaining the organization. As a self-help peer group organization, Synanon has no official staff and provides no formalized treatment plan. Detoxification of new members, when necessary is performed "cold turkey" without the benefit of drug support within the residence. The familial structure of Synanon serves as the vehicle for individual growth and character change. Senior members of the organization are given responsibility for initiating and guiding newcomers. Although the organizational structure is paternalistic and hierarchical, upward mobility is possible, and depends on the individual effecting attitudinal and behavioral changes that are rewarded by the membership. Thus a person may be washing dishes one day, working in a Synanon gas station a month later, assistant manager of the station three months hence, and head of the transportation department nine months after that. However, behavioral change is not necessarily the only requirement for full acceptance into the Synanon community. In return for being allowed to live within the community and become an active member of the organization, individuals are expected to contribute their financial maximum. These contributions depend solely on the individual's resources but often include one's holdings of real property, bank accounts and business operations. The general attitude regarding a person's position within the organization ignores material contributions, and is succinctly expressed by founder Charles Dederich who states that, "Character is the only rank," and Synanon attempts to build character and to "absorb people into the responsible community." [4]

The Synanon "Game" is the primary vehicle for effecting attitudinal and behavioral change among initiates, as well as the principal method for maintaining organizational consistency. Describing the Game is a difficult undertaking because no two are ever alike. They have been described as "attack therapy" [5], yet the attack or confrontive element is only one aspect of the experience. Yablonsky terms Games "an emotional battlefield [where] individual's delusions, distorted self-images and negative behavior are attacked again and again." [5] The process of self-identification, or finding out about oneself and developing a new self-concept, is a primary organizational goal for the drug abuser when entering Synanon, and the Game is designed to challenge the existing self-concept by serving as a social mirror which reflects back to the actor his behavior and attitudes. Since a basic aspect of self-evalution is considering the opinions and behaviors and others [6], a drug users in the unfamiliar circumstances of a Game is likely to turn toward others when evaluating himself and his position.

Most studies of Synanon and the Synanon Game have not comprehensively examined the organization as a whole, but rather have focused attention on specific aspects which, taken out of perspective, can be misleading [5, 7].

While not questioning the validity of such research, it is merely suggested that the Game cannot be understood solely from the perspective of sociological theory, or the theory of group psychotherapy. As Simon has indicated, "it is misleading to think that the Game could be understood in the therapy metaphor alone, any more than it could be fully comprehended as a form of community government or as a religious institution alone. . . where Synanon is described as a drug rehabilitation community only, many of its aspects as a social experiment with communal child rearing systems are neglected. Where Synanon is described as a social movement only, many of its innovations in the field of drug rehabilitation are, overlooked. If a description of Synanon management is offered from the frame of reference of its being a hospital run by an 'administrative staff' only, certain aspects are emphasized and neglected. . . this view in turn emphasizes and neglects certain aspects in relation to Synanon management being described as the 'leaders' of a social movement, or as the 'elders' of a communal society." [8]

The method in which the Game is presented here is designed to provide a somewhat broader perspective of its form and function, though a truly comprehensive description would require a book-length treatment. There is only one formal rule in the Synanon Game, no physical violence and no threats of physical violence. This edict protects the player, ensures a physically safe environment, and restricts all interaction to the verbal medium. Several Game playing guidelines and techniques have evolved during the years that the Game has been played at Synanon, and these can be summarized by concise statements. For example, "*Do not defend* what is said to a person, but support it regardless of one's personal understanding of the message," is one such epithet. It serves the purpose of insuring that important points attempting to be made by the group are received by the recipient as unambiguously as possible and without benefit of compassionate support should the message be unpleasant. In the Game, unconditional support or pity "kills" personal growth.

A second guideline is to "support the indictment," or opening statement that is made about a player's behavior. Indictments can resemble a verbal rapier though some are more like a sledge hammer, and often they generalize a behavior into the larger context of the player's lifestyle. Even if a player disagrees with the opening indictment he should support the statement nonetheless. Though disagreements sometimes arise from a misunderstanding or failure to grasp the general concept behind the original indictment, the indictment is still supported. If disagreement persists, game players are free to talk with the person who formulated the original indictment in an attempt to gain clarification of his message. A third guideline is to "spend only 10-20 minutes focusing attention on any single person. Moving the focus of the Game from person to person allows everyone a chance to be spoken to and allows a player being indicted an emotional recess. Game playing involves several forms in which indictments or general discussion can occur. These techniques are briefly described in order to provide a general familiarity with communication modes most frequently used in the Game. "Engrossment" contributes to the confrontive, attack quality of the Game, and involves exaggeration of the aspect of a person's behavior or character that the group is exploring. The purpose is to make the quality clear by embellishing its proportion and impact. The method of "belittlement" takes something that a player considers an insolvable conflict and makes it appear inconsequential. The intention of this communication mode or technique is to allow the person to see things from a different perspective by stripping away the emotional element of a situation which may be preventing the player from moving toward solution of a conflict and learning something about oneself.

According to Simon "ridicule" is often regarded as the most powerful Game technique [8]. In practice it involves mockery, derision, sarcasm, satire and taunting, and it can be employed either as a tool of attack or as a tool of absurdity. As a tool of attack, ridicule is used for breaking through the defense mechanisms that players employ to support aspects of current behavior and character. As a tool of absurdity, the technique can produce laughter by making the commonplace look logically or philosophically ridiculous. Thus it is useful in encouraging alternative perspectives of life that a player may have overlooked in his tacit acceptance of the status quo.

"Running it or getting into it" refers to an indepth review and discussion of a player's feelings. This mode of game-playing is the exception to the 10-20 minute guideline in that no time limit is set on the span of this exploration of the person. This is an emotional mode of communication which occurs more often with experienced players who no longer need to scream out frustrations, but are able to discuss them on an intimate, personal level. Running it often results in catharsis. "Humor" is also considered to be an important element of the Synanon Game. Games should be humorous and good players know when it is appropriate to interject a humorous note. The Game is not designed to solve problems, but to demolish them. Humor can contribute to this by placing problems in a perspective that makes them look ridiculous. Used in this manner, humor serves an analogous function to the technique of ridicule. However, humor may also be used to release the "pressure from the cooker." Much pent up tension can develop in group interactions, and laughter is an effective, natural way for people to dispell tension and anxiety [9].

Synanon views the drug user as a character disordered individual, much as many modes of psycho-therapeutic intervention do. However, the harsh, confrontive style of the Game is distinctive, and is said to be required to combat the years of development of the actual character disorder in as short a time span as possible. Essentially, the Synanon Games and traditional modes of psychotherapy share a common goal of restructuring the clients character and personality, but they differ in technique and in the span of time deemed necessary and appropriate to effect change. Synanon denies the eventuality of emotional damage resulting from direct confrontation, refuting the "spun glass theory of mind" [10] by pointing to the numerous individuals who have been rehabilitated through their participation in the Game. Of course, it is difficult to unambiguously attribute successful rehabilitation solely to the impact of the Game. The familial residential context undoubtedly contributes to rehabilitation of Synanon members as well, but a precise empirical assessment of which characteristics of the organization bear the most influence has and continues to be unavailable.

The "act-as-if" concept concisely summarized Synanon's therapeutic approach. New members are assumed to have no control over their own lives and are indeed often treated as emotional infants who are beginning a process of relearning. They are told to act-as-if they were mature, responsible adults, under the assumption that eventually they will adopt those characteristics. The confrontive quality of the Game seeks to reinforce the act-as-if policy which is a major inspiration for attitudinal and behavioral change.

The wide variety of response modes available in the Game add to its unique and diverse quality. But this same diversity has been a source of discord among the professionals as it makes the Game difficult to classify and evaluate by current standards and criteria.

HASSELA COLLECTIVE

The most debated issue in Sweden regarding drug abuse is that of force versus free will. The question is whether society has the right to force abusers into rehabilitation or whether it should be a matter of free will and voluntary admission. The Hassela Collective believes that free will among drug users is a contradiction in terms, and that it is that same free will which allows hundreds of people to kill themselves every year with drugs.

Each year approximately fifteen "students" are sent to Hassela from a Stockholm clinic. These students, aged sixteen to twenty years, are described as the most incorrigible of the clinic's patients, and that no other form of societal treatment has been effective in deterring their drug use. The issue of force concerns primarily the admission and retention of students. Hassela students are often wards of the court and must be placed in some sort of institutional care. Consequently, if a student runs away and the staff is unable to find him/her, police services are used to find the runaway and bring him or her back to the collective. In only rare, extreme cases will a student be returned to the Stockholm clinic.

The general program at Hassela is a one year stay at the collective, and then two additional voluntary years of residence at a sister collective while attending remedial school. All students enter the collective at the same time and graduate together. The year starts in the fall when the residential staff and the students experience a full week of hiking and camping in Sweden's northern mountains. The purpose of this excursion is to isolate the students from familiar environments, place them under some form of physical hardship, and let them think and reflect over their new situation. As a deterrent to the students fleeing, the location is selected because of its extreme distance and isolation from any other people. The responsibility of keeping up with the ten mile per day pace, staying with the group, cooking and preparing food, allows for many positive and negative aspects of the individual's personality to surface. The Hassela staff uses the opportunity to obtain information about the people with whom they will live full-time for the forthcoming year. The value of the trip can be summarized in eight general points made by the Hassela staff:

1. Students receive intensive training in collective living.
2. They acquire knowledge about each other.
3. They gain a first insight into their destructive behavior.
4. They learn that a conflict [uppgörelse] is not automatically a catastrophy (learn to handle small conflict situations).
5. They are led on a shortcut to establishing some (hopefully) permanent emotional ties with their peers.
6. They take a first step toward growth-producing self-criticism.
7. They get a new and unique experience to remember and be proud of.
8. They gain an appreciation for some of the home comforts they previously took for granted.

Hassela's daily program is stringent and allows for little variation. A typical daily schedule would be breakfast at 7:30 a.m., work from 8:30 a.m. to 11:00 a.m., physical recreation until 1:00 p.m., lunch followed by additional work until 4:30 p.m., then dinner at 5:00 p.m.

There are three work groups which alternate monthly. The groups encompass all aspects of running the collective, including building maintenance, food preparation, cleaning, and animal care. Evenings are occupied by discussion, debate, political "upbringing" [fostran], dancing, music or general interest activities. Opportunity to leave the collective is made possible by city trips for entertainment, skiing, and community socialization. The Hassela year ends with a group bus trip through the European continent.

The therapeutic framework of Hassela is somewhat obscured because the organization denounced psychology as a "tool of bourgeoise suppression." Hassela accuses Swedish mental health practioners (psychiatrists, psychologists, social workers) of lacking the courage and strength to competently cope with the turbulent and difficult conflict situations of the drug users. It is the same emotional and political passivity of the beauracracy which some have suggested preserves the present structure of Swedish society [11]. Hassela maintains that capitalist society is the basic cause of drug abuse, and the worst enemy of their therapeutic efforts is considered to be the consumer society which works against a socialist oriented upbringing. Hassela believes that technological advances, alienation, and the loss of the collective spirit results from the consumer society.

Philosophically, Hassela refers to their method as an alternative pedagogy rather than therapy. K. A. Westerberg, program founder, states Hassela's pedagogic position:

> Man is a product of his social and economic situation which suggests that those young people who, in their early years fall into the alienation process become adapted to an environment which for them is fatal. In other words, we don't need to rely on any hocus pocus to rehabilitate the students we get up here at Hassela—it's a matter of simple, straight upbringing. Their problem stems from faulty learning where the goals were diffuse, fluid, asocial and where the teachers themselves had adapted to an unhealthy environment [11].

Modern humanistic psychology, according to Hassela, is fixated on inner experiences and inner freedom. It gets lost in interpretations which are too far from the social and economic contexts, and crises, in which we live. Application of the Hassela pedagogy is based on four concepts: Upbringing [fostran], education [utbildning], rehabilitation or correction [upprättelse] and struggle or fight [kamp]. Upbringing entails the correction of "wrong learnings" [felinlärningar] or distortions which are developed during childhood and have since become an integral part of the personality. Drug use has helped to support these characteristics. With critical discussions and encouragement the Hassela method, like parents, tries to consciously steer the students attitudes and manners into becoming softer, more anti-drug, with behavior more in line with social norms (meaning Hassela's norms).

To break through drug users' defenses, discussions and encounters have an honest and confrontive quality. Any moment that conflict appears, be it during work, a night in town, or while cooking, those involved will engage in talk to determine the problem, its causes and possible solution. If a student is especially resistant to having difficulties he might move in and share a room with a staff member so that he will have continual watchful support. Education at Hassela is not restricted to academic disciplines. In the beginning, students learn many practical skills and are slowly introduced to more formal schooling. During the first year schooling consists of remedial exposure to basic reading, writing and arithmetic skills. Hassela stresses the importance of drug-free motivation for any activity, including school and practical work. Understanding that drug users typically have a very negative attitude toward school, academic disciplines are not considered of prime importance in the beginning. As reflected in the daily schedule, work is considered one of the most healthy aspects of living at Hassela, and a full five hours a day are devoted to practical work experience. For young drug addicts who know only the streets of Stockholm, this is indeed a unique education.

Rehabilitation is conceptualized as the rebuilding or renewing of past relationships. For example, parental ties are often stretched to the breaking point with hostility, mutual distrust and resentment. To try and reunite broken ties is meaningless, and it is viewed as better to teach the students to be self-respecting adults on equal terms with the parents. Fight or struggle in the Hassela sense is interwoven with rehabilitation. It is hoped by the staff that the newly awoken insight into the students class situation and their lifestyle as drug users will motivate them to become politically active and fight against the consumerist society in which they live [12]. The Hassela pedagogy builds on the young person's need for new experiences, knowledge, responsibility and friendship. Hassela's therapy is not conducted at group meetings or in individual sessions, though some of the staff are qualified social workers. Nonetheless, no individual psychotherapy is provided. The staff lives fulltime at the collective and serves as continual, round-the-clock role models.

The methods of influence used in Hassela are by no means clearly delineated nor independent of each other. However, the bases of power which appear to be more effective are what Raven refers to as referent and coercive power [13]. Referent and coercive power are two forms of social influence referring to a change in one person that originated in another person or group. Referent power depends upon a person's actual or desired identification with the influencing agent, while coercive power in contrast, depends upon the presence of a threat or punishment.

At Hassela, the staff is older than the students and have never used drugs themselves, though they attempt to compensate for their lack of experience by being very familiar with the students and eliminating "doctor-patient" roles. Staff members will often share living quarters with problem students, and when they address members of the collective they use the familiar Swedish pronoun you [du] rather than the formal pronoun. The use of coercive power is a dominant feature. Hassela must use coercion to retain all of its members in the collective. The staff has coercive influence in that they could send the students back to the clinic where most of them do not want to go.

Hassela concedes that psychotherapy is appropriate for certain people. However, the drug users problems seldom lie on the psychological level, they claim. To this end, Hassela attempts to help drug abusers straighten out their social lives by living within a family structure that has very clearly delineated norms and values, and which does not tolerate deviance from those.

THE VALLMOTORP FOUNDATION

The Vallmotorp foundation was started by Lars Bremberg in 1973, and has in the past five years undergone several dramatic structural changes. In 1976, a tri-mester system was introduced and Transactional Analysis was adopted as the theoretical framework for treatment and rehabilitation. Fall of 1978 marked the introduction of a separate facility (Hemgården) where newly admitted members live for the first two or three months before moving into the Vallmotorp School. The minimum age of the students is eighteen, and the

Vallmotorp and Hemgården facilities have a combined bed capacity of fifty. The fourteen member staff at Vallmotorp consists of psychologists, psychiatric social workers, counselors and teachers, as well as eight interns [praktikanter] who live at the facility each year for advanced training in milieu therapy.

Hemgården

When a student enters Vallmotorp he moves into the induction house, because the staff feels that a continual flow of students into the school is disruptive. New students initially spend time away from the school so that they will be dissociated from a drug using lifestyle, be able to focus on their problems and goals, and have an opportunity to prepare themselves for entrance to the school. Students are not allowed to leave Hemgården unless accompanied by a staff member, and the daily schedule is quite intensive. Typically, a Hemgården day begins at 8:00 a.m. with breakfast which is followed at 8:30 by a morning meeting. Group therapy is conducted from 9:00 a.m. until noon, and again from 1:00 until 3:00 p.m. A one-hour lunch provides the mid-day break, and maintenance work around the facility serves the same purpose in the late afternoon. At 4:00 p.m. an evening meeting is convened which is followed by dinner at 6:00 p.m. Evenings are free of organized activities. Interjected at various times are group sessions led by interns, recreation, and occupational therapy.

Vallmotorp School

After two to three months in Hemgården, students move into the Vallmotorp school during a semester break. The daily schedule is then oriented toward exposure to a variety of academic and occupational experiences, as well as to continuing group therapy.

The daily schedule begins with a morning meeting from 8-8:30 a.m. followed by physical recreation or a study group until 10:00 a.m. For the next two hours until lunch at noon students meet in either work groups or occasionally meet with a counselor for vocational guidance or for taking care of legal and social affairs. From 1:00 p.m. to 2:30 is group therapy followed by a half-hour of free socializing. At 3:00 p.m. individuals take charge of cleaning and laundry until the evening meeting which lasts from 4-5:00 p.m. After dinner at 6 the evenings are free.

Students are assigned to one of five groups when they enter the school, and this group serves as both the therapy group and the work group. Work groups change jobs every three weeks so that all students participate in all jobs during the fifteen week semester. Work details include administration work, kitchen and laundry, outdoor group, a research group and a study group. Research activities are geared toward exposing the students to academic endeavors, such as compiling answers to questionnaires, using library facilities, and creating study projects. The outdoor group has the responsibility of being group-on-duty.

The staff leaves at 5 p.m. and returns at 8 a.m. With a five day work week there is no staff on weekends. The outgroup is then responsible for the grounds at this time.

The therapeutic framework of the Vallmotorp community is described as milieu therapy with a Transactional Analysis-Gestalt orientation. Although group therapy is primarily based on Berne's Transactional Analysis Model [14, 15], many techniques and concepts have been borrowed from the Gestalt school. Transactional Analysis (TA) is concerned with the development of Ego states of parent, child and adult. It is an interactional approach which analyzes the different roles assumed by people. The Gestalt school is known for its emphasis on the "here and now" or the individual's life. This existentially oriented mode of therapy examines how people do things rather than why they do them. In addition, the five core therapy groups do not change membership during the term nor do they participate in any form of "specialty" groups, with the exception of psychodrama which is referred to as creative drama [skapande dramatik].

Vallmotorp believes that group or individual psychotherapy is only one aspect of milieu therapy. It is the combination of social, medical, creative and pedagogic experiences or activities that creates the most effective therapeutic community, and so the community is based on social and psychological concepts. This kind of social psychological orientation creates the following demands regarding treatment programs and patient response:

1. the patient must have opportunities to recognize and define his problems;
2. the atmosphere should be helpful and understanding, and stimulate feelings of security;
3. the atmosphere should stimulate creative thinking;
4. the patient must have opportunities to experiment with alternative behavior, especially connected with experiencing feelings.

Maxwell Jones' structure for therapeutic communities has been adopted for the purpose of achieving these four demands [16, 17]. Implementation involves daily general meetings and daily group psychotherapy. The Jones model is a democratic, non-manipulative form of milieu therapy with a professionally trained staff. No ex-users are employed as paraprofessional peer counselors or teachers.

Because of Vallmotorp's voluntary admission procedure, and the student's stated desire to give up drugs and learn a better way of life, the foundation refers to itself as a school. To the end, Vallmotorp refers to their method as "dialogue pedagogy," with the explicit organizational goal of forming an institution in which everyone take responsiblity for themselves and their development. This is contrasted with an institution in which knowledge is drilled into passive students. TA therapy contains several didactic elements and it suits the staff on several accounts. Vallmotorp wishes to be a school and it views psychotherapy as a way to teach something. Also Vallmotorp believes it can realize an equality between personnel and students in the area of treatment theory and technique which is usually placed outside of the democratic strivings of milieu therapy. Vallmotorp views drug abuse as largely due to societal versus individual factors. In this sense drug abuse is a choice, albeit an often steered and influenced choice. Drug use then becomes a deep rooted habit, and it is only by engaging a new choice that one can alter the pattern. Vallmotorp attempts to offer and encourage a range of new choices.

DISCUSSION

In terms of the structural dimensions described in the introduction, there are several differences and commonalities among the three institutions. (See Table 1.) The range of drugs which are commonly used by new members are the same in all the organizations with only minor differences. A general increase in heroin addiction is found in Sweden in contrast to a decreasing trend in the U.S., while Hashish is considerably more popular than marijuana in Sweden.

Vallmotorp places much emphasis on academic and vocational training, while Hassela believes that remedial work in basic skills is all that is necessary. Synanon requires no formal academic participation of its members, though they are free to pursue any education, vocational or avocational interest they desire.

Apart from the residential experience of the community, Hassela offers no formal therapeutic services to its members. The emphasis is on living a "straight life" and on hard work. Synanon requires all its members to participate in Games which serve a therapeutic purpose, and all residents are assigned jobs within the organization. In contrast, Vallmotorp provides a variety of therapeutic experiences, including individual psychotherapy, psychodrama, group therapy and vocational counseling.

The classification of each organization by its theoretical orientation is extremely difficult. The Hassela Collective does not acknowledge association with any form of psychology traditional or otherwise [11]. Indeed, since no traditional psychotherapy is offered in any form, one can at best say that they offer their students a new, socialist lifestyle. Of the three organizations, Vallmotorp presents the clearest alliance with a formal school of therapeutic thought, blending Gestalt and Transactional Analysis into a unique brand of residential treatment, and rehabilitation [18]. Synanon, like Hassela, provides its members with a very structured living situation, but the vehicle for promoting individual attitudinal and behavioral change, as well as group cohesion, is the "Synanon Game."

The administrative structure of each organization reflects more dramatic differences. Synanon is known for its hierarchical structure within the organization. Older members and those who accomplish much positive behavior change are the recipients of prestigious jobs and status related privileges.

Table 1. Comparison of Three Drug Rehabilitation Organizations

	Synanon	*Hassela*	*Vallmotorp*
Age of residents	all ages	16-20	18-approximately 30
Drug usage	all types	all types	all types
Specific services provided	encounter group, detoxification	work experience	individual therapy, group therapy, vocational counseling
Theoretical label	Synanon Game	"alternative pedagogy"	Transactional Analysis/Gestalt
Administration	communal, hierarchical, paternalistic	communal	democratic
Staff	ex-abusers, live-in	para-professional live-in	professional (Ph.D.), non live-in
Admission	voluntary	court-ordered	voluntary
Program time span	no specified time	1 year +2 year follow up schooling	1 year
Political activity/ affiliation	none	socialist, marxian	none

Synanon defends its patriarchical government on the grounds that "off-the-street junkies" are in no position to make decisions for themselves. Dederich, as a person who claimed to know what was best for the addicts, considered his decisions to be law. Within the Hassel and Vallmotorp groups this philosophy is strongly opposed. Reflecting an egalitarian philosophy, such authoritarianism is fervently rejected. Also, because of the time span of Hassela's program, it is impossible for some members to rise in status above others. In addition, because all of the members enter and leave the collective as a whole group, there are no senior members present when a new group arrives. The Vallmotorp group stresses the participatory democratic functioning of their community. Every morning at a general meeting all members are present, and they vote on critical issues affecting everyone.

Composition of the staff is another difference between the three organizations. Synanon has no staff in the fashion of a true peer self-help group. There are professionals among the residents but they are people who were simply attracted to the Synanon way of life, and, as such, they share an equality with all the other members and are ascribed no special status. The Hassela staff are people who live full-time at the collective and remain there as each group of students enter and graduate. However, they are only para-professional in their academic training and none of them are ex-drug users themselves. Some are qualified social workers, but most are lay counselors who enjoy working with young people and who support the Hassela ideology. In contrast, the Vallmotorp staff consists of counselors and licensed psychologists and health care professionals. They have all received training in the Perls and Berne schools of therapeutic thought, and they spend an eight to ten hour work day at the foundation but do not live on the grounds.

Neither Synanon nor Vallmotorp espouse any political affiliations or aspirations. But a distinction should be made between the apolitical position of Vallmotorp and Synanon's role as a social movement. It is recognized that Synanon has no affiliation with an existing political party of ideology. However, the fact that Synanon strives to be a self-contained community separate from society at large and that the organizational policy is to retain all members and not return ex-addicts to society suggests that the organization is clearly an "alternative lifestyle" contrary in many respects to accepted norms of American society. Hassela considers political thought to be the principal concern of the organization, and drug abuse is viewed as a class problem that can best be erradicated by the advent of Marxian socialism.

Ultimately comes the question of admission to each organization. New members come to Synanon and Vallmotorp on their own initiative, many coming from the streets to join simply because they need and desire a change of lifestyle in order to give up drugs. Though some residents are serving a sentence by living in one of the communities, they are only there because they have chosen it over several other options. For most members of Synanon and Vallmotorp, they are free to leave whenever they wish, though Synanon members who contributed financially to the organization have no means of recouping donated financial concerns.

Adamantly opposed to this doctrine is the Hassela group which fervently believes that free will among drug users is merely a license for suicide. Residents of Hassela have no choice about being there and escape attempts will ultimately result in being returned to the collective. Hassela is able to maintain this policy due to the age of the students and the nature of Swedish Child Welfare laws [barnavardslag].

Statistics regarding the success rate of the three organizations are difficult to obtain, and once obtained, they present a problem in verifying the validity of the reports. The purpose of this study is not, per se, an analysis of the effectiveness of each program. However, to complete the presentation of each facility the available statistics are presented. Bremberg states that of the initial fifty members who come to Vallmotorp, 50 per cent of them discontinue before progressing to the second stage. Of the twenty-five who then continue, a maximum of 25 per cent leave the program prematurely. Thereafter, of those who complete the remaining eight to twelve months, an extimated 75 per cent remain drug free and function successfully in society. The end result is an overall rate of 28 per cent successful completion [19]. The past ten years of

Hassela's operation have seen a gradual increase in the number of students each year. In 1969, six students began the program and now the fall of 1978 there are fifteen new students entering the program. Of all the students who have entered the program seven and one-half out of every ten are said to be socially rehabilitated and drug free. Synanon is antagonistic toward any sort of study regarding rehabilitation effectiveness, and the only published findings are those of Casriel [7]. His conclusions state that 50 per cent of those who enter Synanon stay ninety days, and of those who remain past ninety days, 90 per cent remain drug free. This translates into an overall figure of 45 per cent who remain drug free.

CONCLUSIONS

The intent of this study and discussion was to present alternative examples and techniques in the field of drug rehabilitation. We have attempted to delineate some basic conceptions in therapeutic community methodology and to provide a conceptual framework for different therapeutic strategies. We believe much is to be learned by examining the methods generated by people with a new outlook on the drug abuse program. The Hassela group offers a sound program which is proving to be an effective alternative to traditionally oriented psychological practices. The collective demonstrates what can be achieved by individuals who are without extensive psychological training. With the European model of Maxwell Jones [20] as a foundation and the application of a Gestalt/TA blend to the treatment of drug addiction, the Vallmotorp Foundation appears to be making progress since its inception just a few years ago.

We suggest that there is much room for change in the American tradition of therapeutic communities. Synanon has explored and developed an intriguing method of group interaction which deserves more objective study for its contributions to group processes. The "down to earth" qualities of Hassela appear to be a power influence in changing the attitudes and lifestyles of young drug users. Synanon had supported the concept of peer group self-help movements which play an active part in rehabilitating drug addicts. Holroyd suggests that self-help groups may not provide sufficient confrontation and criticism to promote psychological change [21]. While this is not the case with Synanon, expanding Holroyd's point brings forth a valuable suggestion. The peer self-help groups could in all probability increase their effectiveness, if while keeping within the confines of the particular group's organizational structure and patterns, they included into their programs more psychological applications and therapeutic processes. This is a fundamental contribution of Vallmotorp. They have attempted, through Gestalt and T.A., to blend traditional psychotherapy with a residential community model of drug treatment and rehabilitation. Experiments of this sort are needed for exploring possibilities of achieving increased effectiveness for drug users in residential rehabilitation facilities.

The problem facing the United States today, and other Western European countries is the increase of drug abuse both in the volume and range of drugs that are used. New drugs are entering the market place whose psychological and pharmacological effects are yet to be precisely determined. Yet their effects are experienced in the rehabilitation centers, and the challenge we face is to be prepared for the peculiar sort of maladjustment created by these drugs.

REFERENCES

1. J. Lindberg, The Extend of Drug Abuse, *The Narcotic Drug Situation in Sweden,* Centralförbundet för alkohol och narkotika upplysning, Stockholm, 1976.
2. R. Huntford, *The New Totalitarians,* Stein & Day, New York, 1972.
3. C. G. Batiste and L. Yablonsky, Synanon: A Therapeutic Lifestyle, *California Medicine, 114:*5, p. 90, 1971.
4. C. Dederich, *The Synanon Scene*, January/February 1969.
5. L. Yablonsky, *The Tunnel Back: Synanon*, Macmillan Co., New York, 1961.
6. S. Schacter, *The Psychology of Affiliation,* Stanford Univ. Press, 1959.
7. D. Casriel, *So Fair A House: The Story of Synanon,* Prentice Hall, New York, 1963.
8. S. Simon, The Synanon Game, unpublished doctoral dissertation, Harvard University, 1973.
9. M. Grotjahn, *Beyond Laughter,* McGraw-Hill, New York, 1957.
10. P. E. Meehl, Why I Do Not Attend Case Conferences, *Psychodiagnosis*, W. W. Norton & Co., New York, 1973.
11. G. Englund, *Hassela-tvånget till frihet*, AB Grafiska Gruppen, Stockholm, 1978.
12. J. Mattsson, Hassela-fostran i stället för vård, *Socionomförbundets Tidskrift, 12-13,* p. 24, 1978.
13. B. Raven and J. Rubin, *Social Psychology,* Wiley & Sons, New York, 1976.
14. E. Berne, *Principles of Group Treatment,* Oxford University Press, New York, 1961.
15. ________, *Games People Play*, Grove Press, New York, 1964.
16. M. Jones, *Social Psychiatry*, Charles C. Thomas, Springfield, 1962.
17. ________, *Social Psychiatry in Practice–The Idea of the Therapeutic Community,* Pelican Press, London, 1968.
18. M. James and D. Jongeward, *Born to Win*, Addison Wesley, London, 1973.
19. L. Bremberg, *Vallmotorp*, Bonniers, Malmö, 1978.
20. B. Sundin, *Individ, Institution, Ideologi,* Bonniers Grafiska Gruppen AB, Stockholm, 1970.
21. J. Holroyd, Psychotherapy in Women's Liberation, L. Harmon, J. M. Birk, L. E. Fitzgerald and M. F. Tanney (eds.), *Counseling Women,* Monterey, 1978.

CHAPTER 22
Use of Gestalt Therapy Within a Drug Treatment Program

STEPHEN I. SIDEROFF

An effective therapeutic treatment for drug addiction is still being sought. In fact, it has been pointed out that the traditional approaches are not appropriate with the addict population [1, 2]. Recently there have been attempts to structure the therapeutic encounter and to explore new techniques. Switzer [3] for example, describes a procedure called "feeling therapy" that incorporates aspects of Reality, Primal and Gestalt therapy in working with drug addicts, while Bratter employs a heavy dose of confrontation along with Reality Therapy that he claims to be successful with adolescent drug abusers [4]. The present article describes the basis for using a Gestalt Therapy approach in drug treatment, and an account of its use with individuals and groups within a drug treatment program.

While there are many treatments presently in use, it is possible to reach agreement on some important aspects of the rehabilitative process. In Gestalt terms these appear to be:

1. development of self-support and taking responsibility,
2. dealing with anxiety,
3. avoidance, primarily manifested in lack of contact.

In addition, I believe the relationship between the therapist and patient is a significant aspect of therapy. Although this does not exhaust the list, they will be the focus of the present paper.

THERAPIST-PATIENT RELATIONSHIP

The basic philosophy behind the Gestalt therapeutic encounter lends itself to working with drug addicts. Due to their previous experience most addicts are wary of people in authority. The Gestalt therapist, however, tries as much as possible, to relate on an equal basis, as well as fostering a trusting relationship with the drug addict. By not holding myself up as an authority figure, being completely honest, expressing my own feelings in the encounter, and in general being available to the patient, I am making myself believable as a person who can be trusted.

The Gestalt therapist also relies quite heavily on his own reactions to what is going on. By using myself as a resonating chamber I can tune in to the special way the person interacts. This approach has helped me with my drug patients. For example, I have been aware at times of being uneasy and confused while listening to a patient. Instead of ignoring this reaction I will express it. On some occasions my uneasiness was the result of the patient clouding over his feelings by trying to talk about three things at the same time. Even the patient was confused, resulting in a loss of feeling. As a consequence of confronting him with my feelings the patient became aware of how he avoided dealing with his own.

As a Gestalt therapist, I try to avoid interpretations. I believe that the patient knows better than anyone else, the reasons for his actions. So instead of laying an interpretation on him, I will ask him to tell me. Sometimes I will use this approach in relation to an observed behavior. A recent session went as follows:

Therapist: (noticing patient tapping fist with his hand) What are you doing with your hands?
Patient: (looking down and thinking) Ah . . . I don't know.
Therapist: Would you exaggerate the action.
Patient: (hitting fist harder) I'm beating on it. (he continues)

Therapist: (at this point I might have begun a dialogue between the two hands, with the assumption that they both represent parts of the patient, usually polarities within his personality. Instead the following occurred.) Give the hand a voice.

Patient: You bastard (referring to his other hand). You f_____ bastard. (as he continues to beat his other hand)

Therapist: (after awhile) Who are you really talking to.

Patient: (thinking as he continues to hit). My father, that bastard. He was always giving me shit, he. . . .

Therapist: Tell him directly.

Patient: I'm sick and tired of you dumping on me . . . etc.

I might, on occasion, have a hunch as to the cause of the patient's behavior, and check it out with him; but if he is being honest, I trust him when he says "no." This serves two functions. First, it puts at least part of the responsibility on the patient to understand his behavior and thus begin to break the habit of relying on others, in this case the therapist to interpret his behavior. And it helps to create the equal type of relationship we desire, as opposed to an authoritarian one.

SELF-SUPPORT

Perls [5] has called therapy the process of going from environmental support to self-support. This would certainly seem appropriate for the addict seeking help. Furthermore, the therapeutic process is actually a reflection of maturation, which also transforms environmental to self-support. Unfortunately, most addicts experience some form of early environmental rejection, rather than support. In many cases this has to do with the way they were treated by one or both parents. The patient in the above dialogue for example, referred quite frequently to being abused by his father. As a result, he felt alone and abandoned as a child and was never able to shake these feelings until our therapy. This type of antagonistic relationship exists between a number of my patients and their fathers.

I have found that by not receiving the normal environmental support as a child the development of self-support is inhibited, resulting in low self-esteem. It is like the construction of a building without the foundation. This development results in the addict still looking for environmental support as he becomes a young adult. On the other hand there is the fear and anxiety that what happened with his family and early experiences will happen again. This typically leads to an avoidance of family and other common ways of receiving support. Instead the prospective addict turns to drugs, as well as some form of drug subculture. Here he finds the support he never had: peer relations giving him some sense of security, identity as well as orientation and structure to his life.

He now has structure but still no foundation! As a result he becomes even more dependent on this lifestyle.

In dealing with the support issue and early environmental rejection in particular I frequently work with, or rather uncover, certain pent up feelings. Firstly (after trust has been established–a very crucial ingredient), many of my patients experience anger at one or both parents for abandoning them. As with the patient mentioned above the anger is typically directed at the father (note, all my patients have been men). The Gestalt approach is to have the patient express this emotion in the present. To facilitate this I have them imagine their parent sitting in a chair next to them. This way they can express what they are feeling directly to the parent. For most this is a very difficult procedure at first. Typical problems include: discomfort and self-consciousness talking to an empty chair; not being in touch with their feelings; avoiding the pain of uncovering these feelings; and residual fear of their parents as well as fear generalized to the therapist. And while these problems are common to most people starting Gestalt Therapy, they are a more formidable barrier with the drug addict.

Using the present-centered approach tends to increase the intensity of the addicts response. As a result they are able to more fully and completely experience the anger and get beyond it. What I frequently find at this point is the uncovering of a huge sadness. The patient fully grasping what he was deprived of, feels an emptiness and sometimes a hopelessness. I find that this opening up and expressing their feelings (and needless to say–becoming aware of these feelings) has facilitated a second important process–contact, to be discussed below.

Having the patient get in touch with his feelings and expressing them has the effect of a) releasing much pent up emotion–the unfinished business of Gestalt Therapy and b) start the process of realizing that "I'm okay, I didn't do anything to cause my parent's rejection and lack of love." This is necessary since the original assumption made by the abandoned child is that "I must have done something wrong (I'm bad, not okay) to deserve such treatment."

This is the first step in the acquisition of support. Once the patient is able to release his anger the underlying sadness emerges in full force. This also serves a necessary function. The sadness is the patient's realization that he was really never loved; that he didn't get what he needed from his parents. For me this is a very touching moment. It is the first time that they drop their defenses exposing their "weakness," and their souls, in a sense. Once the patient becomes aware of what he is missing, what his parents didn't give him, we explore ways that are nondrug related in which they can have the same needs for affection and love met.

It is important to note that the patient usually finds it very difficult to express or admit to the need for love and affection. This is due to the fact that their past, i.e., their history, is one of getting rejected whenever they reached out for this. I see part of my role as therapist as being a teacher and model; in this sense I demonstrate my own warmth to the patient and encourage this behavior in the other members of the group. Thus the patients start getting positive reinforcement when they look for support, affection, understanding etc. and realize that this is possible outside of the group also.

On this issue, the therapist has two jobs. First is to help the addict find other types of reinforcement, nourishment and support. This means a) discuss and make the addict aware of various alternatives such as courses, training programs, sports, hobbies etc., b) help the addict discover where his interests lie, c) serve as a source of support and model—the most important aspect being lack of judgment, so fear of failure isn't perpetuated but instead minimized. The second task is to help the addict develop a sense of self-support. This is most important since it is the only type of support that will remain with them. All environmental support is transitory with the risk of being removed, thus placing the ex-addict back at square one. I believe that my patients remain addicted, not because of the physical addiction but primarily because they use the "fix" as their source of support. This was evident in the following interaction during a group session. The patient was describing a scene in which he had scored some heroin. He had prepared a "spoon" and was ready to shoot-up:

Therapist: Okay Bob, I would like you to talk to the needle, to the syringe.
Bob: (somewhat confused) Hey man, don't be crazy . . . talk to the needle?
Therapist: Well, if it wasn't crazy, what would you say to the needle. (after further discussion on this the patient agrees)
Bob: (to the syringe) Hey . . . com'ere. . . .
Therapist: Would you go through the motions as you talk.
Bob: (getting back into it and raising his hand as if the syringe was in it) You're really lookin good. I really need you . . . I want you to warm me up . . . Make me feel good. Yea, make me feel good all over . . . Just get inside me and I don't need anything else.

At this point I spent some time in dealing with Bob's dependence on heroin and use of it for support. Followed by:

Therapist: Do you see the empty syringe lying on the table.
Bob: Yea.
Therapist: I would like you to go over to the table and be the syringe. . . . (he goes to the table) now, talk to Bob.
Bob: (being the syringe) Man, are you a dummy. I just suckered you in again. All you had to do was see me and you fell. You just can't stand on your two feet.
Therapist: Switch back to Bob and respond.
Bob: (going back to his chair, sitting slumped over)

Therapist: What are you feeling.
Bob: Shitty . . . that god damn syringe is right.
Therapist: Well, what do you want to do about it.
Bob: What can I do. (he is expressing his helplessness)
Therapist: How are you feeling toward that syringe over there.
Bob: (looking over, in a low voice) Pissed.
Therapist: You don't sound pissed.
Bob: (agàin looking at the syringe; getting visibly upset) You god damn bastard. What the f____ do you want from me. (he goes over to the table) I'm going to f_____ destroy you. (makes sounds of rage) That's the last time your going to trick me you f_____ Bastard.

This sequence was very important in that the nurturing fantasy of the heroin was juxtaposed with the aftermath or devilish nature of the habit. Also the patient was able to fight back, in a sense, and thus feel some kind of power over a habit that, for many years had all the power over him.

Another helpful exercise I utilize in the development of self-support is to have the patient express what he likes about himself. I find that after some coaxing, most are able to do this–after all, their street skills of hustling, conning, agility etc., when isolated from their role in getting heroin, can be very good assets. By appreciating their own skills and other qualities that they like in themselves they begin to build a support system and develop self-esteem.

ANXIETY

Related to the issue of support is the addict's weak ego development and how this leads to anxiety. The way I describe this in Gestalt "operational" terms is their inability to deal with the "topdog-underdog" conflict. The topdog (TD) in this case is that part of the patient setting up unrealistic goals. The patient then becomes involved in a double bind situation: he wants these goals yet doesn't have the tools with which to acquire them. This conflict leads to anxiety. In Gestalt lexicon, anxiety is excitement without adequate support. The addicts have the excitement, in terms of what they want. But they don't have the support or the tools, background, training etc. to make the goals a reality. In more simple terms, there is energy created without any behavioral outlet. Consequently, the formation of a goal and the attendent excitement produces anxiety. To control this feeling they turn to drugs. Thus when the TD sets up the unrealistic goals, the underdog (UD) sabotages the attempt to achieve them by taking heroin. The heroin makes the addict unresponsible, or "unresponse-able," affording an excuse for not reaching the goal. In addition, the UD uses the heroin as a substitute goal, a way of getting nourished.

Again, the first step in dealing with this problem is bringing this conflict to the patient's awareness. The most straight forward method to achieve this is by having the person initiate a dialogue between his TD and UD. In this process I ask him to switch seats, i.e., in one seat he is his TD while in the other he is his UD. This procedure more clearly delineates the polarities and separate characters within himself. In general terms what is usually realized is the unreasonableness of the TD and at the same time the process used by the UD to sabotage the TD's plans and goals. By not attempting to reach the goal the addict avoids the possibility of failure.

Once the patient becomes aware that his goals are beyond his reach *at the moment,* he can start setting up goals that are more reasonable. The act of successfully seeking and achieving these new goals is the first step in breaking the "excitement-no support" attitude which creates the anxiety. The addict starts to realize he has other alternatives than shooting-up.

CONTACT

The last issue to be discussed is contact. During my initial work with drug addicts I had a very difficult time. While leading my group I felt uncomfortable, yet was unaware of the cause. One day at the end of a session I was quite frustrated and said to myself, "This is like beating my head against a wall." With that statement I discovered that I had been doing just that—beating my head against the invisible wall that my patients had set up between us. The following week, armed with this awareness, I looked for signs of the wall; but the process was a very subtle one. What I finally discovered was that my patients never really made contact with me—that was their invisible wall. Of course when this was mentioned they either denied it or were totally unaware of doing it. After much work on this it became clear that this avoidance of contact helped the addict to escape. Once this was acknowledged, we tried to uncover what they were escaping from.

In the course of this search it became obvious that many of the drug patients saw me, their therapist, as a judge; someone who was going to lay some kind of trip on them or in some way tell them they are no good. This could be expected since that has always been their experience, and it had been their experience long enough so that they frequently made the generalization to whomever they were dealing with. To overcome this I had them describe me and talk about me. This helped them discriminate between me and those who judged them in the past. Their relationship with me thus created the possibility that others might have positive responses to them, and for them to check this out. Again we return to the issue of self-support since this is usually a prerequisite for taking the necessary risk in making contact. Once the patients allowed themselves to believe that they can have positive contact, they began to recall previous instances where they had good interactions.

The personal issue relating to the therapist is just the beginning in approaching the avoidance of contact. The drug addict still has other motives in keeping that wall between them and the therapist. And they have many techniques to accomplish this. Usually as the conversation approaches any type of feelings the patient quickly goes into story-telling and other forms of monologue. By going into the past, or talking about outside events, they avoid their feelings at the moment and avoid contact with me. When I become aware of what they are doing (which isn't always immediately evident) I ask them what happened to our contact. My job at this juncture is to keep them in the here and now, or make them aware of their flights away from the here and now. I am very direct in this approach, telling them "You are not staying with me"–or "Where did you go to." My most difficult task is being firm and not letting them get away with it. One of the most helpful tools I have employed at this point has been the tape recorder. Upon hearing their actual words on tape it becomes more difficult for the patient to deny his avoidance.

Once the addicts are able to acknowledge that they are avoiding their feelings, we begin to look at what was going on just prior to their loss of contact. One patient discovered that he was starting to get angry at his mother when he shifted to another topic. Upon reexamination he realized that part of him thought it was not right to be angry at his mother. In another situation a patient began getting sad prior to his loss of contact. This occurred a number of times, with me, the therapist, asking, "What was happening just before your eyes looked away," (my indication that he literally did go away to avoid the feelings starting to emerge). I could even add, "You looked sad just before you looked away." In this manner the addict eventually learns how he is avoiding his feelings, and the periods of time that they are with me, in contact, gradually increase. As a consequence, they are more able to get in touch with their elusive feelings.

CONCLUSION

I have briefly described some Gestalt therapeutic techniques that have been useful in working with drug addicts. Through this approach the issues of contact, avoidance, anxiety, self-support and responsibility are experienced by the addict in the present and thus become more immediate and intense. This facilitates growth and change in the patients. It should be emphasized that this approach is more than simply a collection of techniques but a unified way of approaching the therapeutic process. This process starts with the patient-therapist relationship, a non-authoritarian approach that employs trust rather than power as the basic motivating factor. It also focuses on the process rather than content. By exploring *how* the patient interacts with the therapist we get an idea of his process in other relationships and in dealing with other situations. This, along with the avoidance of interpretations by the therapist and relying on the patient to take responsibility places the emphasis on self-support which should extend beyond the therapeutic situation.

REFERENCES

1. E. Harms, Two Basic Defaults in the Present Psychotherapy With Drug Addicts, *International Mental Health Research Newsletter, 14,* pp. 1-2, 1972.
2. J. J. Platt and C. Labate, *Heroin Addiction: Theory, Research, and Treatment,* Wiley, New York, 1976.
3. A. Switzer, Drug Abuse and Drug Treatment, California Youth Authority, 1974.
4. T. E. Bratter, Treating Alienated, Unmotivated, Drug Abusing Adolescents, *American Journal of Psychotherapy, 27,* pp. 585-598, 1973.
5. F. S. Perls, *The Gestalt Approach and Eyewitness to Therapy,* Science and Behavior, Palo Alto, 1973.

CHAPTER 23
Issues in the Training of Alcoholism Counselors

ANDRIS SKUJA

INTRODUCTION

The last decade has seen an increased involvement by health and social agencies in servicing the alcohol abusing population. While legislation on national and state levels calls for the development of programs to help people with alcohol problems, there has been a shortage of trained personnel to carry out "front-line" services to alcoholics [1]. Lay alcohol workers have existed for years, but they usually lack formal training. The shortage of competent personnel in the alcohol field has led to increased interest in educational programs aimed at training paraprofessional counselors and upgrading skills of existing workers [2].

Recent efforts towards certification of alcoholism counselors in order to qualify them for public funding as treatment providers has contributed to the emergence of alcoholism counseling as a "new profession" with a relatively distinct identity [3]. The proliferation of training opportunities and pressure

* Currently Chief of Alcohol and Drug Abuse Program at Kaiser Permanente Medical Center, South San Francisco, California.

to upgrade the quality of service personnel has increased the number of persons seeking training.

From the author's experience of eight years with four alcoholism counselor training programs and a review of the alcohol literature, this paper will examine the alcoholism counselors' emotional and ideological problems and their relationship to training. Psychological and social stress which predispose, precipitate and perpetuate emotional problems will be discussed, with attention to the significance that emotional disturbances have in the learning of alcoholism counseling skills. Some recommendations for reducing sources of stress will follow.

WHO ARE ALCOHOLISM COUNSELORS

Alcoholism counselor trainees on the average tend to be older than other therapists, have completed high school or a year or two of college, be active AA members with several years or more of abstinence, have themselves been in treatment and have had some work experience in the alcoholism field (e.g., volunteer, 12-step worker). They perceive alcoholism in terms of AA concepts and their own experience. If exposed to alcoholism training, it is alcohol summer schools and workshops which tend to reaffirm AA-oriented beliefs about alcoholism.

The sparse empirical information about those who become alcoholism counselors suggests the possibility of predisposition to some kinds of stresses. Several studies of recovered alcoholic trainees have reported elevated degrees of psychopathology on various personality measures [4–9]. The findings vary, but tend to point to low autonomy and high social conformity, orderliness, impulsivity and defensiveness. Moreover, these traits do not seem to change as a consequence of training [10, 11]. While far from clear, the findings suggest a degree of impaired personal adjustment and are consistent with evidence that many recovered alcoholics may not function effectively even with sobriety [12–16]. Lessened quality of overall adjustment may increase susceptibility to training stresses.

It may be possible that some persons enter the alcoholism field as a way of dealing with their own emotional vulnerability. The counselor role carries an implicit definition of adjustment superior to that of the client and thereby allows the counselor to deny his or her own unresolved problems by redirecting focus on others. The notion that in helping others one is helping ones self is also reflected in AA self-help concepts.

Alcoholism counselors come into training with a wide variety of life experiences and educational backgrounds. Traditionally, former alcoholics have been the majority of alcoholism treatment personnel. These persons frequently bring with them a high level of dedication, unique knowledge about alcoholism and other strengths. In addition to the stress experienced by counselor trainees in any helping profession they face problems unique to a rapidly changing alcoholism field. Because they are recovered alcoholics in paraprofessional training status they are susceptible to additional sources of stress. Not all alcoholism counselors are recovered persons; but those who are not share many of the stresses of their recovered colleagues. They often had a family member with alcoholism and may have participated in treatment. Non-alcoholics with no personal involvement with alcoholism also have backgrounds and adapt beliefs which predispose them to problems during training.

IDEOLOGY AS A SOURCE OF STRESS

One important source of stress is ideological conflict stemming from the influx of scientific-professional methods and emerging research based concepts in a field long dominated by subjective-intuitive values and traditional alcoholism concepts [17, 18]. Straight forward, simple answers are no longer forthcoming about formerly unambiguous issues such as treatment goals, loss of control and the disease concept.

Most alcoholism counselors follow AA principles and are committed to traditional concepts. They avoid serious consideration of alternative views on the nature and treatment of alcoholism and rarely question their premises in light of new research evidence [19]. Training for alcoholism counselors has tended to avoid challenging existing ideology [20].

When the analytical-objective attitudes of the professional presented in training are not reflected in treatment practicum settings, counselor trainees experience conflict between rational-scientific and emotional-experiential modes of understanding. Where concepts are raised and information presented which varies from traditional ideology, counselor dissonance increases.

The recovered alcoholic is usually emotionally resistant to knowledge that challenges traditional views of treatment [17, 21, 22]. The individual whose sobriety rests on acceptance of AA principles may be personally threatened by information that calls such principles into question. A challenge to traditional beliefs may be an academic matter to be debated and investigated further for most, but for the recovered person the challenge may be viewed as a menace to sobriety and stability. While the recovered trainee may be especially susceptible to ideological conflicts there are indications that the prevailing treatment setting beliefs are shared by non-alcohblic colleagues [23], who also become, to a lesser degree, subject to ideological stress.

Ideological stresses are related to many theoretical, conceptual and practical issues. For example, alcohol ingestion is seen as "the problem" by the alcoholism counselor who is successful if he or she helps the client avoid drinking. However excessive drinking may be perceived as a symptom of underlying social or psychological problems by the professional, for whom client treatment success is not necessarily signified by non-drinking. Other examples are the bias against appropriate use of psychotropic medication, strict adherence to a progressive disease model and insistence on abstinence for all clients.

The counselors' limited frame of reference confines their understanding of alcohol problems and their counseling effectiveness to a narrow range within ideological boundaries. As newer emerging concepts and the complex world of human and social behavior challenge personal ideology and call into question the adequacy of traditional alcoholism treatment formulations, the counselor will face increased stress.

PROFESSIONALISM AND PROFESSIONALS

Counselors often have an anti-professional bias for several understandable reasons. As might be expected of persons bound by self help ideology, they resist being "scientificized" or "professionalized." To do so would erode the shared belief system which forms the social bond of AA and makes for its effectiveness. Professionalism also creates a dilemma when the counselor assumes opposition between being "professional" and a decent, caring person in touch with simple humanity and concern for clients [24]. Trainees tend to minimize their professional identity. For example, one counselor stated his reason for entering training as, "I'm just a drunk trying to learn to help my fellow drunks a little better." While alcoholism counselors want to become "professionals," they may fear becoming too professional.

They are also suspicious of existing helping professionals who are thought of as easily manipulated because they have not had first hand experience with alcoholism. The AA principle of staying free of formal connections with institutions and professional groups further leads to a kind of isolation from professional attitudes.

Counselors often have ambivalent feelings about professionals. Underneath respect for professional workers, it is not unusual to find feelings of resentment based on years of frustrating experiences with physicians and other professionals who had abandoned, misdiagnosed or mistreated the alcoholic. The underlying ambivalent feelings of resentment and respect may be projected on to current relationships with co-workers and supervisors.

Finally, professionals have often enforced a subordinate role for the alcoholism counselor which has tended to reduce the counselor's sense of contribution and status. This is further compounded by wide differences in power and pay between professionals and paraprofessional counselors.

BUREAUCRATIC AND SOCIO-POLITICAL NAIVETÉ

Counselors tend to focus on the individual with the alcohol problem. They enter training without much awareness of the socio-political context in which treatment services take place. They also have little understanding of the social and cultural contributing factors to alcohol problems. Focusing on cultural and institutional factors is viewed as a kind of escape from individual responsibility for one's drinking. Moreover, these counselors have a naive idealism about the workings and goals of institutions and communities. They easily become disillusioned and frustrated when introduced to agency political dynamics and are ill prepared to recognize and deal with special interest group conflicts, complicated double-bind like multiple loyalties to client, practicum, society, training program, etc. [25].

Alcoholism counselors without some prior bureaucratic work experience (e.g., work in settings with expectations similar to those of a professional setting) received less favorable work performance ratings [26]. This finding supports the observation that counselors work best in structured agencies. The relative lack of structure in many professional agencies may constitute yet another source of stress.

DIMINISHED EXPERTISE AND LIFE TRANSITIONS

Trainees must suddenly face a loss or threat to their expertise in alcoholism when they enter training. In the past, traditional concepts, experience with alcoholism and personal recovery constituted a marketable credential for work in the field. Newer concepts which have not been, or cannot be, incorporated into the counselor's own experience may undermine the base of their "expertise." In addition, the recovered person may have built up a respectable sobriety, status and stability through AA. When resuming the role of learner, the counselor's self esteem that accompanied the position of guide and expert to other alcoholics is diminished.

The perspective counselor's sense of adequacy is on the line also because he or she has made a far reaching decision and are beginning a life transition, perhaps leaving a job, changing occupations, or returning to school for the first time in years.

Finally, financial problems, long hours of study and practicum, and emotional unavailability of the trainee may undermine an adequate and stable marriage or relationship. The counselor's frequent upsets, crises and personality changes associated with training may create conflict in the home. The trainee's involvement in personal growth and self-examination may lead to feelings of "out-growing" their spouses who are unresponsive to, unable to understand, or threatened by the counselors new insights and sensitivities.

BECOMING A COUNSELOR

A major source of stress is the trainees struggle to achieve an identity as a counselor. There are many anxieties related to the development of a counselor role, attitudes, ethical and clinical sensibility. Trainees also find themselves with substantial responsibility at a time when their clinical knowledge and skills and self confidence are very limited. A related issue is the trainees quest for being the ideal "good counselor." The "wish to cure" and the anxiety over whether one is doing a good job may lead to a radical self-examination producing more anxiety or depression. The counselors reconciliation to the fact that he or she may not be able to help all their clients and that many will return to drinking and other destructive activities may result in acute stress which may lead in turn to a growth limiting massive identification with the supervisor.

Finally, the trainees tend to over identify with their clients. The clients' problems may become the trainees, especially in the instances of a recovered counselor. Mandell has suggested that counselors with limited sobriety (two years or less) develop a deep belief that their mode of recovery is the only effective and superior one for alcoholics in general [21]. This conviction helps them with their new found sobriety. They may need to repeatedly relive their recovery in order to reassure themselves that recovery is possible. This may explain the intense anger and frustration some counselors experience after their clients resume drinking after a period of sobriety.

PROBLEMS IN SUPERVISION

Frustrations and disillusionment may result from problems with clinical supervision. While supervision is a useful tool in teaching counseling it can also contribute to the emotional difficulties of the trainee. Unfortunately, many individuals who find themselves in supervisory positions are unable to provide adequate supervision because they themselves either lack appropriate clinical skills, have not been exposed to supervision in their own training, or are unaware of the procedures for establishing a program of clinical supervision [27].

Supervisors may find themselves threatened by the trainee who possesses more clinical skills than the supervisor by virtue of training. The practicum supervisor may also be committed to a rigid ideology which may conflict with the more flexible treatment viewpoints taught in the training setting. Not uncommonly supervisors rely on AA, confrontation or some other treatment approach and abstinence treatment goals which are applied to all clients regardless of individual differences. This is complicated further for the trainee because the supervisor is in a position of divided loyalty between the trainee and the agency in which he or she is both educating and evaluating the trainee. The supervisor has realistic power over the trainee's success or failure in the program. Moreover, supervisors unaware of their own counter-transference feelings may fail to recognize emotional stress in trainees or fail to perceive trainee "acting out" as representing unresolved conflicts in the supervisory relationship.

THE ROLE OF SUPERVISORS AND TRAINERS

Emotional difficulties can interfere with acquiring the skills and knowledge for effective alcoholism counseling. This imposes on teachers and supervisors the responsibility to help the counselor with his or her emotional difficulties. The failure to prevent, recognize and treat such disorders may result in further trainee decompensation, resignation or failure in training; or perhaps lead to a cynical, dissatisfied counselor; or possibly contribute to the incidence of drug or alcohol use among counselor trainees.

The failure to identify problems which precipitate personal stress, drop outs or more severe casualties of training may induce guilt in training personnel resulting in a general sense of inadequacy about successfully meeting the trainees' emotional needs and having inadequate screening and selection procedures.

Although a degree of anxiety and depression are probably inevitable in the course of developing competent and empathic counselors, in exaggerated forms these symptoms may be related to premature termination of training, poor training performance and negativistic attitudes towards the field. Typical symptoms found in trainees are psychosomatic problems (especially before tests or in particularly stressful practicum circumstances), depression, anxiety, and family/interpersonal relationship problems.

Some Recommendations for Reducing Stress

Several writers have outlined methods of minimizing and preventing therapist problems in training and treatment settings [28–32]. One approach is to provide primary prevention for emotional problems of mental health personnel in training and is aimed at early detection and intervention [29]. Primary prevention implies a focus away from the individual to the environment in which the trainee works.

Supervisors and trainers awareness – Supervisors should recognize subtle expressions of trainee's concern. The supervisor-trainee relationship is usually conflictual and ambiguous to begin with. Supervisors should be helped to empathically relate to trainees in stress or exhibiting symptoms.

Better screening and selection – Efforts can be aimed at screening out those who are likely to be predisposed to acute stress. This usually includes persons with less than two years of sobriety; with ongoing personal, financial, family or other problems. The use of psychological tests, multiple interviews, and examination of past work performance, emotional and professional stability should be considered.

Trainee awareness – Trainees should be alerted to the possibility of emotional conflicts that stem from identification with clients, treatment failures, and a sense of inadequacy in relation to new responsibilities, etc. Attempts should also be made early in training to familiarize counselors with bureaucratic and community political realities. Speakers from and visits to public and private funding and service provider agencies are helpful in this regard.

Desensitizing ideological issues – Alcoholism counselors should be familiar with the ideological and controversial issues shaping the alcoholism field. No attempt should be made to prescribe any "school" of thought but trainees should be encouraged to formulate their own approach to alcoholism through ongoing and open examination and integration of various models, theories, and research findings with their own past learning experiences. Teaching staff should foster a critical understanding and mutual respect for various orientations to counseling alcoholics. An atmosphere of free exchange of ideas, where it is appropriate to question alcoholism formulations, will expose potential issues and better prepare trainees to constructively deal with controversial matters.

Small group – Peer group competition can be diminished by small group meetings where the trainees can share their anxieties, develop a sense of mutual support and work towards solutions of personal and professional problems [33]. The group may also help the trainee to deal with the ambiguities, and difficulties encountered in the challenge of previously held concepts. The small group leader should be a consultant from outside the training institution. This avoids the evaluator-supervisor conflict and allows the student more latitude and trust in expression.

Upgrading supervisors – Supervision is another area which, if upgraded, may diminish the incidence of trainee dysfunction. Most supervisors need additional training on how to conduct effective supervision. Supervisors should avoid slipping into the attitude of viewing trainees as clients. While supervision involves many psychotherapy like functions and intimate discussions regarding the trainees personal reactions and experiences, a distinction should be made from seeking private personal help and supervision. The focus should be on the trainee-supervisor relationship yet the supervisor should retain the position of being primarily a teacher. It should be kept in mind that no "therapeutic alliance" or "contract" has been entered into and that the supervisor has evaluative functions which conflict with a therapeutic function. It is also possible that countertransference problems of a supervisor may disqualify the supervisor as a psychotherapist. It is best that the supervisor focuses on work related experience and obstacles interfering with the counselors' effectiveness. Once these issues are pointed out; if they are not remediated than a decision for seeking further treatment outside the training institution should be encouraged.

Family support – Finally, the trainee's family should be given some attention. Long hours away from home, stress, financial problems resulting from little pay during the training period, may exacerbate emotional problems and family tension. Attention should be given to spouse groups or social gatherings of an informal nature which may help them share experiences, gain support and decrease isolation and instability felt on the family level while their spouse is in training.

A CONCLUDING NOTE

It was not intended that this paper constitute a conclusive examination of the issues facing the alcoholism counseling field, many of which are controversial and subject to differing interpretations. Some of these issues reflect unanswered questions facing the alcoholism field and are likely to be sources of stress for counselors in training and those working with alcoholics. To that extent, training programs ought to address these concerns which can be used to educational advantage in stimulating healthy counselor self-examination and reflection. This will be possible only if trainers themselves model constructive exploration of controversial issues with the expectation that it will lead to improved training and better prepared counselors.

REFERENCES

1. L. Mitnick, Training Alcoholism Personnel: Goals, Needs and Problems, *Alcohol Health and Research World,* pp. 1-3, Spring 1974.
2. E. Blacker, Training for Professionals and Non-professionals in Alcoholism, B. Kissen and H. Begleiter (eds.), *Treatment and Rehabilitation of the Chronic Alcoholics*, Plenum, New York, 1977.
3. G. E. Staub and L. M. Kent (eds.), *The Paraprofessional in the Treatment of Alcoholism,* Charles C. Thomas, Springfield, Illinois, 1973.
4. E. R. Bonynge and H. Hoffmann, Personality Measurements in Selection of Applicants for an Alcohol Counselor Program, *Psychological Reports, 41,* pp. 493-494, 1977.
5. G. Cooke, G. Wehmer, and J. Gruber, Training Paraprofessionals in the Treatment of Alcoholism: Effects of Knowledge, Attitudes and Therapeutic Techniques, *Journal of Studies on Alcohol, 36,* pp. 938-946, 1975.
6. H. Hoffmann and B. B. Miner, Personality of Alcoholics Who Become Counselors, *Psychological Reports, 33,* p. 878, 1973.
7. D. G. Jansen and H. Hoffmann, MMPI Scores of Counselors on Alcoholism Prior to and After Training, *Journal of Consulting and Clinical Psychology, 43,* p. 271, 1975.
8. L. Morrison, A. Skuja, and J. Berman, *Evaluation of the Alcoholism Counselor Training Institute of Nebraska,* Department of Psychology, University of Nebraska–Lincoln, 1978, Unpublished data.
9. A. Skuja, B. Battenberg, D. Wood, and S. Bucky, The Impact of Paraprofessional Alcoholism Counselor Training, *International Journal of the Addictions, 15:*6, 1980.

10. C. M. Rosenberg, J. Gerrein, V. Manohar, and J. Liftik, Evaluation of Training of Alcoholism Counselors, *Journal of Studies on Alcohol, 37,* pp. 1236-1246, 1976.
11. H. Hoffmann and R. Wehler, Pre and Post Training MMPI Scores of Women Alcoholism Counselors, *Journal of Studies on Alcohol, 39,* pp. 1952-1955, 1978.
12. D. L. Gerard, G. Saenger, and R. Wile, The Abstinent Alcoholic, *Archives of General Psychiatry, 16,* pp. 83-95, 1962.
13. W. M. Kurtines, L. Ball, and G. Wood, Personality Characteristics of Long-term Recovered Alcoholics: A Comparative Analysis, *Journal of Consulting and Clinical Psychology, 46,* pp. 971-977, 1978.
14. E. M. Pattison, B. Headley, C. Glesser, and L. Gottschalk, Abstinence and Normal Drinking: An Assessment of Changes in Drinking Patterns in Alcoholics After Treatment, *Quarterly Journal of Studies on Alcohol, 29,* pp. 1610-1614, 1968.
15. J. Rossi, A. Stach, and M. Bradley, Effects of Treatment of Male Alcoholics in a Mental Hospital: A Follow-Up Study, *Quarterly Journal of Studies on Alcohol, 24,* pp. 1236-1240, 1963.
16. W. Wilby and R. W. Jones, Assessing Patient Response Following Treatment, *Quarterly Journal of Studies on Alcohol, 23,* pp. 1269-1272, 1962.
17. M. Kalb and M. S. Propper, The Future of Alcohology: Craft or Science?, *American Journal of Psychiatry, 113,* pp. 641-645, 1976.
18. E. M. Pattison, Ten Years of Change in Alcoholism Treatment Delivery Systems, *American Journal of Psychiatry, 134,* pp. 261-266, 1977.
19. J. Rossi and W. J. Filstead, Treating the Treatment Issues: Some General Observations About the Treatment of Alcoholics, J. Rossi and M. Keller (eds.), *Alcohol and Alcohol Problems: New Thinking and New Directions,* Ballinger, Cambridge, Massachusetts, 1976.
20. M. Hertzman and L. Mitnick, Ethics, Evaluation and Training in Alcoholism, *Drug Forum, 7,* pp. 145-153, 1978.
21. W. Mandell, Role of the Professional, *Alcohol Health and Research World,* pp. 5-7, Spring 1974.
22. E. M. Pattison, A Differential View of Manpower Resources, G. Staub and L. Kent (eds.), *The Paraprofessional in the Treatment of Alcoholism,* C. Thomas, Springfield, 1973.
23. A. T. Skuja, Counselor's Clinical Attitudes Associated with Alcoholism Recovery, Doctoral Dissertation, California School of Professional Psychology, *Dissertation Asbtracts International, 38,* 1977.
24. P. B. Lenrow, The Work of Helping Strangers, *American Journal of Community Psychology, 6,* pp. 555-571, 1978.
25. S. Saxon and J. D. Blaine, Treatment Binds of Drug Treatment Personnel, *Drug Forum, 7,* pp. 121-127, 1978.
26. H. P. Chalfant, L. Martinson, and D. J. Crowe, Prior Occupational Experience and Choice of Alcoholism Rehabilitation Counselors, *Community Mental Health Journal, 11,* pp. 402-409, 1975.
27. D. J. Powell, *Manpower Needs in the Alcohol Field,* Eastern Area Alcohol Education and Training Program, Bloomfield, Connecticut, 1977.

28. H. J. Fruedenberger, Staff Burn-Out, *Journal of Social Issues, 30,* pp. 159-165, 1974.
29. E. M. Waring, A Preventive Approach to Emotional Illness in Psychiatric Residents, *Psychiatric Quarterly, 49,* pp. 303-315, 1977.
30. C. Maslach, The Client Role in Staff Burn-Out, *Journal of Social Issues, 34,* pp. 111-124, 1978.
31. A. Pines and C. Maslach, Characteristics of Staff-Burnout in Mental Health Settings, *Hospital and Community Psychiatry, 29,* pp. 233-237, 1978.
32. L. Sank and M. F. Prout, Critical Issues for the Fledgling Therapist, *Professional Psychology, 9,* pp. 638-645, 1978.
33. A. Skuja, W. Ford, S. Scott, and D. Ellis, ACTION: A Community-University Partnership for Training Alcoholism Counselors, *Journal of Alcohol and Drug Education, 25,* pp. 41-47, 1980.

CHAPTER 24
Drug Program Evaluation: Outcome Measures

JOHN W. MURPHY

STATEMENT OF THE PROBLEM

At this time drug abuse agencies are beginning to fall into the trap of using methods of client evaluation that are not at all congruent with the environment of treatment that prevails in most drug programs. That is, drug programs in most cases are out-patient, community based facilities in which a client can most certainly be considered to be successfully treated while still being associated with a rehabilitation program [1].

This out-patient treatment philosophy therefore appears to be that which is underpinning most drug abuse treatment programs. Out-patient treatment is theoretically supposed to be a crisis intervention support service, which enables the client to maintain a functional existence in the community while still in treatment. At this time an evaluation method is being endorsed by the Government that is not at all consistent with the treatment philosophy that accompanies the use of the out-patient treatment environment [2]. This particular outcome measure is generated through the "reason for discharge" variable that is present on every Client Oriented Data Acquisition Process (CODAP) form.

The Client Oriented Data Acquisition Process, more commonly known by the acronym CODAP, is the management information system used by the National Institute on Drug Abuse (NIDA) to collect information on clients entering and leaving federally funded drug treatment programs. In order to perform this function a CODAP admission form is completed on every client entering treatment, while a discharge form is completed on every client who is terminated from treatment. Accordingly, a matched admission and discharge report is assembled for every client which passes through treatment, thus allowing for a client historical file to be established. This type of historical file theoretically allows for a client's treatment to be monitored in terms of entry to discharge behavioral change. Most of the information collected by these CODAP forms is demographic in nature, yet some of the data items can and are being used to assess the treatment effectiveness of drug treatment programs. These evaluative items relate to such variables as drug use patterns, employment status, and a generic assessment of a client's discharge status. This latter variable is operationalized in terms of a question specifying the reason for discharging a client from treatment.

The CODAP discharge form that is completed on every client discharged from a NIDA funded drug program specifies nine possible reasons for which a client might be discharged from a drug program. Two of these reasons are used to delineate the parameters of a definition that is thought to adequately detail the status of a "successfully discharged" or successfully treated client. These criteria for defining a successfully treated client, however, presuppose that the client is no longer actively being treated. Accordingly the implication here is that only those clients who are not in treatment can be assessed relative to their treatment status. Such an approach to program evaluation totally violates the basic theoretical assumptions of the out-patient approach to treatment. Does this CODAP definition of successful treatment also imply that a client is dysfunctional until he/she has been discharged from a treatment program? The specific type of support service supplied by the out-patient treatment facility was originally developed to be on-going while the client actively continued to participate in community activities. Therefore, this type of support service could theoretically be supplied to a client throughout his/her life. If a client leads a functional social life while remaining in out-patient treatment, how can such a client be counted as a treatment failure? According to the cost/effectiveness criteria currently being suggested for use in evaluating drug programs by the Government, a drug program that never discharged a successfully treated client would surely receive a poor evaluation. This method of evaluation is appropriate for a treatment regimen substantiated by the concept of therapy adhered to by in-patient hospitals, and not out-patient mental health clinics.

Anyone who has ever worked in a drug abuse program, however, knows that many clients come into treatment and change their lives drastically. What these clients needed was the supportive environment which a drug program can and does provide. Likewise, many of these clients when they are discharged from a program experience an emotional let-down which eventually contributes to their renewed drug use. Yet a program must discharge these clients who are doing well while in treatment if it is to "look good" to program evaluators who only look to successful discharge rates as the major indicator of a program's overall effectiveness. This pressure to discharge clients many times results in a clinic prematurely severing its therapeutic relationship with a client. Therefore, in order to adequately assess the effectiveness of out-patient drug programs a success indicator must be employed that also takes into account a client's movement through various stages of treatment. These treatment stages, moreover, should be indicative of behavioral change on the part of the client, so that movement through a program would be illustrative of client improvement. Using this type of method as a supplement to the successful discharge measure might actually allow for a more accurate assessment of the effects of drug abuse treatment that is substantiated by the idea of out-patient, supportive therapy.

METHODOLOGY

In order to supplement the present criterion of "successful discharge" for program evaluation in drug abuse treatment, the following model might be employed for the purpose of charting a client's movement through a treatment regimen. The type of treatment categories to be used in this type of tracking model, for example, might be as follows:

I. using methadone; looking for work or working; therapeutic counseling sessions; no illicit drug use; no court contacts;

II. using methadone; working to become job ready; minor drug use (e.g., two "dirty" urines per month); cooperative counseling sessions; minor court contact (e.g., no present legal involvement, but maybe working off an old case through probation, etc.); and

III. using methadone; unmotivated for straight work (still clinging to street life image); indifferent counseling rapport (e.g., belligerent, deceptive manipulative, irritable, evasive, etc.); actively involved in illegal activities; illicit drug use (e.g., three or more "dirty" urines per month).

The use of this type of evaluation typology allows for a client to be assessed while still remaining in treatment, thus being congruent with the treatment philosophy underpinning the use of the out-patient treatment environment. Of course only categories one (I) and two (II) of this typology would be viewed as being indicative of treatment success, in that most clients at the time of entry into treatment would fall into category number three (III). Using this typology a client could be classified at the point of entry to a program and at a variety of times thought to be appropriate while in treatment. In this sense it would be up to a program's staff to determine how long a client should be in a program before any behavioral changes should be witnessed. Following this technique would allow for behavioral change to be monitored while a client remains in treatment, while also allowing for the calculation of a statistic which attempts to provide an indication of the behavioral change ratio of a program.

The point of this new strategy for evaluating drug programs is that no longer would a program be forced to discharge its "best" clients with its "worst" clients so that it will not appear as if that program is only producing treatment failures. For example, if a program continues to treat its really responsive clients and for the most part releases its failures, it would certainly appear as if it were having no appreciable treatment effect. Using this method all the clients that a program services can be included in any particular evaluation, thus providing an overall picture of a program's effectiveness. Accordingly, this method would balance the findings of an evaluation generated through the utilization of the successful discharge as an indicator of treatment success, for *during the life* of an out-patient clinic this discharge category in most cases will not accurately represent the immediate treatment effects of a program. The long-term effects of treatment, like always, would have to be measured in terms of post-treatment follow-up.

According to this new strategy, however, how can a client's behavioral change be measured? In a decentralized, out-patient clinic it is almost impossible without an extremely large staff to measure the actual impact that a program has on a client, for to obtain this type of information would require the implementation of a rigorous experimental research program. The CODAP impact variables were designed with this shortcoming in mind, in that they do not purport to be able to factor out and measure actual program impact, but instead only make the claim to provide a crude index of behavioral change. Likewise, this new strategy for evaluating out-patient programs cannot assess actual program impact. Yet, this strategy does use change indicators that do allow for a more accurate assessment of change to be made than is possible with the CODAP data collection procedure. For example, the question might be asked, what percentage of the clients categorized at program entry in category III have progressed after ninety days of treatment to groups I and II? Accordingly, a question can be asked such as what percentage of all clients entered in all admission categories moved in a positive behavioral direction during the course of treatment? A simple 3x3 matrix, for instance, would allow for the tabulation of data in a manner which would provide an answer to this latter question (see Table 1).

Table 1. Performance Level by Entry Level
90 Day Performance Level

	Groups	*III*	*II*	*I*	*Total*
	III	0	(5)	(5)	10
Entry Level	II	0	5	(5)	10
	I	0	5x	5	10
	Total	0	15	15	30

All a counselor would have to do is to first assess his/her caseload in terms of a client's behavioral status at program entry, and enter the appropriate number in each evaluational category in the total column on the right side of the chart. For example, a caseload might consist of thirty clients, ten of whom are classified as being in each of the three admission categories. Once this is done, every client in each entry level category should then be sub-divided into the appropriate ninety day treatment category. For example, after ninety days in treatment the ten clients originally placed in category II fell into categories I and II, with five of the original ten clients falling into each of these two ninety day performance categories. The same type of client distribution is present among the clients who were originally classified at admissionin category I. What this ninety day treatment distribution illustrates is that 50 per cent of the clients in treatment witnessed a positive behavioral change (circled numbers in Table 1), while 17 per cent of the clients digressed from their original entry level classification status (number marked with an "x" in Table 1). As such, the overall change rate is 33 per cent. However, 100 per cent of the clients in treatment are considered to be having a successful treatment experience, while only 50 per cent of these clients could theoretically be considered candidates for successful discharge from a program.

SUMMARY

Admittedly this evaluation method is not as comprehensive as is desired for assessing the actual impact that a program has in effecting behavioral change on the part of the client population it serves. Yet if the administrator does not have the capability to conduct on-going experimental research in order to assess actual program impact, and must resort to the use of "quickie" methods to monitor behavioral change, this method is certainly more accurate than that provided by the use of CODAP discharge forms.

It is suggested that particularly out-patient programs should employ this type of evaluation technique, for it is consistent with the treatment philosophy that underpins the use of that style of treatment environment. Because of this it will provide a more accurate evaluation of the behavioral change that occurs in the out-patient treatment environment than will an evaluation methodology that does not take into account the specific treatment philosophy of that therapeutic environment.

REFERENCES

1. *National Drug Abuse Treatment Utilization Survey, Executive Report,* DHEW, Washington, D.C., 1978.
2. *Analytic Approaches to NIDA Information Systems: A Management Report Series, Report No. 4, Evaluation of Treatment Programs and Client Outcomes,* Richard Katon Assoc., 1977.

Contributors

ALLES, WESLEY F., Ph.D. Associate Professor of Health Education and Coordinator of Community Health Education at Pennsylvania State University. Primary interest is in professional preparation in health.

ATKIN, CHARLES K., Ph.D. Professor, Department of Communication, Michigan State University. Professional activities and interest areas include research on the impact of mass media on society—including effects of health campaigns and alcohol advertising.

BASKERVILLE, JON C., Ph.D. Research consultant with Baskerville Associates. Interests include biostatistics, epidemiology, clinical trials, and survey research.

BENTLER, PETER, Ph.D. Professor of Psychology and Director, UCLA Center for the Study of Adolescent Drug Abuse Etiologies. Interested in personality and social development, individual differences and psychometric methods.

BRUNO, JAMES E., Ph.D. Professor, Graduate School of Education, UCLA. Teaches courses in the application of quantitative methods to educational policy issues. He is the author of *Educational Policy Analysis: A Quantitative Approach*.

CHNG, CHWEE LYE, Ph.D. Assistant Professor, Division of Health Education, North Texas State University, Denton, Texas. Has authored many articles on drug education and drug education strategies.

DEMBO, RICHARD, Ph.D. Associate Professor of Criminal Justice, University of South Florida, Tampa. He is the author of numerous publications in the fields of criminology, mass communications, mental health and drug use. His current research efforts include the etiology of psychosocial behaviors and drug abuse prevention.

DOSCHER, MARY-LYNN, Ph.D. Assistant Research Psychologist, Department of Psychology, UCLA. Current work includes application of log-linear and causal modeling techniques to forecasting in the area of drug abuse.

DOUGLASS, FRAZIER, M., Ph.D. Clinical Director, South Central Alabama Mental Health Center. Currently interested in rural health and mental health, and community treatment of the chronically mentally ill.

EISEMAN, SEYMOUR, Dr.P.H. Professor and Chair, Department of Health Science, California State University, Northridge. Current interests in the area of primary prevention of drug abuse through educational models.

FERNÁNDEZ-COLLADO, CARLOS, Ph.D. Director of the Communication Research Center, Universidad Anáhuac, Mexico. He received his Ph.D. in sociology and his M.A. in communications.

GOODSTADT, MICHAEL, Ph.D. Head of Education Research Section, Addiction Research Foundation of Ontario, Canada. A social psychologist with special interest in communications and social influence. Research has concentrated on the experimental value of alcohol and cannabis education programs.

GRAEF, DAVID is a Graduate Assistant, Department of Communication at Michigan State University.

GREENBERG, BRADLEY, Ph.D. Professor of Communication and Telecommunication, Michigan State University, East Lansing. Active in research on the social effects of the mass media, with particular focus on the social role and social behavior/learning by children and minorities from TV.

HUBA, GEORGE, Ph.D. Associate Research Psychologist and Associate Director, UCLA Center for the Study of Adolescent Drug Abuse Etiologies. Has an interest in drug use as it is related to psychosocial functioning, psychometric methods for causal modeling, adolescent development.

JOHNSON, DAVID W., Ed.D. Professor of Educational Psychology, University of Minnesota. Primary interests in prevention of antisocial behavior, prosocial development; social development; conflict resolution; group dynamics; organizational development and change.

KHAVARI, K. A., Ph.D. Professor of Psychology, Department of Psychology University of Wisconsin, Milwaukee. Past director of the Midwest Institute on Drug Use of the University of Wisconsin-Milwaukee. Current member of the Scientific Committee of the Wisconsin Alcohol and Drug Research Institute. Research focus on human alcoholism and drug addiction.

KORZENNY, FELIPE is a State University Assistant Professor, Department of Communication at Michigan State University.

LEFCOE, NEVILLE M., M.D., F.R.C.P.(C). Professor of Medicine, University of Western Ontario. Professional activities and areas of interest are teaching, research, and pulmonary diseases.

MANN, ROBERT, M.A. President of Teamm Resources, Inc., a drug rehabilitation agency providing residential treatment of adolescent drug abusers.

MITIC, WAYNE, Ed.D. Assistant Professor, Health Education Division, Dalhousie University, Halifax, Nova Scotia. Presently involved in a study which investigates the relationship of drug use among adolescents and stressors in their lives.

MONISMITH, SAMUEL, M.S. Instuctor in Health Education, The Pennsylvania State University, University Park. Teaches a variety of health education courses on topics such as stress, weight control, consumer health, and smoking education.

MURPHY, JOHN W., Ph.D. Assistant Professor of Sociology, Arkansas State University, Jonesboro. Professonal activities include past Project Coordinator for the Health Careers Opportunity Project at Ohio State Medical School and Program Evaluator in drug/alcohol abuse.

PEDERSEN, LINDA, Ph.D. National Health Research Scholar, Health and Welfare, Canada. Assistant Professor, Departments of Medicine, and Epidemiology and Biostatistics, University of Western Ontario. Primary focus of research in the area of the development, maintenance and termination of cigarette smoking. Additional experience in evaluating smoking cessation techniques.

SHEPPARD, MARGARET, M.Ed. Research Associate in Education Research Section, Addiction Research Foundation, Ontario, Canada. Primary activities include developing and researching alcohol and drug education programs with particular emphasis on prevention programs in schools.

SHUTE, ROBERT E., D.Ed. Associate Professor of Health Education, The Pennsylvania State University. Areas of interest include health behavior, especially in smoking, drug, and alcohol abuse.

SIDEROFF, STEPHEN, Ph.D. Faculty member of the Department of Psychiatry, School of Medicine, UCLA; Director of Stress Management Programs; Clinical Psychology practice in Gestalt Therapy and Behavioral Medicine with individuals, families, and groups.

SKUJA, ANDRIS, Ph.D. Chief of the Alcohol and Drug Abuse Program, Department of Psychiatry, Kaiser/Permanente Medical Center, South San Francisco, California. Current professional and research interests include clinical training in alcoholism and the use of short-term dynamic psychotherapy with alcohol and drug abusers.

ST. PIERRE, RICHARD W., Ed.D. Chair, Department of Health Education, Pennsylvania State University. Activities and interests include smoking and health research with an emphasis on lifestyle adoption and change.

TENNANT, FOREST, M.D., M.P.H. Executive Director, Community Health Projects, Inc., and Associate Professor UCLA School of Public Health, Los Angeles, California. Research interest in drug dependence.

TURNER, CAROL J., Ed.D. Assistant Professor, Counseling Psychology, Graduate School of Education, Rutgers University, New Brunswick, New Jersey. Interested in the development of reliable and valid measures of educational psychological variables, i.e., self-esteem and quality of relationships.

WEPNER, STEPHEN, Ph.D., Director, Research on Drug Abuse Prevention Techniques Program. Primary interests are in the area of research, evaluation, program design and staff development in substance abuse prevention; staff training in adult education and human resource development; and application of case studies and simulations to in-service training.

WILLIS, ROBERT, J., Ph.D. Psychotherapist and consultant. Board of Psych. Examiners for New Jersey. Consultation on values in health care, consultant in religious psychology. Primary interests are psychology of contemplation and peace.

WINGARD, JOSEPH, Ph.D., Research Scientist, System Development Corporation, Santa Monica, California. Interested in research related to functional models for drug abuse prevention.